WEB-BASED HUMAN RESOURCES

The Technologies and Trends That Are Transforming HR

Edited by

Alfred J. Walker

Towers Perrin

McGraw-Hill

New York   Chicago   San Francisco   Lisbon   London
Madrid   Mexico City   Milan   New Delhi   San Juan
Seoul   Singapore   Sydney   Toronto

Library of Congress Cataloging-in-Publication Data

Web-based human resources : the technologies and trends are transforming HR /
Alfred J. Walker, editor.
    p. cm.
    Includes index.
    ISBN 0-07-136515-X (hc.)
    1. Personnel management—Computer network resources. 2. Internet. 3. Information
storage and retrieval systems—Personnel management. 4. Management information
systems. I. Walker, Alfred J.
    HF5549.A27 W43 2001
    658.3'00285'4578—dc21   2001030860

McGraw-Hill

*A Division of The **McGraw-Hill** Companies*

*The sponsoring editor for this book was Richard Narramore, the editing supervisor was
Maureen B. Walker, and the production supervisor was Charles Annis. It was set in
Janson by Matrix Publishing.*

Printed and bound by R. R. Donnelley & Sons Company.

The publication is designed to provide accurate and authoritative information in
regard to the subject matter covered. It is sold with the understanding that nei-
ther the author nor the publisher is engaged in rendering legal, accounting, or
other professional service. If legal advice or other expert assistance is required,
the services of a competent professional person should be sought.
—*From a declaration of Principles jointly adopted by a Committee of the
American Bar Association and a Committee of Publishers*

McGraw-Hill books are available at special quantity discounts to use as premiums and sales promotions, or for use in corporate training programs. For more
information, please write to the Director of Special Sales, Professional Publishing, McGraw-Hill, Two Penn Plaza, New York, NY 10121-2298. Or contact
your local bookstore.

 This book is printed on recycled, acid-free paper containing a minimum
of 50% recycled, de-inked fiber.

Contents

PART II
DESIGNING AND IMPLEMENTING WEB-BASED HR

PART III
OTHER KEY TRENDS AND TECHNOLOGIES
CHANGING HR

Preface

Steve Fein

HUMAN CAPITAL has become the last competitive advantage in business. As management of this critical resource grows in importance, the nature of Human Resources management is changing dramatically. Human Resources management is no longer just a single entity, but an array of disciplines, plans, processes, products, and services, each with its own opportunities for adding value, and each with its own inherent risks.

Providing this vast array of services and products is no longer possible without Web-based technology. The Web allows the delivery of "mass-customized" products and services to "customers" within an organization, and supports HR's ability to function as a proactive business partner with senior management, in the pursuit of business goals.

Steve Fein is a Principal at Towers Perrin, and the Firm's global director of the Technology Solutions business. He is located in the Stamford, Connecticut, office.

Stamford office address: One Stamford Plaza, 263 Tresser Boulevard, Stamford, Connecticut 06901-3226.

The Web provides the long-sought-after technology for systematically integrating multifunctional HR departments, and for improving the effectiveness of each HR process or function. But technology does not in itself create world-class HR practices that also address the strategic business needs of a specific organization. That's where people come in, to shape the technologies to fit the situation. Web-based HR implementations will, therefore, naturally differ from organization to organization.

Thus, the first section of this book, following editor Al Walker's comprehensive introduction, focuses largely on what Web-based HR looks like in practice, and what this technology brings to HR's most critical functions. After the key chapters on Web-based employee self-service and Web-based manager self-service, experts discuss the specific impacts of Web-based systems on benefits, recruiting and staffing, performance management, compensation, training and development, and knowledge management. The authors convey the basic principles and state-of-the-practice concepts driving these functions in leading-edge organizations.

Next, beginning with Chapter 10 on creating a business case for your organization's Web-based HR initiative, the focus is on the design and implementation of Web-based HR systems, including issues regarding the transformation of the HR function, setting the HR technology strategy, workflow, service centers, and service center implementation. In these chapters, authors who have been key participants in helping major organizations develop HR technology strategies and implement them in the real world, share their findings and lessons learned, and present the reasons why the Internet and other new technologies are driving fundamental changes in HR service delivery.

The final section, on other key trends changing the world of HR management and its technology, includes chapters on outsourcing, which is already being vastly transformed by the phenomenal growth of application service providers (ASPs); and a chapter on how HR is being changed internationally by the World Wide Web.

Web-Based Human Resources is a practical compendium of knowledge, principles, and best-practice approaches to effective

HR management, with an emphasis on how Web-based technology provides the infrastructure for fully implementing these principles and practices.

One final note about the structure, breadth, and value of this book to managers and HR and HR technology professionals: Any one of these chapters could have been a book in itself, and necessarily summarizes much of what the authors and their colleagues at Towers Perrin might have included. We have included contact information for each of our authors, who will be glad to respond to your inquiries for further information relevant to your own efforts to transform HR using Web technology. Your comments will also be welcome, and can be directed to me, Al Walker, or any of the authors.

Contributors

Lynn Adamson Consultant, Towers Perrin, San Francisco, CA (*Chapters 2 and 3*)

Brian D. Beatty Managing Consultant, Towers Perrin, Chicago, IL (*Chapter 11*)

Joseph Bender Consultant, Towers Perrin, Parsippany, NJ (*Chapter 14*)

Jack Borbely Principal and Director, Towers Perrin, Valhalla, NY (*Chapter 9*)

Stephen C. Brescia Consultant, Towers Perrin, Voorhees, NJ (*Chapter 15*)

David Cohen Principal, Towers Perrin, Los Angeles, CA (*Chapter 5*)

Cynthia DeFidelto Principal, Towers Perrin, London, England (*Chapter 17*)

Joanne Dietch Principal, Towers Perrin, Los Angeles, CA (*Chapter 4*)

Elaine M. Evans Principal, San Francisco, CA (*Chapter 6*)

Steve Fein Principal and Global Director of Technology Solutions, Towers Perrin, Stamford, CT (*Preface*)

Diane Gherson Principal and Leader, Towers Perrin, Irvine, CA (*Chapter 7*)

Joseph Gibbons Consultant, Towers Perrin, New York, NY (*Chapter 8*)

Stephen J. Gould Principal, Towers Perrin, Boston, MA (*Chapter 9*)

April E. Hartness Principal, Towers Perrin, Atlanta, GA (*Chapter 15*)

Allen P. Jackson Principal, Towers Perrin, Stamford, CT (*Chapter 7*)

Thomas Keebler Principal, Towers Perrin, Philadelphia, PA (*Chapter 16*)

John G. Kelly Consultant, Towers Perrin, Boston, MA (*Chapter 13*)

Lori G. Lanzelotti Consultant, Towers Perrin, Philadelphia, PA (*Chapter 12*)

Jennifer Lego Manager of Technology Solutions, Towers Perrin, New York (*Chapter 10*)

Iain Slater Consultant, Towers Perrin, London, England (*Chapter 17*)

Alfred J. Walker Senior Fellow, Towers Perrin, Parsippany, NJ (*Introduction, Chapters 1 and 12*)

J. Alec Wilder Practice Leader, Towers Perrin, Philadelphia, PA (*Chapter 12*)

Robert Zampetti Consultant, Towers Perrin, San Francisco, CA) (*Chapters 2 and 3*)

Introduction

How the Web and Other Key Trends Are Changing Human Resources

Alfred J. Walker

Importance of Portals and the Web

Today's new browser-based HR portal technology, with point-and-click ease of use and combination of text, data, and video, is changing the way we manage human resources. This technology is the new vehicle by which critical information about people is now captured, edited, stored, retrieved, and shared with others who need that information. Managers and employees can now directly access this information and make on-the-spot decisions about employment, development, and pay, without involving the HR function and without using antiquated paper-based processes. This information sharing also takes place between systems, new or legacy, whether it's via the Internet, corporate intranet, or extranets, and a premium is placed on useful data structures.

Alfred J. Walker is a Senior Fellow in the Towers Perrin Parsippany, New Jersey, office. He specializes in the use of technology to improve the effectiveness and efficiency of the HR function.

Parsippany office address: Morris Corporate Center II, Building F, One Upper Pond Road, Parsippany, New Jersey 07054-1050.

The biggest development over the past several years on the technology front, enabling direct employee access, is the Web-based HR information portal. An HR information portal is a set of applications that provides users with a single gateway to customized and personalized information. These portals bring together information from sources within and outside the organization. They are also the underpinnings of the new "HR store" and e-commerce HR, where employees can directly shop for discount travel, home mortgages, and other items such as child care and elder care. Yet even more significant is the ability to use Web-based applications through HR portals for knowledge management, organizational learning, and distance training. Companies are now combining classroom teaching with other learning forms, such as real work projects and knowledge databases using the Internet as a delivery channel. Individualized instruction programs can now be made available at any place, at any time.

This description of cutting-edge Web-based Human Resources all starts with access to a Web-based HR home page (see examples of an HR home page in Figures I-1 and I-2), which brings together the company's plans and programs for the user.

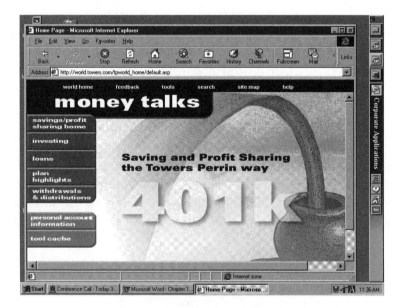

Figure I-1

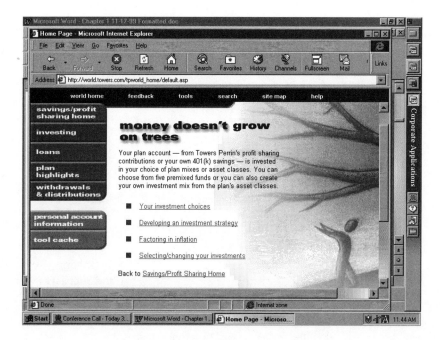

Figure I-2

HR home pages and their links represent the end products of an HR strategic technology planning and transformation process. The transformation process integrates the various components of HR service delivery for dramatically improved ease of customer use and lower overall cost, compared with most of the earlier HR technology systems.

Along with Web technologies, employee self-service is another basic idea that makes possible the new HR portals. Although self-service does not require HR portal or Web technology, it greatly enhances the capability of self-service. Self-service enables employees and managers to directly access information for decision making and to make updates to their data from their PCs or workstations. This capability is especially useful for dealing with complex HR transactions such as career planning, retirement calculations, handling open enrollment, and stock options. These and other new technologies are leading the way for transformation of HR work as depicted in Figure I-3.

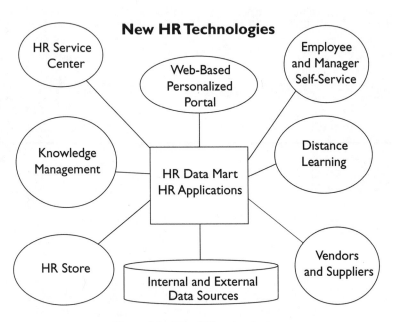

Figure I-3 New HR technologies.

Recent HR Information Systems History: How We Went from Legacy Systems to Enterprise Resource Planning (ERP) to the Internet

In the early 1990s client/server systems became the ideal configuration for most companies, and they began the somewhat arduous task of migrating their legacy systems to these new packages designed with a more advanced structure. They offered users advantages in functionality, storage capacity, and performance, and a new look and feel, and gave companies an opportunity to reengineer and streamline their HR processes at the same time.

Reengineering in the early 1990s was all the rage since it was based upon many of the same principles and ideas as the quality initiatives, which proved so successful in the manufacturing and supply chain areas. The plan was to apply those quality techniques to the HR area. So the approach, strongly backed by the IS professionals as well as the HR folks, was to redesign the HR processes before they put in the new technology. In that way they would fit the new technology to the new process and not have to change it later. It seemed to make great sense, and the newer client/server products were marketed with this in mind. In fact, another initiative in the systems world was contributing to this thinking as well: ERP systems.

The need for these systems was caused by the fact that most companies were dealing with an increasing number of systems containing inherent differences, and system maintenance and upkeep was absorbing an inordinate amount of the IS resources, both human and financial. The systems had different software languages, different hardware platforms, and different data structures, and perhaps the time had come to replace most if not all of these separate computer-based systems with a single suite of integrated applications and modules. These new ERP systems were designed and built to work in harmony—with a single set of databases, and common processes and standards, which would apply throughout the enterprise. Leading the pack were global software vendors such as SAP, PeopleSoft, Oracle, Lawson, and Baan, which expanded their client/server product lines to compete in this market. They offered applications in all major areas of business, including manufacturing, purchasing, logistics, finance, and HR. So the HR and IT departments thought it made perfect sense to abandon the older HR systems they had been using and to move to the newer products and reengineer their processes at the same time.

However, history tells us it did not quite work out as planned. The complexities of business are such that tackling a full-scale ERP project for a midsize or large organization was a massive undertaking, affecting almost every department's work, and requiring dedicated resources from user departments and IS far beyond anything they had tried before. Many companies are still in the midst of determining how far they want to go with this enormously expensive and time-consuming effort. And the HR modules are usually somewhere lower on the priority list, since the manufacturing and logistics processes are worked on, and in many cases are still being implemented. Thus many ERP projects may never get to work on the HR needs.

Even where HR was able to acquire a client/server product and install it as a single project, not connected with an ERP initiative, the road has not been smooth. It turns out that there are so many processes and subprocesses to work on in HR, that the projects were being delayed for years while process teams tried to figure out how they wanted processes to be handled with the new technology. Many abandoned the reengineering work and moved on to installing a "plain vanilla" HR system. It often took years, and millions of dollars, for some companies to fight their way through the development and implementation phases, with or without reengineering. This was far beyond what the companies thought it would take at the start, and often these projects were so costly that any benefit from the implementation was gone. The client/server toolkits, which promised to be easy to use for HR novices, became so complex that IS professionals were needed in order to employ them. The software programs, applications, and databases that composed the systems turned out to be extremely difficult to load, modify, and put into production. This was not entirely the fault of the software companies. Users demanded more functionality in the products before they would buy them, and legislation and compliance demands grew over the years. The combined effect of the complexities and unsatisfactory track records of many good companies was enough to put fear into almost any IS manager's heart. As a result, many companies have halted their plans to install such systems.

Web-Based Systems to the Rescue

With this brief history, we can see more clearly why the Web-based technology appears so attractive. Implementation times for applications run into weeks or months, not years. The systems are visually appealing, HTML, Visual Basic, and SQL logic are fairly easy to understand. But Web-based systems cannot easily replace all HR systems functionality, and still are not equipped to fully replace the complex nature of HR processing, for example, as in a multistate payroll system. Therefore, organizations still must spend significant sums to maintain and upgrade legacy HR applications until technology finds replacements cost effective. But companies are exploring alternatives to costly client/server ERP projects and are finding some answers.

Some people question if, at the end of the day, this Web and HR portal technology has really helped the HR function, and the employees and managers all that much. Is this not just repackaged retrieval and analysis and better screen design? The reason Web and HR portal technology is a dramatic advance is not because of the technology by itself, but because the Web has been effectively integrated with self-service, HR service centers, and other Web applications. The result has been that the services available to employees are much more advanced then ever before. So from a customer service and usage standpoint, HR portals are a big step forward.

From an implementation point of view as well, Web-based systems are easier to build and implement, and the major vendors have now expanded their ERP product lines to include these capabilities, putting themselves in a better position to compete with the vendors of Web solutions. Use of this technology for decision-making purposes, sharing data, and performing routine transactions will increase dramatically in the years ahead and perhaps be as important as the telephone as a communication device, as bandwidth grows. It's easy to use, can handle multimedia, is accessible virtually anywhere, and is relatively inexpensive. Difficulties in security have been overcome with firewalls and encryption. Most companies are using their corporate websites to advertise jobs, collect resumes, and complete employee and manager transactions, including accessing sensitive data over the Internet, not just over the corporate intranet.

This means that technology is finally reaching the end users faster, and also directly, without intermediate or derivative applications. The employees and managers are the *targeted* users, and the systems are not just being used as a tool to help the HR function, with a side benefit for the others.

What the New HR Department Looks Like

Due to the impact of these technologies and fundamental business changes, the Human Resources department as we knew it is gone. No longer do we have a single group of people who know all about the benefit plans, salary programs, and career opportunities in a company. Today's companies are simply too diverse in terms of their products and services and their global reach, to be able to operate under a common set of HR programs, administered locally, the way organizations were able to do in the past. And with this business diversity came a bewildering array of new compensation and plans, training and development programs, union agreements, and relocation policies to contend with, just to mention a few.

Another large influence on HR complexities is a growing scarcity of skilled workers, especially "knowledge" workers. These people, able to understand and build the systems of the future, demand a changed employer-employee relationship. Pension plans based on working for one company for 40 years no longer have much appeal. And authoritarian management styles, outdated compensation plans, and overly strict employment arrangements don't fit the needs of the younger, computer-literate workforce either. The very relevance of the HR function itself, as well as the HR programs offered, has also been challenged by management. It is no wonder then that traditional HR plans and programs, and the traditional HR function, are becoming obsolete.

What we are dealing with now in most companies is an HR function undergoing profound transformation to adopt a new mode of operation: the ability to offer individualized HR plans and programs to each employee. HR plans and programs need to be streamlined, tailored, and packaged to meet the specific needs of each employee, similar in concept to the customer-driven model that businesses have adopted. And, using the latest HR portal technology, new HR programs must be able to deliver and administer their plans in a self-service mode, which enables faster, individualized service at a much lower cost. In sum, the HR function is dramatically changing its focus on several fronts.

New Technology Transforming HR

From	To
Local	Global
Administration	Self-service
Internally delivered programs	Outsourced delivery
Transactions	Business information
Employer-oriented plans	Individualized employee and manager plans

It must be remembered that today's Human Resources departments are still required to deliver a myriad of plans and services to the managers and employees of an organization, and beyond those groups, to dependents, as well as to retirees and applicants for employment. Further, these plans are required to comply with legal regulations and contractual agreements. The number of such HR plans and programs that need to be administered cover a wide range of subjects, such as

Health and welfare plans—including short-term and long-term disability (STD and LTD)

Pension and investment plans

Compensation—salary administration, bonus and incentive plans

Payroll administration

Expatriate administration

Performance appraisal

Separations

Diversity and EEO/affirmative action compliance

Training and education

Employee communications

Employee development

Management development

Employee relations

Organizational effectiveness

Succession planning

Labor relations

Recruiting and sourcing

Safety and environmental health

Transfer and relocation

Executive resources

The challenge is in how to enable HR to deliver Web-based plans in a cost-effective manner. And shifting the work while it is ongoing is not easy. The plans must be continually administered in an efficient manner; however, the plans themselves change due to changes in regulations and plan design, and the technologies are also always evolving. So merely having a desire to improve and a vision for how to use technology to handle some of the work is not sufficient. We need well-thought-out methodologies on how to bring about successful change.

New Roles for HR Professionals

The following is a graphical depiction of how new HR technologies will alter the structure of the HR function and change the role of the HR staff as they interact with the various user constituencies. Note that the business consultant role, and other face-to-face HR roles and services are not meant to be supplanted by technology.

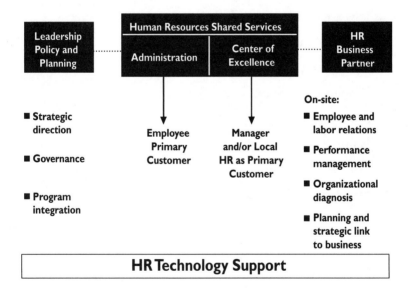

Figure I-4 HR technology alters the roles.

The New Model for HR Service Delivery

At the center of the interaction with technology are the Web-enabled HR portal and self-service network, as shown in the above figure, which will provide access to the Human Resources information database system and to other major internal and external systems.

Also prominent in the delivery picture is the Human Resources service center, which handles day-to-day inquiries from employees and managers regarding plans and policies, as well as specific questions around such issues as compensation, open jobs, payroll, and benefits. In the future it is envisioned that such service centers will also be used to handle deeper management inquiries such as those involving performance management and staffing, whereas today those interactions are best handled by the HR business partner.

The HR work itself within the new model is redesigned and repackaged into three basic types, and the allocation will change depending upon where the work is performed. The three types of work and the new roles for the HR staff in the new model will be as follows:

- *Strategic partnering* with the line businesses
  - ◆ At a leadership and senior level
  - ◆ At the local, generalist level
- *Centers of expertise* housing the required HR functional specialists
  - ◆ Can be centralized or localized
- *Service center* administration
  - ◆ Is centralized

For some of the current HR staff, work after e-engineering will remain mostly the same as before the transformation. Primarily this applies to the work of HR strategists, policymakers, and generalists. However, this will be a minority of the HR workers. Most will find that their work has been altered in some fashion.

Some will find that the work they were doing has been shifted to technology and is being handled through the portal or self-service, or the work has been outsourced to a vendor. Perhaps it will have been physically transferred to another site in the country or region, or out of the country altogether. Where once HR staff were the focal point for an activity, they may no longer be. That component of their work will simply be gone.

Some of the HR specialists will move into centers-of-excellence units, perhaps within a shared service organization.

The following is an outline of the positive impacts on several of the HR roles under the new HR model:

Professional HR Staff Impact

HR vice president and senior managers

> Implement new HR plans and programs more quickly.
>
> Develop new service delivery pathways with vendors and suppliers.
>
> Permit faster access of information to customers.
>
> Develop standard HR programs and processes and deploy them more quickly and at less cost.
>
> Access meaningful HR enterprisewide business information on productivity measures, key dashboard data, and process results.
>
> Provide a key component for developing a best-in-class HR organization.
>
> Focus on growing and developing organizational strength across business units and geography.

HR business partners and consultants

> Provide senior business managers with information about the entire organization, regardless of organization or business boundaries, quickly and easily.
>
> Respond quickly to line management and customer needs.
>
> Standardize and monitor programs/processes within business units (if not enterprisewide).
>
> Shift focus from transaction-based work to value-added work.

HR directors and HR business heads

Spend time working on business issues and activities, instead of becoming distracted by having to support corporate activities.

Access other HR systems resources, global and regional.

Access expertise in centers of excellence.

Access specialty resources and solutions (e.g., automated applications such as those provided by Oracle, PeopleSoft, SAP, SAS, Authoria, and Kadiri).

Use common tools and systems that reduce maintenance and support costs.

Shift focus from transaction-based work to value-added work.

HR functional specialists

Standardize and deliver HR programs and processes more quickly and at less cost.

Access global and regional HR systems resources when needed.

Access expertise located in centers of excellence.

Access specialty resources and solutions.

Use common tools and systems that reduce maintenance and support costs.

Shift focus from transaction-based work to value-added work.

Essential to this model is that the key HR staffs within the business groups and the corporate and regional offices work in close contact with senior management to help ensure that the HR plans, programs, and the delivery of services are aligned with the overall business objectives.

Other changes to the work will take place as well. With the growth of outsourcing and the introduction of shared services units, it becomes necessary to reexamine supplier activities that could be managed centrally or regionally. Additionally, with the

HR work now redesigned, a new role has taken shape: that of handling more complex employee inquiry tasks. And all involved are dependent upon technology, where there will also be new jobs.

New Vendor Manager Role Emerges

A role that is still emerging is HR vendor management. The purpose of this role is to oversee the growing list of outside suppliers to HR, including the various contracts and service-level agreements (SLAs) that have been signed and put into place. This is where the process measurements are key, since many of the vendors are now monitored by such metrics. Many if not all areas of HR could potentially be outsourced, with such areas as payroll, staffing, relocation, benefits and disability management, HR service centers, and HRIS operations among those most likely to be affected.

HR Service Center Customer Service Representatives' Key New Role

The HR customer service representatives handle a wide range of inquiries from the various groups they support: employees, retirees, managers, and outside suppliers and vendors. They are trained to either handle the incoming calls or e-mails directly, or walk the customer through the transaction on the spot. They have access to an HR database, a case management tool, and applicable policies and practices through a knowledge base. Whatever they need, within reason, to enable them to perform their jobs, is provided. Appropriate time for follow-up and completed documentation regarding the transaction is built into the position.

Expanded HR Technology Positions Crucial

Technology is the underlying foundation upon which the new HR organization will operate. The traditional HRIS positions such as analysts, programmers, and database administrators will be needed, as well as telecommunications, LAN, PC, and Web specialists, to develop, maintain, and keep secure the various HR, payroll, and benefits systems. These roles will continue to be shared with the information technology organization. However, several new technology roles have been added to support the new HR model. These include the following:

- A knowledge base specialist to build and maintain the needed policies, practices, and procedures, to support the employee and manager self-service initiatives in a way that allows employees and HR staff to access the applications via the portal or service center in the appropriate manner
- An overall HR information manager, who will establish and maintain with the subject matter experts the standard definitions, usage, access privileges, and privacy rules for all HR data elements
- Service center technologists, who will deal with supplying data to the shared services unit; handling case management systems, CTIs, call paths, etc.; and tying that unit to the HR portal and other HR functional units
- Portal communication specialists, who build and maintain the portal and websites, and who create and transmit to the various groups the important HR information messages and content relating to ongoing activities and change management programs
- Enterprise data mining and data mart experts to build and support needed templates and information sets of HR and mixed HR–business and productivity data for managers and HR users
- Field systems analysts, including global and regional representatives, to define the needed local and regional HR data needs and to support the users in their locales
- E-engineering analyst and business process redesign (BPR) consulting capability to integrate and streamline work processes that maximize both cost savings and the power of technology through the Web, workflow, self-service, and collaborative transaction systems
- A quality control and measurements capability to maintain the desired level of data cleansing, accuracy, and customer service

The incumbents in the new global roles and positions must be able to deal with the varying levels of technical sophistication found in other countries, as well as various legal and privacy regulations. Certainly these changes demand new competencies for the HR staff to fulfill their new roles. In the future there will be an increased emphasis placed on interpersonal skills, consulting skills, "pure" HR functional knowledge, business savvy, and technology. Global awareness and experience will be at a premium.

Summary

The emergence of HR portals and self-service technologies has created a major new opportunity for the HR function. With these solutions, and the associated reengineering and e-engineering methodologies, organizations can at last alter the HR structure and roles to provide more support to the line businesses, reduce HR delivery costs, and develop new and exciting services for its customers. At the same time, HR can give its customers more personalized plans and programs. Organizations moving to the new model of operation will have a strong competitive advantage since they provide new business information to managers, reposition HR professionals to build more productive workforces, and unleash powerful new tools to increase learning and education.

PART I

Web-Based HR: What It Looks Like

Best Practices in HR Technology

Alfred J. Walker*

HUMAN RESOURCES (HR) TECHNOLOGY must accomplish several objectives to be considered successful:

Strategic Alignment must help users in a way that supports the goals of the business.

Business Intelligence must provide the user with relevant information and data, answer questions, and inspire new insights and learning.

Efficiency and Effectiveness must change the work performed by the Human Resources personnel by dramatically improv-

*Alfred J. Walker is a Senior Fellow in the Towers Perrin Parsippany, New Jersey, office. He specializes in the use of technology to improve the effectiveness and efficiency of the HR function.

Parsippany office address: Morris Corporate Center II, Building F, One Upper Pond Road, Parsippany, New Jersey 07054-1050.

ing their level of service, allowing more time for work of higher value, and reducing their costs.

If your organization has been involved in technology deployment for the HR function, hopefully all three of these objectives will be achieved. But as it turns out, few HR technology projects have been fully successful with high marks in all areas. This is in spite of major Enterprise Resource Planning (ERP) projects, establishment of HR service centers, outsourcing, new Human Resource Information Systems (HRIS) applications and Internet usage, and often millions of dollars of investment. Why haven't they been more successful?

A–Shortfalls with Some HR Systems Installations

It has become clear over the last several years that to accomplish the goals that have been set for HR technology projects, dramatic changes have to be made in the work that HR performs. The savings and efficiency objectives as we well know by now cannot be achieved by merely downsizing and cutting the HR head count. The work still remains. Companies need to reengineer and streamline their activities with technology, not merely put new technology on top of old processes.

What about other methods of changing HR, such as outsourcing or reorganizing? Have these initiatives helped? In fact, they have not helped a lot. Outsourcing the 401(k) plan for most companies was the right thing to do, as were removing claims administration work, security guards, and cafeteria duties from the HR functions, since these activities were not considered central to developing the human talent in an organization. Can more of HR be outsourced? Probably, but if it's not done carefully, the result will be a lack of coordination of function and facilities overrun with vendors all using out-of-date and incomplete data. And not too surprisingly, many outsourcing initiatives have not saved money. They have, however, improved the quality and level of service to the customer, and in a few instances they have displaced some work, enabling the HR staff to concentrate on more important matters.

But even with these outsourcing arrangements and reorganizations, and the infusion of technology, the ratio of HR staff to employees, a key issue, has increased over the past ten years. According to survey data more HR staff are needed today to manage the HR business than were needed from the early 1990s. Most of the work that the HR staff does on a day-to-day basis, such as staffing, employee relations, compensation, training, employee development, and benefits, unfortunately remains relatively untouched and unimproved from a delivery standpoint.

How then can we achieve and sustain real improvement in HR work? I believe that the newer technologies hold the answer. Most companies are realizing that by intelligently utilizing a set of Web-based and service center technologies within HR, guided by a well thought out HR strategic technology plan, and delivered by good project management, the goals can be reached if not surpassed in many cases.

B—Process Reengineering Must Come First— Then E-Engineer the HR Work

Before we can implement any technology, we must streamline the work itself, redesigning the delivery to gain the efficiencies we seek. This is done by first categorizing the HR work into a set of processes that will be examined by reengineering teams, customers, and users. At a high level, these categories can be placed into groupings such as acquiring resources, compensation, benefits, training and development, moving and transferring, and so forth. Each of these in turn is further divided into subprocesses. For example, the acquiring of resources could encompass such activities as hiring exempt/nonexempt employees; college recruiting; hiring temporary employees; and so forth. What emerges is a set of processes—some of them not currently being performed— that need to be reengineered. These processes will then be fully analyzed and examined by the team users and customers. They will be redesigned based on criteria developed by the reengineering team so they are better aligned with the organizational goals, streamlined for cost effectiveness compared to the "best in class" examples, and better integrated with other processes.

What should emerge is a new set of processes reflecting the way HR work will be performed in the future. HR Portals, new roles and responsibilities for line managers, employees, vendors, and HR staff will be developed, resulting in the improvements necessary to achieve the project goals. In almost all of the successful HR reengineering cases that we have seen, a major factor enabling the changes has been a better use of existing technology, or new technology itself. And the changes usually have not been resisted in these cases: customers, HR staff, and process stakeholders alike, generally chose technology as the preferred solution over organizational realignments ("realignments" involve passing the same process to someone else on the internal staff or outsourcing it to a vendor).

HR Portal and Self-Service Technology Overview

There are several technologies, some of them fairly new to the scene, that are enabling these new methods of delivering HR work, all of which should operate in a fully secure and confidential manner. These will be described in greater detail in later chapters.

Workflow. With this technology, users are directly involved in a process, using their computer terminal, where they can access employee records or initiate an event by entering key data, and then submitting the work to the next appropriate person for further action or review—*all electronically*. It can be thought of as e-mail with a database and built-in intelligence. Prescribed chains of events are set up based on user-defined roles and on reengineering changes that ensure that the transaction is routed properly. Reengineering will also ensure that the process conforms to security and audit rules. Using a salary example, a manager would submit a salary change to his or her boss for approval. The system knows who works for whom, and who has the authority to approve such changes. Further, the HR department may want to review all salary increases above a certain percentage, or those that are submitted either under or over acceptable time guidelines. Under workflow, the paths the transaction takes and the actions needed at each stop are always governed by the company rules.

C–Manager Self-Service

At the front end of the HR Portal and workflow is a set of fully functional desktop applications that permit line managers to view and change their employees' records; access policies and procedures; gain opinions from others (including HR staffers) relating to personnel problems; and perform many of their duties as managers on their PCs. Some of these applications enable the managers to rate their employees, model the salary increase budgets, grant employee salary increases, and enroll employees in training courses and the like. HR Portal technology will "push" important information to managers and alert them to upcoming due dates.

D–Employee Self-Service

Similar to the manager's self-service, employees are able to become more self-sufficient with respect to many items previously handled by the HR staff. These include such activities as making changes and additions to their own benefits program, participating in annual benefits enrollment, selecting training programs and development plans, investigating job opportunities and postings, handling payroll deductions, and participating in retirement planning. Also, the employee can alter selected portions of their base records such as marital status, address changes, and dependent data, as well as have access to company policies and procedures. Portal technology will personalize this information further and "push" relevant data to them as well.

E–Interactive Voice Response (IVR)

One form of the employee self-service, albeit a lower-tech version than HR Portals, is to permit many of the changes to benefits, payroll, and some aspects of job postings to be made over the telephone utilizing push-button features. The telephone is quite a bit less expensive, more widely available, and often easier to use than the computer-based options. Although limited to simple transactions using sensibly designed scripts, quite a few applications such as verifications of employment, accessing job openings, and enrolling in training can all be handled by phone.

F—HR Service Centers

Using centralization concepts complete with a set of new technologies, the establishment of service centers has become one of the favorite solutions in Reengineering or E-Engineering HR work. Service centers are set up to handle inquiries, customer transactions, and to resolve routine problems. Internal telephone calls, e-mails, or on-line inquiries are channeled to operators via an automatic call path if the caller needs to discuss an issue or if the transaction was not covered by the service center's telephone script. The operator would access the caller's record via Computer Telephone Interface (CTI) technology and answer questions based upon predetermined Q&A's. These are referred to as scripted protocols, brought on-line so the operator can refer to them. Here a knowledge base, usually hypertext driven, is employed, allowing the operator to key in the issue/question. The knowledge base brings on-line the relevant policy text and/or answer for the service center representative to explain to the caller. For complex issues, or those not covered by the script, the problem can be referred to a supervisor, using workflow.

When the call is completed, faxes can be generated and sent to the caller. In addition, other materials/forms can be supplied automatically, as well as instructions to the caller on how to complete a transaction or take other steps to solve a problem. A record of the call is made for future reference, using case management technologies. Statistics on call volumes, speed of response, and levels of knowledge base access are stored. The results have been very well received by most companies, who report that they are providing more consistent answers, faster service, and lower costs.

G—HRIS Systems/Databases

The HRIS System is the primary transaction processor, editor, record-keeper, and functional application system which lies at the heart of all computerized HR work. It maintains employee, organizational, and HR plan data sufficient to support most, if not all, of the HR functions depending on the modules installed. It, along with IT-provided infrastructures, also supplies the backbone network, architecture, and communications support for HR, enabling reports and information to be available to those who need them. These systems, although often legacy systems, supply needed information to the data warehouses and data marts supporting the HR Portal.

H–HR Stand-Alone (Bolt-on) Applications

A wide variety of HR applications have been developed that go beyond mere record keeping and extend the power of the HRIS systems. They can be applications that are linked to an HRIS, or they can be used as complete systems in their own right. These include applicant tracking, succession planning, 360 assessment and appraisal systems, retirement planning applications, and the like. Usually they can be attached, though not always easily, to the HRIS, enabling a process to be more completely automated. They should share a common database with the HRIS, but most do not. They too feed the HR Portal Data Mart. Issues on standard data structures and data accuracy must be resolved when combining data sources.

I–Data Marts, Warehouses, and OLAP

The concept of Data Marts and Data Warehousing has been a part of HR systems for years, under a different banner—that of retrieval and analysis. These are large collections of information, usually stored in relational databases, which then can be accessed by analytical tools for business information purposes. Data must be collected, transformed into usable information, perhaps cleansed, and stored. Then information access tools, such as ad hoc query programs, Decision Support tools, or On-Line Analytical Processing (OLAP) programs are able to bring the data to the end users. The term *Data Mart* usually applies to information that might be from a single source, i.e., HR, while *Data Warehouses* refers more to collections of data from mixed sources, such as financial data, production, supplier, and HR sources.

Web-Based HR Must Be Guided by an HR Technology Strategy

A–HR Technology Strategy Rationale

Literally thousands of Internet and computer-based products, as well as related service centers or outsourced services are available to handle the myriad of tasks confronting companies as they deal with the hiring, deployment, and administration of their employees. And most companies have purchased a good number of these products in the hopes of delivering better service to their employees and managers.

What we also find, however, is that there is no overall plan for the acquisition and use of such technology or services in most of these companies. And without a master plan there is often no direct connectivity among the products, resulting in duplicate databases being installed to support these products, each perhaps with differing data descriptions and with overlapping functionality and service offerings. The result is that there is no true benefit to the organization, and in fact there is an increase in costs due to the support and maintenance required.

The ultimate goal of HR technology is to help the organization meet its business goals and objectives today and in the future. See Figure 1-1. And in most companies this can be done in a number of ways, such as

- Helping managers deploy their workers more effectively
- Ensuring that workers receive proper training and development

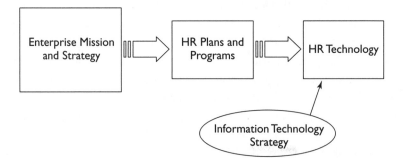

Figure 1-1 Enterprise mission and strategy primary driver for HR and HR technology.

- Offering new insights on how to increase productivity
- Enabling employees and managers to receive needed information faster
- Reducing HR administrative costs
- Assisting with better employee assessment and selection

There are hundreds of such examples that can be offered, some of which were most likely used to justify the purchase of a particular HR product. But again, in the absence of an overall HR technology strategy, it is a piecemeal approach.

B–Single HR System Strategy Fails

An HR technology strategy was not really needed prior to the mid 1990s. Until that time, there was no Internet per se in widespread use for HR work; nor were HR service centers being employed for any functions other than for 401(k) or 403(b) administration, and outsourcing arrangements were limited for the most part to payroll, relocation, and administration of some of the benefit plans. Applications products for the HR area were also limited to a few areas due to cost constraints. The vendors understood the economics of the situation since the cost of developing a top-notch solution, marketing and selling that product, and supporting it had to be substantially less than the expected revenue they would receive. This was a difficult proposition over the long term due to the fact that the major HR systems vendors at that time (such as PeopleSoft, Oracle, Tesseract, GEAC, and SAP) were embedding similar functionality within their product lines.

Therefore, the only thing a company thought it had to do was merely choose one of the major systems vendors, and that vendor would supply most if not all of the applications the HR function would need. The vendors either had applications that were close enough to what most users wanted, or they had development plans to include that functionality in later releases. The choice of vendor, in fact, became their HR technology strategy. But this strategy proved far too simplistic.

For starters, just choosing an HR major systems vendor does

not guarantee that you will have an overall strategy. There are still a number of questions and issues that need to be thought through, such as what specific modules of the system or applications get deployed, in what sequence, and by whom? What modifications are needed to the base product? What time and effort are required from the HR user community? What are the roles of the Human Resource Information Technology (HRIT) group in conjunction with the IT group?

Next comes an even more difficult set of issues surrounding HR processes. Are we to have a common set of HR processes within the organization, or can every business unit modify the product to conform to the way that it perceives that it needs to, in order to deliver a particular HR plan, performance management, or compensation, for example? What is our overall strategy here?

Making the case for an overall strategy even clearer is the question of the choice of delivery mechanisms. Which specific technology solution does one choose if there are overlapping technical (or manual) capabilities? Do we always use Interactive Voice Response (IVR)? Or do we favor the Net for plan and policy delivery to employees? How and when does one decide? Is there a framework for making such decisions?

And how about transforming the HR function itself, in order to make it more proactive and less of a transaction and administrative group? Where does this initiative fit on the priority list for the HRIT team? Most HR organizations have had streamlining HR's work as a goal for a number of years, and again, just picking an HR system's vendor does nothing by itself to ensure the HR work is altered sufficiently to turn the majority of the HR staff into strategic partners within the organization.

Lastly, new players arrived on the scene: the Internet; HR service centers; and strong multicapability outsourcers. The combination of these service alternatives now not only makes a single vendor strategy overly simplistic and obsolete, but also highlights the need for an overall strategic plan for the development and deployment of technology to assist with the management of an organization's human resources.

C–Comprehensive HR Technology Strategy Needed

As Figure 1-2 shows, the influences on developing an HR technology strategy are many. For example, the strategy must map to the organization's IT policy and direction. But the dominant voice here is the HR voice. How the HR plans and programs are delivered at the end of the day is HR's call. This function's management must decide on the methods, timing, and priorities of the programs, and how they will be disseminated throughout the organization.

Items such as finding and developing the proper employees, retaining the intellectual capital of the company, building the organizational capabilities, increasing employee productivity, assessing the managerial talent, and developing the appropriate total rewards structure must be high on HR's agenda. These items go to the heart of the business-partnering role, which line management cares most about. And most HR functions are constantly reorganizing to achieve greater effectiveness, with the role of the HR generalist now enhanced to one of business partner. A major challenge facing each HR business partner is how to coordinate and connect the business needs with the HR products and services, many of which will be provided on a regional or nationwide basis. The HR organization as a whole needs the ability to act on a global basis

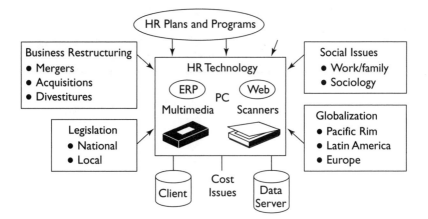

Figure 1-2 The HR technology strategy must consider future changes.

and still have the capability and sensitivity to respond to local issues and needs.

In order to address many of the above concerns, any change in HR structure and service delivery should, of course, utilize advanced work design principles such as service centers, and employ technology to save money and deliver high-quality service. But the key objective is to bring the HR staff closer to their customers, and to ensure alignment of HR programs with the business requirements.

Web-Based Employee Self-Service

A Win-Win Proposition for Organizations and Employees

Robert Zampetti and Lynn Adamson*

THE CONCEPT OF HR self-service has become the goal of most Web-enabled HR systems. HR self-service involves the use of interactive technology by employees and managers to obtain information, conduct transactions, and essentially "shortcut" processes that previously required multiple steps, paperwork, the involvement of HR staffers, and all the delays such processes are heir to. Using secure corporate intranets that limit users' ability to change or initiate data—while providing unprecedented self-

*Lynn Adamson and Robert Zampetti are consultants in the Towers Perrin San Francisco office where they specialize in the design and implementation of employee and manager self-service applications, and HR service centers. Robert also has a strong Health & Welfare benefits background and led the development of Towers Perrin's vendor management system.

San Francisco office address: 525 Market Street, Suite 2900, San Francisco, California 94105.

sufficiency, immediacy, and information access—HR self-service provides the "customers" for HR's products and services with the ideal delivery system to meet their changing, individually variable needs. And the benefits to the organization—from efficiencies realized when employees change their own HRIS data and "serve themselves," to more informed, effective decision making by managers—support a transformation of HR's role within the organization. The role will change from an essentially administrative function to a strategic business partnering function where HR personnel contribute to bottom-line results.

Sound revolutionary? It is. Consider what HR departments have been doing for the last 20 or 30 years as their "products and services" have proliferated and expanded: They have been keeping up with change by adding new data, programs, and specialized software. The idea that this functionally rich, data-intensive, continually changing part of business operations can now divest itself of almost purely administrative work is in itself a radical proposition.

Web-based systems take the revolution a quantum leap further, however, by "adding value" to the organization's bottom line, in effect increasing what employees get in the employment exchange and improving managers' effectiveness as managers. When designed and implemented around the concept of self-service, such systems not only move work out of the HR department to employees and managers, but they also improve the quality of the entire process. Furthermore, self-service HR eliminates the nonvalue-adding administrative tasks that can be handled automatically by the system.

As discussed in the sections that follow, these value-adding benefits of Web-based self-service are somewhat different for employees than for their managers. In all cases, however, the time, cost, and quality improvements enabled by a self-service HR website add value to the organization. Not only are HR department and HRIS administrative expenses sharply reduced, but employees and managers using a well-designed self-service system spend "less time doing more" for themselves, their colleagues, and the business.

Most Commonly Planned or Implemented
HR Self-Service Applications

For Employees	For Managers
HR communications	Personnel changes
Benefits services	Salary actions
Personnel data updates	Job requisitions
Job postings	

Employee Self-Service: Benefits beyond Efficiency

Web-enabled employee self-service, in which all employees have access via a Web browser to information residing on HR systems, means employees can update the personal information they "own" as individuals. Using self-service, employees can also apply for or enroll in the full range of HR products and services available to them as HR "customers." HR self-service provides benefits to the organization and its employees that go well beyond the elimination of both HR paperwork and much of the purely administrative HR work. Moreover, as the costs go down, and the delivery mechanisms of providing Internet and intranet access to all employees continue to evolve from kiosks, IVRs, and desktop computers to Web TVs, handheld devices, and phone attachments, employees' use of Web-based HR systems is likely to become as commonplace and widespread as the morning coffee break, and much more productive for the company.

Already, some of the world's largest employers (including Ford, Delta, and Cisco) have invested huge amounts to ensure total access among employees, by providing them with hardware, software, and Internet access in their homes as well as at work. In these organizations, the benefits of Web-based employee self-service have been recognized as outweighing even today's PC costs—costs that will diminish drastically with the coming of new Web technologies that provide Internet access without a personal computer.

The benefits of employee self-service include, but are not limited to, the elimination of middlemen between the employee and the HRIS. Studies have shown that as much as 50 percent of HR staff time has been spent on making changes to personal data, forwarding forms, and other "administrivia" that can be eliminated by self-service. This is reason enough for the popularity of the concept; but other critical goals of effective HR management are also addressed by employee self-service; including

> **Personal data quality,** vastly improved when employees themselves, the "best source" of personal information, enter and validate this data

> **Employee empowerment,** including new levels of control over their own careers, development opportunities, conditions of employment, options in the rewards system, and other HR programs and services, and access to unprecedented amounts of information that supports informed choices

> **Process improvements** that not only eliminate work in the HR function, but speed delivery of HR products and services to customers, whose wants and needs can be highly time-dependent and varied (for example, the need for medical leave time, cash from a savings plan, or the answer to a question about sexual harassment policies)

> **HR integration at the employee level,** where in some respects it matters most, through the one-system integration of related HR programs such as training, development, succession planning, staffing, and other competency-based programs with common definitions and unified strategic business goals

Personal Data

As the most volatile and individually variable subject matter ever put in a computerized database, information on people, including their attributes has always presented challenges in the data collection area of HRIS design and use. The fundamental principle of collecting data from the "best source"—the person or function in the best position to know and the first to know of any change to the data—requires that vast amounts of HRIS information come directly from employees. This information not only includes addresses, new dependents, outside educational achievements, and other factual data, but in the modern database also includes preferences and other changes of mind caused by as many factors as there are people in the organization. A decision to move from a technical career track to a management track, a switch in medical coverage, a decision to put retirement savings in a different mutual fund, a new willingness to relocate, and other changes affecting personal data "owned" by the employee can be caused by anything from a whim to a spouse's new job. Employee self-service on a Web-based HRIS permits any employee with access to the system to instantly change all data that is personal to the employee, and change it again at another time, ensuring the quality of this information in a Web-based HRIS.

Empowerment

Employee or "customer" self-service for HR products and services via the Web transforms the word *empowerment* from a slogan to a reality, permitting employees to literally help themselves from the full panoply of offerings available on the HR website. Business rules and policies differ among organizations, but some of the offerings employees/customers can at least ask for via self-service are shown in Figure 2-1.

Conducting self-service on the Web generally begins with accessing an HR home page (see example in Figure 2-2).

Many examples of employee self-service exist, since organizations' plans and programs differ, and their delivery philosophy also varies. Self-service programs vary depending on the scope of an organization's HR program and how many of the employee-oriented programs would be pushed to an "employee empowerment" model made possible by an interactive, integrated HR website. For example, when selecting from and enrolling in a flexible benefits plan, an employee might be able to access large amounts of on-line information on the following:

- Costs and benefits of a range of different health care providers, down to details such as the names, bios, and locations of physicians in different HMOs

Select from Flexible Benefits Plan Menu
Schedule Vacation Time
Apply for New Position
Change Address, Dependents, Other "Life Event" Data
Enroll in Training or Development Activity
Model Impact of Change in Savings Plan
Revise Retirement Planning Portfolio
Participate in Computer-Based Training
Respond to Employee Opinion Survey
Assess Colleagues in 360-Degree Assessment
Order Discounted Products/Services
Get Answers to Questions on
 −All HR products/services available
 −The employee's own coverage, eligibility, etc.
 −The company

Figure 2-1 Examples of employee self-service on the Web.

- Descriptions of dozens of different savings and retirement planning programs, with the ability to probe deeper into historical data such as the performance of different mutual funds
- Models of the cost impact of employee-built benefit plans that include scores of different variables, from paid time off to long-term disability insurance

Figure 2-2 From this HR home page, an employee would click on the word *employee*, and be directed to the employee home page. See example in Figure 2-3.

Figure 2-3 As the application is role-based, the other options would not be permitted.

By using the virtually limitless capacity of the Internet and navigational tools that guide users, such systems empower informed choices rather than mere choices.

Similarly, the example noting that the employee can "Apply for a New Position" on the interactive website only hints at the level of empowerment this can provide to employees, especially in an integrated system that incorporates process improvements in staffing procedures.

Process Improvements

As a revolutionary platform for eliminating paperwork, linking previously separate databases and processing, and enabling instant concurrent information flows and transactions, the HR website can deliver products and services to employee customers at unprecedented levels of timeliness and cost-effectiveness. Not only is there no waiting for information, forms, or an HR staffer's response, but an integrated HR website permits the employee to complete a full continuum of related tasks that lead to an objective at the employee's own pace.

For example, an employee with a new baby at home can use

the site to update a dozen or more systems and HR programs all at once and with essentially the same entry. Payroll, benefits, the family leave program, a new insurance beneficiary, a college tuition fund, even a birth announcement in the company newsletter—all use essentially the same information, eliminating previously isolated data collection issues.

Even more important than process improvements that make HR processes more efficient simply by eliminating tasks, the integration of HR functions on an HR website used by employees provides the modus operandi for the full integration of HR services and products at the *employee level*, where it may matter most.

HR Integration

Self-service systems used by individual employees can provide a single, unified view of naturally related HR programs, policies, and processes. The value of this functional and technical integration at the employee level cannot be overestimated, because it not only saves time for both the company and the employee, but it helps to achieve strategic and operational business goals that often require employee participation.

For example, no amount of "top-down" direction will ensure that employees are developing to their full potential, with full commitment to gaining or improving the competencies needed by the company. Individual motivation to learn and grow varies not only among employees, but also for the same employee at different times.

An integrated, browser-based staffing and development system provides the means to make all employees capable of taking control of their own development, whenever and as aggressively as they wish. On the same site and in the same session, the employee can do the following:

- Learn about current and future job openings in the company, the job's skill or competency requirements, other qualifications, location, reporting relationships, and pay ranges.
- If the open position seems to match the employee's wants and qualifications, the employee can submit an on-line

resume resident in the system, which has been prepared and updated by the employee.

- If the employee doesn't understand or is missing a position requirement, it is possible to click on the item for further explanation and for training or development options. The employee can then do the following:
  - ♦ Enroll in a training/development activity
  - ♦ Transfer to another position
  - ♦ Take an on-line test or schedule a test
  - ♦ Apply for tuition aid for education
  - ♦ Apply for any of a range of mentoring, project team assignments, or other developmental activities linked to the staffing requirement in the integrated system

Obviously, the employee using a Web-based system to make a choice about benefits, development, vacation time, or other matters within his or her discretion does not need to make a decision in "real time," in the same session on the intranet. As much or as little information as needed can be printed or sent to the employee's home, or e-mail can be used to set up a counseling session with a "live" expert. But the mere fact that employees *can* "serve themselves" to HR products and services at any time they wish, from anyplace in the world with a Web browser, changes forever the delivery paradigm for serving HR's customers.

Web-Based Manager Self-Service

Adding Value to the Work

*Lynn Adamson and Robert Zampetti**

F OR THE FIRST TIME in the history of HR technology, the question now is not *how* to provide line managers, department heads, and other non-HR managers with the tools to manage their own people, but *what* it is that managers should be doing in the HR arena. Today, virtually every manager in an organization can access intranet websites capable of providing both the information and transactional or process capabilities to manage the full range of HR programs. But how much autonomy, and which HR activities, should be in the hands of these managers?

In organizations where managers have always had primary HR responsibilities such as hiring people, organizing the work, man-

*Lynn Adamson and Robert Zampetti are consultants in the Towers Perrin San Francisco office where they specialize in the design and implementation of employee and manager self-service applications and HR service centers. Robert also has a strong Health & Welfare benefits background and led the development of Towers Perrin's vendor management system.

San Francisco office address: 525 Market Street, Suite 2900, San Francisco, California 94105.

aging performance, and setting the terms of the employment exchange, the process improvements enabled by Web-based technology offer clear and immediate advantages. For example,

- No more waiting for forms, policy guidelines, HR department approvals, or an employee's job history
- Self-sufficiency in changing an employee's status or terms of employment
- Instant, enterprisewide delivery of requests for knowledge, information, people, or best practice—followed by on-line, instant response through knowledgeable systems, and electronic delivery or subject matter expertise resident in the system or prepared by HR staff experts
- The overall improvement of the manager's leadership competencies, which includes the ability to think and act strategically, to act promptly and decisively in response to new and changing business needs, and to use analytical capabilities supported by the system's "what if" modeling features

In other organizations, where some of the functional applications described below have not been within the manager's job description in the past, a cultural change within the organization may be the first order of business. In general, managers' responsibilities for people management in the modern organization include participation in all or most of the HR aspects shown in Figure 3-1. In certain of these areas, as discussed next, the benefits of Web-enabled expansion of managers' responsibilities are such that whatever cultural resistance to change may exist is only temporary. Self-service not only helps managers do more HR work faster and better, it also leaves them more time for their "real" jobs.

Value-Adding Applications

Certain HR functions are best performed by managers themselves in a self-service system. These are the functions that offer the best opportunities for both reducing administrative costs and significantly improving the effectiveness of all HR functions, while

Selected HR Aspects of a Manager's Job
- Defining roles and job duties
- Interviewing and selecting staff
- Performance management
  - Development and training
  - Compensation recommendations
    - Employee/labor relations
  - Controlling time and attendance

Commonly Planned or Implemented Manager Self-Service Applications

Personnel changes	Salary actions	Recruiting
Supervisor changes	Salary changes	Requisitions
Job grade	Bonuses	Offer letters
Dept. changes	Stock management	Skills matching
Transfers		
Location changes		
Terminations		

SOURCE: Towers Perrin
HR Service Center Survey 2000

Figure 3-1 Selected HR aspects of a manager's job.

achieving the business goals of the organization. HR functions best performed by managers typically have these characteristics:

- Either they involve information that the manager is in the best position to know due to proximity to the work and workers, events, or conditions that require immediate attention, or they involve the manager's skills and experience, the very essence of that person as a manager.
- The process involved is one that requires initial input from the manager, such as a job requisition or a performance appraisal, which in the past would begin a back-and-forth exchange with the HR department and its subject matter experts.
- They are part of the manager's responsibilities, for example, turnover control, budgeting, production goals, quality, train-

ing, and workforce productivity—functions within the manager's domain but guided and informed by enterprisewide business goals, policies, and standard procedures.

Because Web-based technology permits the integration of a multiplicity of different functional applications at the same user interface on the corporate HR intranet, a browser-based workstation used by individual managers can carry a broad range of HR management functions with multiple levels of decision-making capabilities and control options. The system can be designed to reflect the organizational structure and the work itself, so that managers have access on a need-to-know basis, for as many or as few employees as required, and transactions are performed based on managers' defined responsibilities. The overall objectives of manager self-service then include the following:

- Improve the delivery of HR services
- Eliminate process steps, approvals, and forms
- Speed up and streamline workflow
- Reduce administrative costs
- Improve manager access to vital data
- Provide more time and enable strategic HR

Using the Web-based manager self-service approach, a manager would access the manager home page and then be presented with a screen that might look like Figure 3-2.

With this capability available, manager self-service should not be used as a way to shift as much HR work to managers as possible. Further, one size doesn't fit all companies or even all applications in the same company. Still, the advantages of Web-based manager self-service for many HR functions can still be recognized as nothing short of revolutionary. Self-service systems already operational or under development at leading employers include Web-based systems for **compensation, performance management, staffing and recruitment, time and attendance,** and **training and development.**

Compensation. The distribution of compensation information to managers and the provision of interactive self-service that per-

Figure 3-2 Web shot of typical manager's home page.

mits managers to be involved in pay decisions represent two apparently conflicting goals of HR technology. In the first instance, the company wants consistency—everybody complying with corporate policy, working within budget guidelines, following the same procedures, and aligning with business strategy. Getting managers fully involved in pay decisions, however, calls for the provision of technology that supports individual autonomy among managers, permits discretionary decisions, and encourages managers to use what they know about their own people and their operational goals to match pay to individual contributions. Interactive Web-based systems with unprecedented capacity for delivery information and calculating power can resolve this paradox.

Depending on organizational structure and the overall compensation plan design, managers' responsibilities for establishing pay levels can range from divisional or local salary planning and the determination of incentive pay, to recommendations for individual salary changes. In a growing number of organizations, however, the trend is to have managers do more in compensation decisions because they are in the best position to know employees' contributions. Furthermore, managerial responsibilities also include the need to motivate workers with tools, including the rewards system.

The benefits to managers of Web-based self-service in compensation functions fall generally into two areas: First, information and process access is administratively efficient—fast and easy, compared with paper-dependent processes, which only the most compensation-oriented managers were glad to use. In salary planning, for example, paperwork or disks would come down from the corporate compensation group with departmental or local budgets and guidelines, and would be returned the same way, with managers' recommendations. On the Web, by contrast, the manager simply logs on the salary planning module, views all corporate information and individual records, makes recommendations, and clicks on an approval or recommendation for change.

Second, the capacity of Web-based systems provides unprecedented modeling capabilities that permit managers to fully utilize their discretionary powers as self-sufficient participants in compensation decisions. The salary changes that the manager wants to make are informed not only by standard salary increase guides, but also by their overall impact on the manager's salary budget, as well as other spreadsheet factors that can include local market pricing. Modeling, or "what if" capabilities, encourages the manager to consider the big picture in salary changes or recommendations and support the company's goal of making all managers more strategic.

The on-line delivery of calculating power that makes modeling fast and easy for managers is especially valuable when manager self-service includes the planning and apportionment of incentive pay. Especially in organizations where numerous measures and criteria determine incentive pay, where different formulas apply in different functions, and where both teams and individuals are eligible, incentive pay can be an administrative nightmare and a function most managers would rather leave to the compensation professionals at headquarters.

Yet, managers with direct responsibilities for the day-to-day and annual performance and productivity of their people are almost always in the best position to know whether and how much incentive pay is warranted. Further, the people working for the manager who has discretionary power to award incentive pay *know* that the manager has this power.

In a Web-based incentive compensation application, managers

can be given an overall "pie" to be apportioned, corporate goals and measures to use as guidelines, the opportunity to suggest new measures or formulas, and the ability to automatically calculate any number of different scenarios.

Performance management.   Manager self-service systems that provide interactive access to a range of related HR data and processes on the corporate intranet provide the enabling technology that puts performance management where it should be, in the hands of supervisors and managers. This keeps them in direct contact with the people they manage, holds them responsible for the operational objectives of work, and uses managerial understanding of the strategic business goals to help define performance. In the area of performance management, all managers are human resource managers, with responsibilities for motivating, guiding, and continually improving the work of those they manage, along lines consistent with business objectives and goals.

Web-based manager workstations that supply links to previously separate databases and functions provide the technology needed by managers to use all the tools available to improve individual and team performance. In modern organizations, increasingly populated by "knowledge workers" and employees who bring a diversity of wants, needs, and values to the workplace, these tools can and should include much more than incentive compensation linked to financial measurements or other objective data. In performance management, for example, the manager can also do the following:

- Learn about the successful structuring of project teams or other team organizations that represent "best practice" configurations for achieving certain goals
- Learn how to conduct a performance appraisal, learn the specific criteria and measurements of given positions or roles, see examples or models of effective appraisals, and enter performance appraisal results when completed
- Access training and development systems to identify the courses or other developmental activities available that will address an individual's needs

- Learn how to conduct and evaluate potential assessment
- Identify future opportunities for advancement of individuals in the organization, and help the employee shape a career plan
- See historical data on individual employees, including past appraisals, developmental activities, and resume data

Perhaps most importantly, information available to the manager on the corporate intranet provides the manager with an understanding of what "performance" involves, and what it is that the manager should be motivating and improving. Especially in modern organizations with competency-based definitions of work and workers, this is not a "given" to be taken for granted. Companies have different ways of identifying and communicating competencies, ways that are often a mix of credentials, experience, and observable behaviors, and managers serve as the implementers of competency-based HR.

Other performance management information and processes available to managers on an integrated, Web-based system can include noncash awards and recognition programs, information about the employee assistance program (EAP), policies and processes for giving paid and unpaid leave time, and the full range of HR programs and policies affected by employment law—from sexual harassment investigations to termination procedures. This self-service access to information and processes allows managers to act when they should act, making informed decisions without waiting for HR staffers to return a call or schedule a meeting.

Recruitment and staffing. In organizations where the demands of work require increasingly competent employees, where business requirements for people are volatile, and where human capital has become the last competitive advantage, the manager's role in timely, effective staffing and recruitment has assumed new levels of importance to the company. Line managers and others "in the trenches" of the organization, from sales managers and production foremen to department heads and office managers, are in the best position to know the competencies they require, when they need them, what they can afford, and what the business impact will be if they do not get the human resources they need. Using a Web-based self-service system that includes staffing and recruitment functions, these managers now have unprecedented abilities to both contribute their managerial knowledge to this process and get what they need to put the right people in the right jobs when needed.

Both staffing and outside recruitment functions in a Web-based HRIS use an on-line job requisition created by the manager. The requisition typically includes a job description with skills and competency requirements that are uniformly defined throughout the organization, as well as other qualifications, such as degrees, licenses, and relevant experience. If the manager is creating a new role or position to be filled, this fact is noted on the requisition, initiating an on-line approval process.

With a fully integrated, Web-based system, the creation of the job requisition can be much more than just checking boxes or clicking on data fields in the position description fields of the HRIS. For example, the manager can also do the following:

- Access the performance appraisal system to understand the "levels of proficiency" identified for each competency, which may be a crucial factor in a given job.
- View statistics from staffing and recruitment systems to see what's available in the applicant marketplace and perhaps adjust the requisition's requirements accordingly.
- Check training and development data for data showing people "in the pipeline."

Depending on corporate policies, the same job requisition can be instantly forwarded to others via a job posting system as needed such as to staffing professionals at headquarters, recruiters, managers of other business entities, and employees throughout the organization. Either through the service center or directly, employees can "submit themselves" on-line, using resumes that include the uniformly defined competencies.

The rules of the game for manager's participation in staffing and recruitment can vary enormously, but most business policies, union rules, and regulatory requirements can be built into the system and verified by subject matter experts in HR.

Further, all of the "administrivia" associated with staffing and recruitment in the past, such as offers, wage or salary calculations, interview scheduling, background checks, and so on, move out of the manager's domain and are handled electronically, outsourced, or managed by HR specialists using the system. The net result, in a well-designed system, is that the manager is doing more to get the right people in the right jobs at the right time, but spending less of his or her time doing it.

Time and attendance. In an economy where the average employer spends over 50 percent of its operating budget on employee costs, and where alternate work schedules, disability costs, and the use of contingent workers are escalating, oversight and management of employee's time on the job has become an increasingly critical management responsibility. Today's time and attendance (T&A) systems, linked to the manager's HR website, can do more than forward the right information on overtime or docked pay to payroll. They can also provide the data and self-service capabilities the manager needs to do the following:

- Analyze current and historical relationships between productivity and such factors as the makeup of teams, worker competencies, location, or scheduling.
- Review "best practice" models from other parts of the organization, showing optimal project team structures, schedules, costs, and other employment practices.
- Match time off for sickness and disability analysis.
- Compare performance and productivity of individuals and teams over time.
- Analyze the costs of alternate work hour schedules and the use of contingent workers against measures of performance and productivity.

Using an on-line T&A system, the manager has adequate time to perform these analytical and strategic activities, because such routine matters as vacation scheduling, time reporting, and the forwarding of data to payroll are both paperless and instantaneous.

Training and development. Managers' responsibilities for training and development have escalated in modern organizations, where the skills and competencies of workers require continual expansion and improvement just to maintain current levels of performance and productivity, much less to achieve world-class competitive advantage. Managers are already in the best position to know the developmental needs of their people and the competency requirements of the work, and a Web-based system provides both the information they need to help their people address these needs and the tools for tracking and managing development.

For all developmental activities, from basic skills training to succession planning, individual managers using such a system have on-line, interactive access to data and processes that include the following:

- Information linking competencies to specific developmental activities, such as an internal training course for JAVA programming or a local school's course in accounting
- Information about employees' developmental needs, including past appraisals and assessments, as well as information on what employees are now doing and plan to do to improve themselves
- Human resource planning information, including management succession planning, showing overall strategic HRD goals, anticipated surpluses and shortages, developmental opportunities in other business units or localities, and other corporatewide perspectives on HR development
- Other communications and transactional capabilities, ranging from identifying and assigning mentors, to the scheduling of performance reviews, to requests for extra tuition aid funds

In the past, the manager's role in motivating, informing, and helping employees select and pursue the development they need has been constrained by time and space. The basic format of this role was formerly an in-person performance review or career counseling session, and if computers were used, everyone had to be looking at the same screens at the same time. Now, an employee at a kiosk, desktop, or home connection to the Web-based system

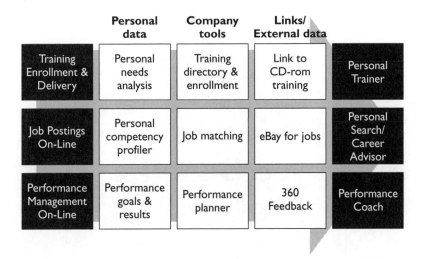

	Personal data	Company tools	Links/External data	
Training Enrollment & Delivery	Personal needs analysis	Training directory & enrollment	Link to CD-rom training	Personal Trainer
Job Postings On-Line	Personal competency profiler	Job matching	eBay for jobs	Personal Search/ Career Advisor
Performance Management On-Line	Performance goals & results	Performance planner	360 Feedback	Performance Coach

Figure 3-3 Employees as HR customers.

can work with a manager concurrently, or whenever each has time, from locations throughout the wired world. See Figures 3-3 and 3-4. And the amount of information that technology can bring to the table in a browser-based system is unprecedented, permitting genuinely informed choices among managers and employees jointly engaged in individual growth.

	Workforce data	Manager tools	Links/External data	
Workforce Data	Staffing size and mix	Strategic staffing system—link to posting	Link to finance	Workforce Planner
Job and Competency Data	Work tasks, profiles, competencies	Performance/ Development system	Link to benchmark data	Work Designer
Performance Management On-Line	Performance metrics/ productivity	Performance management & rewards	Link to customer & stakeholder data	Performance Coach

Figure 3-4 Managers as HR customers.

CHAPTER

Web-Delivered Employee Benefits
From "Why?" to "Wow!"

Joanne Dietch*

AFTER YEARS OF frustrating experiences trying to create a holistic appreciation and understanding of benefits, human resource professionals are looking favorably at putting benefit information on the Web. Experience has shown, however, that few early-generation benefit websites are performing up to expectations. Employees are still calling with benefit questions, still confused about their choices, still unable to grasp a broader rewards perspective, still failing to take responsibility for their current benefit choices and their future security, still feeling entitled and still separating benefits from the business—its realities, competitiveness, and survival. In other words, little has changed.

HR initially reacted with a sense of resignation—perhaps the

*Joanne Dietch, a Principal at Towers Perrin, is an award-winning communicator living in Los Angeles. She is the Director of the firm's Global Innovation and Learning Lab, dedicated to developing leading-edge web solutions.

Los Angeles office address: 1925 Century Park East, Suite 1500, Los Angeles, California 90067.

Web was not going to be the magic bullet that could pierce long-standing employee ennui with regard to benefits. Others in HR aren't quite buying that, basing their gut reactions on

- Personal experiences on the Web
- Continuing pressures to find administrative efficiencies, connect with multiple constituencies, and drive desired change

These e-benefit pioneers aren't ready or willing to give up on the promise of a benefit website that works.

In fact, benefit websites that undergo rigorous and honest scrutiny regarding their effectiveness have taken a major step toward performing up to—or beyond—expectations. HR professionals should assess whether a benefit website is providing

- The immediacy of MSNBC.com
- The fact-finding convenience of popular search engines
- The "you-can't-blow-this" transactional ease of Amazon.com
- The interactivity of selecting an e-ticket on Travelocity.com
- The collaboration of an AOL chat room

If the website is not reaching this level of quality, what will it take to get the website there? What is the vision for future generations of the benefit website?

Without the self-service level (for information as well as transactions) that is found on the Web, it is difficult to build the critical audience mass considered necessary to make the site a good investment. Users may visit the website once, but they are not likely to return if they get lost, bored, or disappointed. The benefit website experience must prove to be more than the same old, same old in a new venue. After all, the same old, same old isn't any more enticing on-line than it is on paper, the phone, or videotape. Moving on-line the mistakes made in benefit print and video media doesn't eliminate any problems. Page upon page of information becomes scrolling screen after scrolling screen of information. Nobody cares to read either. Quickly needed facts, buried deep in benefit booklets or lengthy summary plan descriptions, become even more difficult to retrieve in an unstructured, unintuitive Web environment.

It is refreshing that organizations are scrutinizing their benefit websites to see if the sites are working or not. The same level of attention was rarely accorded predecessor benefit communication (i.e., booklets, worksheets, employee meetings, annual statements, interactive voice response systems, five-part forms, benefit video and slide shows, and planning software). The fact that organizations just shoveled out benefit information for years without demanding (or even envisioning) the best possible performance is one of the reasons why much of what was done in the past failed to work very well.

Organizations experiencing success in the more traditional media are the ones that step back and acknowledge that things can be done better. Organizations that look to advertising and other mass media techniques to sell their benefits, get people's attention, and brand their benefits have been far more successful than those that churn out information without an appreciation of human interests or attention spans. The same holds true with organizations that use a benefit website.

When you consider all the activity and effort that a benefit website can replace, the need for it to be well planned and well maintained is apparent. The new e-platform must not mirror the haphazard and disconnected view of benefits represented by the current hodgepodge of communication and administrative channels. If it does, the e-platform fails to achieve its purpose.

All the things that make the Web powerful—its ability to lead users to the information that is of immediate interest to them, interact with users, provide a personalized view of information, and effect efficient transactions—have to be the benefit website's goal on an ongoing basis. Breakthrough benefit websites are replicating what is best on the Web. These benefit websites are reaching end users, creating interest, generating knowledge, and effecting behavioral change as it relates to benefits.

Creating a Benefit Website That Works

The transition from a "why?" to a "wow!" benefit website requires attention to the following issues:

- Planning
- Metrics
- Information presentation
- Knowledge creation
- Content management
- Access issues and technology
- Empowerment and its implications

This list is just the beginning. Who knows what e-benefit applications will emerge in six months or a year? Who knows how these advances will impact the communication and administration of benefit plans? This changing environment is both exciting and challenging. Nobody really knows what is coming next or what it will mean to benefits—and nobody knows how it will affect the employee/employer relationship itself.

Planning

Sitting down to begin the benefit website planning process is much like planning for a dinner party. Picture a bare table surrounded by empty chairs. Then ask

- *Who is going to be invited to the party?*   Answer: Your guests, the website's audience. Know who they are. Understand their individual needs and preferences. Find out if there are access issues involved in getting them to the table.
- *How will the table be set?*   Answer: With matching china, glasses, and flatware, appropriate for the meal that is planned. For the website, a comprehensive long-term site map coordinates the delivery of information in an ordered, attractive format. Once seven blue glasses have been placed on the table, adding a red one for the eighth guest just doesn't fit. That's why planning ahead keeps things coordinated in terms of navigation, content, functionality, and design.
- *What will be served?*   Answer: Anything from soup or nuts to a light meal. Whatever the content, the information is best served in highly digestible pieces that make the user look forward to the next course.

- *What will get people to the table?* Answer: A website promotional strategy and migration plan, bolstered by the value and relevance of the information on the website. A good website sells itself. The opposite is also true: All the hoopla in the world does not make a poorly conceived benefit website work for the organization or its end users.
- *How is success measured?* Answer: Guests come back and ask for more. They also tell their friends about the experience they've had and generate interest in others to make a visit to the website.

Planning starts with visualizing what the benefit website can be in three years' time.

- How can the website create benefit process improvements for the organization and the end user?
- From a systems or access perspective, what has to be in place to accomplish the vision and by when?
- What relevant external links to vendors, subscription websites, or administrators can enhance the website?
- How should the website be phased in, keeping in mind the interest of those using the site, the constraints on the resources for planning and implementing the site, the benefit communication and administrative needs confronting the organization, and other corporate initiatives that can impact the delivery of the website?

Answer these questions in the beginning of the planning process. Good planning can prevent the need to redo or rethink parts of the site at a later date. Creating a road map for site development takes time and patience but can provide a big payoff in the long term.

Metrics

Developing metrics for the entire website and for specific applications is an important part of the planning process. Website metrics connect planning and performance. As the website matures, the attainment of these metrics can demonstrate a return on investment to management. This ensures continued financial support for the benefit website as well as for the development of new applications and added functionality.

Carefully craft the metrics. Think through what the website can achieve and set "STAR" metrics that are

- Stated clearly
- Tied to a timeframe or event
- Aligned with the organization's objectives
- Realistic in that they can be reasonably accomplished

Metrics help verify that the website is benefiting both its users and the organization. They quantify how the site is generating savings in money and time (e.g., less printing and mailing, HR freed for more strategic activities) or creating desired changes in your users' behavior (e.g., lower call volume, better decisions on benefit choices, greater knowledge of benefit choices).

Consider an organization that is using a benefit website to introduce a new stock ownership plan to all employees. One metric for the site could be: *We want 50 percent of our users to enroll in the new stock option plan within the first year.* This metric is stated clearly, tied to a timeframe, aligned with the organization's objective of broadening employee ownership, and realistic based on the organization's knowledge of employees and its belief in the website as an agent for change.

The application used to introduce the stock ownership plan should be developed to maximize the likelihood of meeting the established metric. This introduces a new level of thinking and planning in benefit communication. The site developers should consider the following questions:

- How will the website focus employees' attention on the new program?
- How will the information be structured so that the user can quickly assess the value of the program?
- What tools can be developed to let the user interact with the "value" of purchasing the stock?

- How will the website make it easy for a user to purchase stock?
- How will the website monitor the purchase of stock?
- When will HR assess the level of enrollees and visits to the site?
- How will HR find out what is impeding progress toward goals?
- Should HR modify the delivery of the information on the website to better reach the stated metric for success? For example, should HR publish mass-customized messages to employees about the program, or should HR target messages to those individuals who haven't acted on program opportunities or ever entered the site?

With website applications, benefit communication becomes far more strategic than in the past. Good benefit communication has a specific goal. It has order. And it can be changed or enhanced at any time to help the website achieve its STAR metrics.

Information Presentation

What's important is no longer what *you* want to tell users (which in the world of benefits has usually meant everything); it's thinking from the users' perspective and not making assumptions about what users want, when they want it, how they want it, or whether they want it at all. This shift means significant changes for those responsible for communicating and administering benefit information.

Forty-eight-page benefit booklets about an enrollment haven't worked yet. Why should the same level of content, presented in the same format, work any better on-line? In fact, it doesn't. It may even work less effectively.

What *does* work is rethinking the information's presentation and categorizing it for placement on the website. This exercise leads to a pyramid of information that starts at the top and works down in the following fashion:

- **What the user *really* needs to know**—the essentials for users to do what they must do on a timely basis

- **What the user should know**—facts for users who want more than headlines and directives
- **What would be nice for the user to know**—background and perspectives for those who are interested
- **What doesn't matter for most users to know**—the grueling details for those who need the fine print about a benefit provision

Assessing content in this manner takes time and courage. HR has to fight the forces within that yell, "Tell 'em everything!" Telling them everything means telling them nothing at all. HR has to think through what needs to be communicated and segment that information into layered content.

HR has to let go of the old paradigms of benefit communication. Think about what works on the Web. Think about why employees passed over the benefit booklet for *USA Today*. Why they doze through employee meetings on major benefit changes but watch hours of reruns on television each week. Think about what lessons HR can learn from the media, from the Web, and from advertising, and apply those lessons to benefit communication. Then figure out how the benefit website can be a valued experience for the end user.

Users don't casually go on-line to read about benefits. When they think about benefits, it's because they have a benefit need. The object is to get them to the website and to the information they want—fast.

Using a life events focus at the top of the information pyramid wards off innumerable phone calls and directs users to the specific events that are affecting their lives and their benefits. More and more the life events focus (e.g., marriage, birth, death) is being expanded to a work event purview (e.g., change in active employment status, layoff). Information about the work/life event—what is required of the employee, what benefits are affected, what the employee should be thinking about, and links to relevant informational sites—is a first stop for many end users. Sophisticated sites link users to on-line forms used to effect changes in coverage, provide evidence of insurability, and add or delete dependents. Ideally, there is no need to surf for an answer on a plan-by-plan basis, no need to make a call, and no need to wait for the mail. Informational and transactional self-service directly meets the needs and concerns of the end user.

Always remember that the Web is a conduit to information. It is not the place to explain things in a linear fashion. Navigation should be clear. Required clicks should be limited. Minimize user effort and you maximize the effectiveness and utilization of the website.

Knowledge Creation

A benefit website can go beyond providing the user with information. It can also create knowledge. Interacting with facts to see how they are personally relevant helps cement them in the user's mind. The value of saving isn't hard to understand. For instance, the need for a thirty-year-old to save is difficult to get across. But an easy-to-use projection tool can paint an instant picture that thousands of words fail to adequately convey.

From users' perspectives, a good benefit website provides accurate information expediently and enables them to interact with that information. Consider what a benefit website can do for users interested in investing in Fund A of the 401(k) plan. Through the website, users can

- See the makeup of Fund A in relation to other funds
- Determine if his/her level of risk adversity and time horizon make this a potentially beneficial fund
- Track the fund's performance
- Compare that performance to those of other funds over various time periods
- Model "what if" scenarios that include investing in Fund A
- Direct contributions into the fund

The amount of time and the number of persons involved in making any of these actions possible for the user would be far greater without the benefit website. In fact, it would be difficult for a user to manage such a range of tasks without the flexibility and interactivity that the benefit website provides.

Until recently there hasn't been a way to effectively engage users in

- Determining their levels of risk adversity or their time horizons
- Showing them the impact of future inflation on their savings and retirement income
- Helping them visualize the difference between an equity and a bond

Yet organizations are increasingly expecting employees to take a greater role in saving aggressively and investing judiciously, particularly as do-it-yourself 401(k) plans replace we'll-do-it-for-you defined-benefit pension plans. The Web isn't a "nice-to-have" in this regard. It's a "needed-to-have."

A good benefit website allows employees to access sensitive information on their own. It serves as a reliable, confidential source of information about health conditions, work/life concerns, and retirement and termination plans. For those hesitant to ask or call for information, the website helps avoid unnecessary confusion, lack of appropriate health care, or misinformation from unofficial sources.

Creating benefit knowledge influences benefit plan performance. In the area of health care, exposing plan participants to information about disease or demand management can be empowering, giving them the ability and confidence to make better choices and spend health care dollars wisely. A change in the behavior of enough health plan participants—use of more generic drugs and appropriate preventive screenings, fewer unnecessary office visits, or more self-care—can impact an organization's bottom line in the long run.

New benefits such as concierge services are finding a home on a growing number of benefit websites. Concierge websites provide access to on-line products and services, often with negotiated employee discounts. Employees pressed for time can preserve weekend and evening hours by buying gifts, necessities, and vacation services on-line. Concierge sites also link to vital information and services such as e-health sites, health plan vendors, child/elder care referral services, estate planners, and business travel resources. The sites bring to life a work/life benefit plan geared to *everyone* in the organization.

Content Management

Content databases take longer to develop than html pages but take less time and effort to maintain. Content management tools tied to databases allow HR to make changes without the intervention of information technology personnel. There is less time spent waiting in the queue to update the benefit website and there is less ongoing cost.

Even in a database environment, someone must always be responsible for the validity of the content on each screen. Ensuring content validity can be an awesome task. Users assume that the benefit website is more current and accurate than other media. It should be. Meeting this standard, however, requires keeping the database up-to-date. What is new should go up as soon as possible. What is old should come down. Content owners are expected to keep their screens up-to-date, and scheduled reviews are a must.

Content should stay fresh for accuracy's sake as well as to give users a reason to check back with the site. A benefit home page that never changes doesn't give the user much reason to check what's new.

Site administrators should create ongoing interest through refreshed content, news based on personal preferences, calendars, pulse surveys with immediate results, bulletin boards, tools, and personal data. Get the user to visit the site even when benefits are not the reason for the visit. A variety of attractors build critical audience mass, create return visitors, and engender familiarity. Then, when benefit information is needed, the user knows where to go.

Content ownership also drives the need to develop guidelines for who can publish on-line benefits information within the organization. It is not unusual for homegrown websites to spring up within an organization. To maintain the value of the benefits communicated on the corporate website, the site must be established as *the* source of benefit information. Divisional or location websites cannot be allowed to communicate benefit facts or interpretations thereof. If they are, consistency of information is likely to be lost.

In a global organization or one in which more than one set of benefits exists, there are additional challenges to ensuring accuracy and control across the board. Technology can help direct users to the right screens; however, technology is not ultimately responsible for the information itself. The task of managing information on multiple sets of benefits is one more item to add to HR's "to do" list.

Access Issues and Technology

How are users connecting to the benefit website? Not all organizations have 100 percent access, whether through desktops, laptops, or kiosks, but the situation is changing. It has to. Once an organization goes on-line and is committed to investing in a benefit website that works, it becomes too expensive and unwieldy to maintain separate print communication for a dwindling number of nonconnected plan participants.

Likewise, setting up access to a benefit website only through the organization's intranet cuts off a host of key audiences that can be reached only through the Web and misses an opportunity to provide important services to these audiences:

- **Recruits**—highlighting benefits as an important part of total compensation
- **New hires**—enrolling these users and getting their data into the system *before* their arrival on the job
- **Active employees**—offering benefit information, modeling, and transactions 24/7
- **Spouses and significant others**—giving family members access to plan information and recognizing their role in benefit utilization, particularly health care
- **COBRAs and LTDs**—providing enrollment and other pertinent information and notices
- **Retirees**—responding to the retired population's many benefit-related inquiries

Access issues require creative solutions. Organizations are setting up PC stations in such places as airport ready rooms, factory break rooms, lumberjack huts, and movie soundstages. Other organizations are subsidizing employees' PC purchases.

Once employees are wired, access issues should be taken into account in designing the site. This means

- Offering multiple views of the site on the home page (e.g., graphics- or text-only for those connecting remotely)
- Assessing how quickly screens pull up and designing graphics that enhance rather than detract from the user's experience
- Programming the site so that it works in Internet Explorer, Netscape, and AOL
- Setting a browser release standard that allows for the interactivity and functionality needed to meet success metrics
- Understanding the technological underpinnings of the website

Technology can deliver the right screens to the right people. It can create screens based on users' preferences. It can provide users screens with personalized information and allow them to make plan transactions. It can remind users to do what they need to do within given time frames. It can provide database-driven content and search features that allow users to enter keywords and be whisked to the appropriate plan provisions.

Every box on a site map represents not only the content or functionality of a screen but also the technology needed to deliver it. The infrastructure of an organization's systems and the ability to make interfaces, go through firewalls, link to vendors, and provide necessary levels of security are essential to the delivery of a highly effective benefit website.

Empowerment and Its Implications

Empowerment is as close as an employee's desktop, kitchen table, or airplane seat—it is wherever an employee armed with a PC might be. Organizations are quickly realizing that empowerment as a concept is far less intimidating than empowerment as a reality. In fact, empowering people through the Web poses a host of unexplored concerns and challenges for management.

The greatest backlash against the e-benefit revolution is coming from management and not from end users. Out-of-the-box progress is often impeded by in-the-box thinking. Would you be surprised to hear HR mulling over questions such as the following?

> How can we keep people focusing on their jobs if they can surf the benefit site or, worse, connect to the Internet? Should we monitor utilization—where people are going, how long they're on-line? By monitoring, do we diminish the value of the site to its end users? What happens if we monitor the site and find that someone is abusing it? If we give everyone a PC or help them purchase one for home, do we want them to use it for purposes other than connecting with the company? Should we care if they do?

With the e-benefit revolution, the comfort zone for HR is being invaded. Empowered employees mean redefined work for HR. That's perceived as a plus. Empowerment also means less control for HR. That's perceived as a minus. Empowerment requires putting trust in employees to do what's right and perhaps giving them more credit than is ordinarily accorded them.

It's wise to keep things in perspective as e-benefit services move forward.

- Are employees likely to spend hours surfing a benefit website? Benefits may be your life, but is it theirs?
- If employees spend hours on the Internet (accessed through the benefit website), isn't that a performance management issue rather than an e-benefit issue?
- Hasn't HR wanted employees to pay attention to their benefits? Now that this might actually happen, why is HR so upset?

The same employees who abuse the Web are the ones who have been abusing the system all along. Availability of the benefit website—and even of the Internet—is unlikely to turn good employees into slackers. Why diminish the possibilities for the majority because of concerns about the minority?

The Benefit Website Links to the Business

A good benefit website creates a framework of understanding. The framework should be structured in an easily understood manner. For example: "This is the corporate website on benefits. The benefits are provided for these reasons by and for the business. The benefits relate to one another in this way. The benefits are funded in this way, and here is how this funding relates to the business and the decisions it must make."

The link between business and benefits has not been effectively and consistently delivered in the past. Without connecting business and benefits, changes in benefits are immediately perceived to take away employee advantages without just cause or reason. An evolving benefit plan becomes an exercise in waiting for the other shoe to drop. Consider how the website can encourage users to stop thinking, "What is the organization going to do to us next?" Consider how users can be encouraged to ask, "What is the organization doing to provide reasonable benefit choices along with reasonable cost sharing so that it can stay competitive?"

Benefit websites can make the vital connection between business and benefits by tying the presentation of benefit information to the business on a consistent and ongoing basis. It is not uncommon to see stock prices and corporate news on the benefit home page or to find a positioning statement aligning the business with its benefits. Such a statement says, "Yes, employees, there is a link between our ability to succeed in the marketplace and our ability to share our profits with our employees." It's not magic. It's economics.

Benefit websites are also effectively taking economic messages a step further by providing employees with ways to preserve and expand their capital. They are teaching users how to make decisions about the right levels of health, disability, and life insurance, how to utilize health care more wisely and cost-effectively, and how to save and invest more proactively. In doing so, benefit websites support organizations' strategies to develop more self-responsible and knowledgeable workforces. In effect, the website is a major step in helping employees visualize the "deal" that they have with their organization.

To reap these advantages, careful orchestration and attention to detail are a must. Strive for a website that is

- Constructed in carefully planned stages, avoiding the need to redo screens or reconfigure the structure of the site
- Built on a strong base of information sharing and knowledge management, adding features and functionality to create ongoing interest in the site
- Structured to serve as a cohesive source of information about all the plans offered to an organization's various constituencies
- Designed to minimize administrative costs and hassles while maximizing communication
- Tied to the business and the impact of its success on employee rewards

Also, know who the audiences are (and will be), where the development is going, what interfaces are needed to tie to vendors and administrators, and what factors define success. Make certain that the website has active owners. As a final measure, constantly assess the website's performance to see if it is driving desired behavioral change, getting users to visit the site, enroll on time, invest more wisely, focus on health and well-being, and appreciate the alignment between the business and their benefits.

Web-Based Recruiting and Staffing

David Cohen, Ph.D.*

T HE WORLD WIDE WEB can vastly expand an organization's ability to search for talent and present itself as an employer. Thanks to the Web, we can put more company and job information in the hands of job seekers than ever before. Moreover, job seekers can now, for the first time, act on this information instantly. Your organization's website can create that valuable first impression and set the tone and the ability of an organization to attract and even retain the right people.

As recently as 1997 only about 11 percent of U.S. employers were using the Web for outside recruiting, a figure that has reached 80 percent today and is expected to approach 100 percent in the next few years. By 2003, an estimated 124,000 companies will be

---

*David Cohen is a Principal in the Los Angeles office of Towers Perrin, specializes in helping organizations find and place the right people, including the development of strategies for Web-Based recruiting sites.

Los Angeles office address: 1925 Century Park East, Suite 1500, Los Angeles, California 90067.

recruiting on-line. Their use of the Web runs from a simple description to commercial job boards to the development of an interactive recruitment website with extensive information about the company and an opportunity for an applicant to self-assess against its competency requirements. Most on-line recruiting is supplemented by traditional methods, especially for hard-to-fill positions at the top of an organization or low-skill entry-level work, where much of the market is not on-line.

The applicant's perspective drives the information provided. For the growing number of people in the world who are on-line, however—several million new users a week—Web-based recruiting does much more than just save time or the cost of a newspaper or postage. To a degree not feasible in the past, passive job seekers (those who are happy with their jobs but open to other opportunities) who would be interested only in certain kinds of companies, working conditions, or other selling points in the recruitment message can easily and safely browse the on-line advertisements. In an economy where some companies are experiencing 70 percent turnover rates among their technical professionals, where unemployment is at a 30-year low, these passive recipients of on-line recruitment information represent a major target to fulfill staffing goals.

Your organization's employment website can uniformly describe what you need and can collect and process applications from thousands of applicants at once, including many who are passively seeking jobs by just surfing the Web. Corporate intranets permit employees to take charge of their careers by permitting on-line applications for transfers, promotions, or development activities related to their individual careers.

Staffing used to mean placing people in open positions, when they become open. As labor markets changed, it evolved to attracting the right people. Today it is attracting and retaining the right people using

- An understanding of a company's business strategies
- Knowledge of a company's employee competencies
- Information on current and future labor markets
- Insights into the people it wants to attract

It takes more than just filling a position when it becomes available to ensure that a company has the right number and mix of people

- With the right competencies
- In the right places
- For the right duration
- At the right cost
- Engaged and committed to doing the right things to create a great organization

Staffing has six components, each of which is designed to address a critical staffing issue. Although the Web does not impact the components equally, they are sequentially linked, so the Web does impact them all. The six components, and the questions each organization needs to answer to move on to the next, are

1. *Workforce analysis and planning.* What talent do we need?
2. *Sourcing and attraction.* Who has the right talent, where are they, and how do we get them interested in joining our organization?
3. *Assessment and selection.* How do we identify, evaluate, and select the right people?
4. *Hiring.* How do we make the offer that attracts the candidate and closes the deal?
5. *Deployment.* How do we move people into, around, and out of the organization?
6. *Retention.* How do we engage the talent for the right duration of time, keeping that talent invested and engaged in the organization?

See Figure 5-1.

Staffing links a company's vision, mission, and business strategy to the process. The organization defines what it must be capable of doing to win in the marketplace against the competition and the competencies employees need to be successful.

Workforce planning and analysis has been less impacted by the Web, per se, than it has by the shear volume of information

Figure 5-1 The six components of staffing.

that the computer enables you to analyze. Simply put, the Web enables you to put a lot more information into the mix to help you make decisions.

Sourcing and Attraction

Let us look at what the Web has done to revolutionize the process of sourcing and attraction, the area most directly impacted by its technology.

Companies need to address the issues surrounding the creation, maintenance, and use of a continuously flowing pipeline of external and internal candidates for open and future positions. They need to determine the best sources for the people they need and how best to access them. The solutions are invariably company-specific, but the Internet has revolutionized this phase of the staffing process.

Web-based technology has, in effect, created a global employment office for companies seeking applicants from outside the organization, and from internal staffing. Intranets permit electronic posting of open positions and automate a full range of employment processes for both internal and external candidates. Websites and specific electronic advertisements can now generate tens of thousands of resumes for a single position! This is where cool technology leads the way and content follows. People are accustomed to be entertained by websites, so they want company websites to do the same thing. Features become important, like the ability to go live to the office of the company to see virtually what it's like to work there! And people want to be enticed and engaged. Self-assessment tools (do I pass?), mini-quizzes (can I pass?), and calculators (can they afford me?) keep people stuck to the site.

But there is so much more to it. Companies ought to think "sticky." They should ask themselves, What is going to keep people "stuck" to the site, and better still, get them to recommend the site to others? Every visitor to a site becomes an ambassador for, or a saboteur of, that site. The answer is, interesting information "done up in pictures," because as good as the words might be, they are visually boring. And in this high-tech world there is one thing that hasn't changed: A picture is still worth more than the 1000 words that should not, and fortunately will not, fit on the screen!

Leading-edge websites contain a lot of information arrayed in a very clear manner. They have

- Press releases from corporate public relations
- Articles on hot topics by noted scholars (internal and external) with information that current and potential employees want to know
- Reference centers with links to important topics

- Regularly scheduled chat rooms with key company executives, politicians, scholars, or well-known company spokespeople
- Recruiting events and other employment-related information
- Tips on how to interview, what to wear, and what to do
- Chats with new employees and live views of offices
- Bios and points of view of key executives
- Who the competition is and how we compare with them
- Community investments
- Information about what the future holds
- What positions are available and how to apply

Make it easy for applicants to access information concerning what positions are available anywhere in the system and whether or not they have the qualities desired by the organization. One major soft drink manufacturer that wants to be known as innovative, fun, and exciting has a great-looking site (movement, pictures, cool information about celebrity spokespeople, hip language geared to its target population), but where to apply is lost in tiny print. If you want to find out about their corporate culture, you get lost in a sea of words communicating, "We don't have an innovative, fun, exciting culture; we have a boring, stodgy, old-fashioned culture." The potential applicant says: "Bingo, I'm outta there, and the likelihood of me coming back is not very good. And now I become the saboteur you fear, not the ambassador you encourage."

Finally, make it oh-so-easy for the applicant to apply to, or contact, the organization with questions, even if frequently asked questions (FAQs) are answered on your site. And always infuse the site with channels for two-way communication, so that applicant and organization have all the information each needs to make the right choice.

Still, application volume and on-site applicant retention alone do not necessarily translate into applicant quality. The mere automation of job postings, resume collection, and other employment processes—no matter how much faster and more efficient—

does little to ensure the continuous flow of qualified applicants necessary for dynamic organizations. If all the Internet is doing is getting the company more people to assess, and managers still complain about the quality or the uneven flow of applicants, the net result of on-line recruiting is that it creates more problems than it solves. In order to be effective, Web-based approaches must give the company and the individual all the necessary information about the other.

This begins the all-important courting phase, and it is still the only opportunity to make a first impression! And the first impression had better be good. If you say you're an innovative high-tech company, your website had better scream innovation and high-tech, and if nothing is moving on the page, it is not as high-tech as it needs to scream. It must have functionality to impress, allowing applicants to go wherever they feel the need. If you want people who are comfortable in a fast-paced environment, they must be able to move quickly and easily around the website without getting lost. And if you want them to apply, all roads must lead to what is available and to an easy on-line application allowing a candidate to cut-and-paste a resume, respond to a few important questions, click, and apply. And since everyone is getting used to the speed of the Internet, the organization's response had best be quick and provide a rationale for whatever decision has been made. Remember, if you want to scream high-tech, then a 24-hour response lag becomes a very long time to wait.

One of the advantages of the Web is that applicants can screen themselves in a confidential and safe environment. Let us say that working in self-empowered teams is crucial to the success of the organization. A simple and short questionnaire will enable the applicant to determine if he or she has the qualities desirable to the organization. No one should be precluded from applying for a job based on a short screening questionnaire, but it will allow applicants some pause to consider if they have what the organization is looking for beyond the technical skills. Most organizations select on the basis of some set of competencies. Defining competencies as well as company values on the site goes a long way toward helping people decide whether or not to apply.

But attracting candidates on the Web requires much more than information about the company or related knowledge. The website needs to catalog everything a job seeker wants to know. The site needs to take the job seeker to all the community and other regional information that might be of interest. But watch out—make sure the site brings them back and does not leave them at a real estate site that is more intriguing than the one they left. Keep your visitors coming back.

Web-based technology provides the delivery mechanism for enterprisewide—yet "customer-specific and user-friendly"—recruitment and staffing. While traditional sourcing methods (job fairs, print ads, local employment offices, and personal references, most of which can be announced on-site) will play a role for the foreseeable future, the benefits of using an integrated, globally accessible, information-intensive, Web-based approach are already making them merely supplementary sources of input documents for the Web-based system.

Companies today want to know how to become an employer of choice, both for the most qualified job seekers in the external marketplace and for career-minded internal candidates. This used to require the development of a credible, cogent "message" as to why the company is a good place to work. In today's increasingly electronic world, the medium of the Internet—with its vast capacity for text, graphics, interaction, and multimedia presentations depicting the company in its best light—is a substantial part of the message, especially for applicants who want to work for organizations at the leading edge of e-business and e-commerce. So don't *tell* them, "This is a great place to work," show them! Make *them* tell *others*. One site has a live video-cam in its office to show how cool it is to work there. Other sites introduce you to new employees and even provide an opportunity to "meet" them through chats or through other direct methods of communication. The site should allow applicants to *see* what a great place of employment you have, not simply inform them of such.

To be credible and cogent, however, the messages must include more than rosy projections of the company's future and its idyllic working environment. It must present specific information about the working environment, educational and developmental opportunities, competencies being sought by the organization, when and why they are needed, how success will be measured, how employees are rewarded for performance, and whatever collateral information the company wishes to list.

The media that should be employed for attracting people depend on what market research tells the company about its marketplace for people in demand, and what those people see and read. The company's website is becoming the foundational medium—it can be referred to in print or broadcast ads and can be updated easily, as needs change. It can provide links to job boards, schools, and other websites to further extend its reach. The Web's huge capacity permits the inclusion of information on employee benefits, training and developmental programs, financial performance, strategic business plans, and corporate leadership, as well as links to other sites describing and showing what it's like to live in locations where the company has vacant positions.

Internal Sourcing

Web-based external recruitment systems can be readily integrated with intranet staffing systems, conceptually and technically, bringing both strategic cohesion to these traditionally separate sourcing functions and huge efficiencies through the elimination of redundant, duplicative work. The internal sourcing process typically follows business rules of its own, especially in organizations where broader opportunities play a key role in retention or collective bargaining agreements impose union rules or restrictions on staffing. However, these two naturally related functions are driven by the same business imperatives and share numerous procedures and information requirements best handled by a single, integrated system.

For example, a job requisition can go simultaneously to external and internal markets for applicants. Even if business policies dictate that current employees get "the first shot" at answering the job advertisement, the same job requisition can later go to recruiters, the service center, and eventually the world at large.

There are other business-based rules and policies differentiating external and internal sourcing in most companies: the employee/applicant may need a certain amount of time in a current position, a current manager's approval, or a certain level of performance, or background checks may be required for external applicants. The hiring manager needs qualified candidates and the information to make the right choice promptly and without additional paperwork or back-and-forth policy memoranda. The qualifications, when built into the system, allow only those people who have met the internal or external requirements to meet the hiring manager.

Assessment and Selection

Assessment and selection rely on competency requirements identified by the organization. For the assessment process, Web-based systems have helped with automating scores of previously time-consuming processes, from scheduling of tests and individual psychological assessment(s) to analysis of past performance evaluations. Some organizations already use the Web to conduct on-line skills testing or critical competency validations for external applicants. Assessment of an applicant's "fit" with the organization can also be determined. An internal staffing system can include not only the employee's self-written resume, but performance appraisals, salary history, and e-mail addresses of current or former managers and colleagues. And at any given point in time, the individual can find out exactly where he or she is in the process. Technology may never replace face-to-face meetings between hiring managers and job applicants, but videoconferencing has made such "virtual" meetings more acceptable.

In a well-designed strategic staffing approach, all *applicants* are considered, all *candidates* are assessed, but only some are selected to be *employees*.

The end result of this component is the creation and filling of a qualified candidate pool—people who have the competencies and attributes needed to fill a specific position and contribute to business goals. Depending on the depth and breadth of competency requirements and other factors, including the terms of the employment exchange, the pool of qualified candidates may be large or small. In Web-based staffing and recruitment, given the reach and capacity of the Web, the pool is likely to be immeasurably larger than ever before, despite more rigorous competency requirements for many types of work.

Selecting the right people from these invariably larger pools of candidates for increasingly demanding jobs requires the identification and implementation of the process to match individual competencies with business needs and organizational culture. What do you do when two or more candidates for the same position seem to have identical competencies? Taking the one with lower salary requirements may not be the best approach.

The selection process differs between organizations and within organizations by type of work, but increasingly it is viewed as optimal when a broad range of managers and HR staffers can participate. On-line systems permit the process to include the advice and recommendations from many individuals without slowing down the process, even when only one makes the final selection decision.

Hiring

The hiring process should not be taken for granted as a mere formality in the staffing framework, especially in an era when the best and brightest candidates with in-demand competencies are likely to have multiple job offers. Web-based technology automating and integrating numerous hiring activities (and providing technology that eliminates others) can effectively streamline hiring processes by making them faster, more efficient, and less costly. Timeliness is critical, to both the candidate and the company, and unnecessary delays while paper is being routed or data are being entered into numerous systems are clearly targets for improvement of the process. Good candidates are lost by unnecessary delays.

Web-based staffing supports the involvement of all participants in the hiring process at the same time, following the same guidelines, business policies, and other "rules of the game," including compliance with employment law. It includes not only the hiring manager, but also HR partners, the compensation function, staffing and requirement specialists, benefits managers, outsourcing providers, payroll, and of course the candidate being hired, and his or her family or informal support network. It provides, in the truest sense, virtual participation by all key people with a stake in the matter. And the support network, family in particular, might have a different set of interests in the information when advising someone to accept or reject a job. Younger applicants might want to know more about the people with whom they will be working, but their parents might want to know more about the benefits being offered a son or daughter. Different needs, same decision.

The huge capacity of Web-based systems permits on-line communications or system-generated material in a job offer that is personalized, unambiguous, and as comprehensive as may be useful. The package might include not only traditional information on pay and benefits, but also information about the community. The flip side, however, is that access to other websites allows comparison shopping.

From a human resources administrative perspective, Web-based technology permits workflow improvements that streamline or eliminate many time-consuming, and often redundant, activities in hiring, from the scheduling of tests and interviews to background checks and EEO reporting. In some well-designed systems, applicant data instantly and painlessly become employee data in the company's HRI system on the day the candidate is hired. That preliminary filling out of forms will not take a day anymore.

Deployment

The effective placement of people in and throughout the organization is in many ways the central issue of a successful staffing process, Web-based or not. Intranets permit rapid responses to changing business needs by providing managers and employees with the information they need to make staffing decisions.

People are less likely to get lost in the "electronic system." Management can also identify employees who do not fit into the company's long-range plans and help them make meaningful transitions out of the organization, thereby keeping people employable by helping them build their competencies and find employment with a better match for those competencies.

Web-based reporting tools can be linked to data warehouses with virtually unlimited capacity for carrying historical, current, and "future" data related to HR deployment, including performance information. This means that the kinds of information which managers at all levels can receive and analyze are limited only by managers' and others' imagination.

Retention

On-line recruiting and competency-based staffing may have increased the flow of applicants and qualified employees, but the quest for talent remains an urgent priority, as the flow of people leaving the organization may be increasing as well.

Web-based HR systems—featuring controlled and secured employee access to appropriate need-to-know information and self-service capabilities that empower employees in areas such as staffing, training and development, flexible benefits selections, and other decisions affecting their lives at work and at home—play an increasingly important role in retention programs. Employees' control over appropriate areas of their careers is a must in a Web-based environment. The value of Web access as an employee benefit is not lost on companies like the U.S. automaker that is offering free at-home hardware, software, and Internet access to its 350,000 employees throughout the world. Companies gain a direct pipeline into their employees' homes, so that dad and the kids can see why mom finds it to be a good place to work.

One cautionary note warrants repetition. The time it took to make hiring decisions in the past is tantamount to the time it took for the first ships to cross the Atlantic Ocean. We're at the speed of cyberspace. The speed for making decisions has to catch up. When people are offered a job on the spot, no one should be taken by surprise.

Internet-Age Performance Management

Lessons from High-Performing Organizations

*Elaine M. Evans**

EVERY YEAR, Human Resources departments discuss improving their performance management systems, and at any given time, at least one-third of business organizations in this country are reviewing or redesigning their programs. Yet despite this effort and attention, effective performance management remains the Holy Grail of HR management, a process easier to visualize and talk about than to actually implement.

However, there is light at the end of this particular tunnel. For the first time, a body of knowledge based on what high-performing organizations have done, and the systems for implementing these principles, aided by the emergence of the Web, has

*Elaine M. Evans is a Principal in the San Francisco office of Towers Perrin. She specializes in helping HR and line managers build great organizations through programs that provide the right people, doing the right things.

San Francisco office address: 525 Market Street, Suite 2900, San Francisco, California 94105.

emerged. This body of knowledge has been driven by the need to get answers to critical questions such as these:

How can we identify our best performers in order to focus our retention programs?

How can we improve performance and productivity across the company?

How can we ensure that our managers develop employees so that we can build needed marketplace capabilities?

In addition, all organizations are seeking to have their performance management systems operate in a more holistic manner, integrating a number of processes and components to achieve the intended program objectives, which include:

Creating lines of sight between individual actions and company strategies and goals

Establishing standards of performance

Establishing and communicating performance measures

Providing midcourse correction and ongoing feedback

Identifying developmental opportunities for employees

Providing information for career management, high-potential identification, and succession-planning systems

Establishing the foundation for merit increases, variable-pay plan payouts, and stock allocation

Serving as a reference point for reductions in workforce, disciplinary actions, and the like

These are serious and critical objectives, which relate to the very heart of whether or not the organization will be nimble and resilient enough to succeed in today's business environment.

The sections that follow will focus on the underlying principles and systems design features that have been found to be effective in achieving these objectives, and they will explore:

1. Performance management systems and approaches used in high-performing organizations
2. Fundamental design considerations that transform "average" or "good" systems into "great" systems
3. The role of technology in supporting performance management systems

Performance Management Systems and Approaches Used in High-Performing Organizations

After many years of debate and discussion, we have finally reached a consensus regarding the fundamentals of performance management. Certain factors are now consistently used in most countries where performance management is practiced:

A plan-do-check model, which involves preplanning or discussion of work to be done, with periodic assessments against actual performance.

A supervisor-initiated process, with either one focal point review or a review conducted on the anniversary date of the employee.

Employee input into the process, often through an informal memo or streamlined edition of the employee performance appraisal summary form used by managers, supervisors, and team leaders.

A summary performance rating, which is used as input into a variety of HR systems and programs. The summary rating is used, along with other variables, to determine merit increases and, in some cases, other rewards, such as stock allocation or variable pay.

An annual cycle, with quarterly feedback encouraged, but not monitored or required to be submitted formally in writing.

Recent Trends

These design elements have been constant for the last decade or so. In the last five years, several trends have begun to take hold,

One Example of Impact of Net Technology: 360-Degree Assessment Administration

Among the performance management processes that have been vastly improved by automation on the Web—even "made feasible" in some large organizations—is 360-degree or multisource assessment. Especially in organizations where numerous competencies and ratings are used, multisource assessment can quickly become an "administrative nightmare" without effective automation. Consider the data collection, reporting, and tracking requirements introduced when a company moves to multisource assessment:

- Instead of one supervisor conducting assessments, multisource assessment by definition requires the participation of peers, subordinates, the employee, and sometimes customers as well, and the raters may comprise a different group for differently situated individuals or teams.
- For organizations using assessment enterprisewide to improve competencies at all levels, the number of people being assessed usually multiplies.
- Hundreds of different competencies may need to be defined in the system, with a dozen or more applicable to individuals or positions, and each competency has its own ratings scale that should include six to nine levels.

The 360-degree assessment process requires the timely, informed participation of hundreds if not thousands of employees "new to the process," people who have never done this before, and their understanding of and commitment to the process requires continual communications, support, and "prompting."

The ubiquity, interactivity, contact capacity, and on-line timeliness of the Web, together with a "portal" approach to assessment system design that presents each user with just what he or she needs to participate effectively in the process, provide a path out of this administrative quagmire. For example, 360-degree assessment conducted on a corporate intranet—or delivered by a Web-based outsourcing firm to all participants with browsers—can provide:

- Consistent information simultaneously delivered to all participants, according to their "roles" in the process, including competency definitions (with examples, e.g., of what it means to "think and act strategically")

(Continued)

- Rosters of colleagues whom the assessor will evaluate, with applicable competencies and a schedule with deadlines for assessments
- Self-assessment information, including both the competencies associated with an individual's position or role and his or her "importance" to the organization—a key component of a performance management system that is at least partly designed to ensure that people know "what is expected" of them in their jobs and what matters most to the organization
- The on-line automation of a range of administrative activities, from data collection to feedback reports, including the ability to automatically "remind" participants of deadlines and the importance of meeting them

For organizations seeking to take full advantage of the benefits of a robust, widely used, competency-rich multisource assessment system, the Web provides the enabling technology needed to "demystify" the process for new users and effectively manage their ongoing participation.

and are now being viewed less as best practices to aspire to and more as basic fundamentals that should be built into any system. They include:

Measurement of "how" things are done, as well as "why." Typically this is accomplished through the use of competencies, either organization-wide or job-specific.

Informal or loosely structured compilation of input from peers, subordinates, and customers prior to finalizing the performance evaluation summary. In some leading organizations input is gathered through a formal, structured process.

Increased focus on ensuring that organizational performance objectives relate to overall business objectives.

Increased participation from line managers in designing the final system, through either participating in design team meetings or participating in focus groups.

Increased attention from senior managers as they lose patience with the pace of change within their organizations, and view performance management as one of the methods that they can use to help reorient employees and managers toward swifter action.

These trends clearly indicated that sophisticated companies have accepted the reality that performance management systems in and of themselves are not the answer to increasing organizational performance and employee commitment. Rather, the key to success lies in using the performance management system as the springboard to creating and sustaining an organizational climate and culture that values and sustains performance. Thus, just as an acrobat can spring into the air twice as high by using the leverage of another individual, organizational success can skyrocket if the performance management system is used as leverage—rather than the outcome itself.

The slow yet steady fruition of viewing performance management as organizational leverage, rather than as a program, is

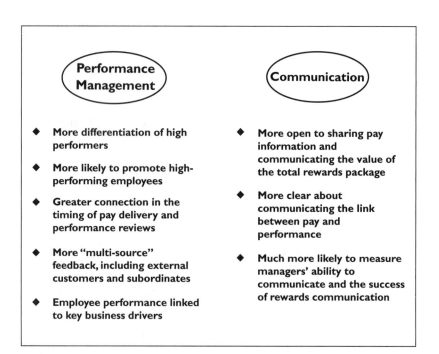

Figure 6-1 What are high-performing companies doing differently than other companies?

evident when we look at the practices of high-performing companies. In 1999 Towers Perrin conducted the Compensation Effectiveness Survey (CES) to assess the effectiveness of various compensation and compensation-related systems. A portion of the study explored performance management systems.

A total of 771 North American companies participated. A subset was defined as high-performing companies, those with total shareholder return in the top quartile, based on a three-year comparison. These crème-de-la-crème organizations report clear differences in the design and execution of the performance management systems in a number of areas (see Figure 6-1). This study shows that careful attention to the individual components of performance management systems can and does make a difference in organizational performance. Further, the high-performing companies are three times as likely to view their performance management systems as effective.

Fundamental Design Considerations That Transform Average or Good Systems into Great Systems

Our research indicates that there are seven factors that must be considered in creating a performance management system. The difference in moving from good to great lies in the details of design and implementation. The seven factors are shown in Figure 6-2.

Taken independently, they provide an audit tool for measuring the competitiveness of your existing system against competitors for customers or labor. Taken collectively, they indicate whether you are creating a performance-driven culture or simply another performance management system. Further, taken collectively these seven factors let you know whether your performance management system is providing organizational leverage or simply taking up time and resources.

To set the stage, it is important to view the historical progression of performance management and where leading-edge companies, such as those described in the prior section, are directing their attention. Figure 6-3 contrasts the history and evolution of performance management systems over the last few decades and points to a clear future.

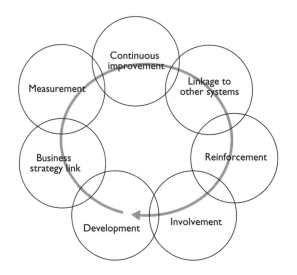

Figure 6-2 Seven factors to consider in a performance.

Many companies report that their current practices still reflect stage 1, performance appraisal, despite their efforts to transform themselves into high-performing companies. In such cases it is important to consider the culture of the organization that must be changed along with the introduction of the new performance management system. If it is not, the new performance management

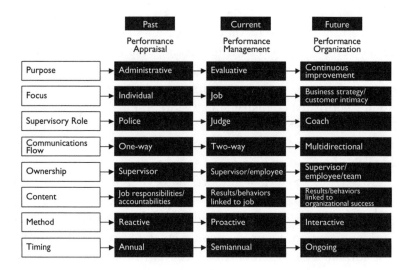

	Past	Current	Future
	Performance Appraisal	Performance Management	Performance Organization
Purpose	Administrative	Evaluative	Continuous improvement
Focus	Individual	Job	Business strategy/ customer intimacy
Supervisory Role	Police	Judge	Coach
Communications Flow	One-way	Two-way	Multidirectional
Ownership	Supervisor	Supervisor/employee	Supervisor/ employee/team
Content	Job responsibilities/ accountabilities	Results/behaviors linked to job	Results/behaviors linked to organizational success
Method	Reactive	Proactive	Interactive
Timing	Annual	Semiannual	Ongoing

Figure 6-3 Issue: The current system emphasizes performance appraisal for individuals—which does not improve overall organization performance.

system will be rolled out with full fanfare, accompanied by glossy communications brochures that are quickly filed in the lower right-hand drawer of the manager's desk, not to see the light of day until the desk is cleaned out. Only through addressing the culture and the system simultaneously will the organization achieve synergy and leverage.

The seven factors are apparently simple, yet are quite complex to design and execute. In our experience, the companies that have made the most progress in this area look at each of the seven independently, in order to assess the "state of the union," and collectively, to see if the overall system is creating leverage.

Business Strategy Link

CEOs and senior managers are clear in their expectations. A well-run performance management system will be linked to, and increase performance against, company objectives. Accomplishing this requires adherence to several fundamental design principles:

> Goals utilized in the performance planning process are linked closely to business strategy or objectives.

> Goals are cascaded from the top, and the aggregate of all individual goals provides real resources and muscle toward the accomplishment of company strategies.

> The goal-setting processes for the organization and the individual are linked.

Several simple analyses will help to determine if your organization is effectively linking performance management and business strategy. Ask yourself the following questions:

> Does the annual operating cycle include references to the performance-planning process?

> Have managers received training on goal cascading?

> Do they understand how to take a macro-level goal and translate it into employee requirements?

> Select a random sample of completed performance evaluations for the prior year, selecting employees from various

types of positions as well as from all levels within the organization's hierarchy. How many specifically refer to company goals for the prior year?

When is the last time senior managers discussed overall business objectives in light of the performance management system?

If you are like many companies, the answers will surprise you. Even the high-performing companies that responded to the CES indicate that they have a ways to go in increasing the linkage between business strategy and individual performance.

Measurement

Historically, managers have struggled with applying measures to performance management. "How do I know what measures to set for different individuals or for different positions?" they ask. "Is it appropriate to set the same measures for everyone?" "How do I reflect the fact that two people can accomplish the same task, and one achieves results in a way that offends others while the other builds bridges and relationships?" In addition, since the annual planning process and its related communication often lag behind the performance year for various reasons, managers often struggle with how to set measures in an environment where final goals for the corporation or business unit are not yet clear.

These issues have led to the three relatively new practices that have brought substantial rigor to the often-subjective process of setting performance expectations:

Aligning measures across all performance improvement programs. Often, in our efforts to avoid "double-dipping" of rewards, we end up under-rewarding some measures of success, or omitting them altogether. A thoughtful review of all performance measures, companywide, contrasted with existing systems often yields surprising omissions.

Measuring not only "what" is done (i.e., results) but also "how" it is done (i.e., competencies). In some firms this has led to the creation of specific behavioral expectations for pivotal roles; other firms measure overall performance against company-wide expectations, or what Lucent Technology refers to as "Citizen Competencies," those skills that one must exhibit to be a citizen of Lucent.

Using a blend of measures, including a balanced scorecard, wherever possible to ensure that performance reflects operational, customer, and employee measures, as well as financial outcomes.

The migration to competencies has been fitful, as companies have explored a multitude of different methods to integrate competencies into the various Human Resources systems. Although the migration is by no means over, increasingly, organizations are willing to explore and implement programs that measure competencies as well as results. In the CES research, nearly 100 percent of the high-performing companies either are already measuring competencies or plan to introduce such a change within the next few years. Thus, the question is no longer "should we?" The new question is "*when* should we?"

The performance measurement issue is fueled by increased corporate attention to setting and measuring performance. Organizations such as the Conference Board have researched processes for measuring organizational performance. In addition, business schools such as the University of Michigan offer four-day programs on stakeholder value creation, roles, and functions of performance measurement systems, performance attributes, linking measures, and developing a measurement culture. This broad organizational focus on measurement fuels the desire for more accurate and comprehensive measures for performance appraisal and performance management.

Involvement

As stated earlier, performance management is still largely a supervisor-initiated process. However, many companies have adopted innovative methods to increase employee involvement in their performance management systems, such as involving employees in the goal-setting process by having them develop first drafts of goals and receive corresponding training. In addition, numerous companies have integrated customer input into the appraisal and evaluation process by using multisource feedback. In some cases, such processes are informal and casual; in others on-line questionnaires and databases are linked in.

At Towers Perrin, for example, the Change Management Practice utilizes a roundtable discussion to gather input. Since the firm is highly matrixed, with professional employees working in virtual teams around the world, merit and incentive recommendations are discussed by the regional and practice leaders for each region, who provide input from a wide variety of perspectives, both internal and external. Thus, the "halo" or "horns" effect that can occur with a single perspective is mitigated. This information is balanced against an annual competency assessment that considers the individuals' skill sets against the requirements for the Change Management line of business. Many high-tech and engineering companies use similar approaches.

In our experience, the use of multisource feedback within performance management systems has several clear advantages:

1. It is increasingly important to differentiate various levels of performance in order to allocate scarce resources. Multisource feedback allows a manager to better differentiate between an "A−" and a "B+" player.
2. Skewed summary distribution practices have led many companies to introduce control measures, such as forced ranking and forced distribution systems. Although such systems may be initially resisted and are controversial, they are an effective method to ensure that managers have the required hard discussions with others so that people who are only "B" performers are challenged to raise the level of their game—if only to keep up with an ever-increasing performance standard. Customer input and employee involvement help to keep the standards level for everyone.
3. Multisource feedback reflects the rhythm and realities of today's workplace. Limited interaction with supervisors, ongoing contact with teams, and rolling from one initiative to the next with limited downtime is the new reality. Intro-

ducing multisource feedback reflects that reality and improves the supervisor's ability to correctly identify performance deficiencies and opportunities.

That is not to say that multisource feedback has been accepted as a fundamental of all performance management systems. Many companies use multisource feedback for developmental purposes initially and then integrate the results into various other HR systems, such as performance management. In our opinion, use of multisource feedback as part of performance management assessment is more than a trend. We are seeing the beginning of a fundamental change, which should become more prominent over the next decade. We would not be surprised to see this area move from being considered state of the art to state of the union.

Development

In the zeal to measure and improve organizational performance, many organizations have paid scant attention to the developmental needs of their employees. However, doing so leaves the organization vulnerable to significant retention problems. Highly marketable employees have made it clear that they value training and development and are no longer as willing to forgo such opportunities. Thus, numerous companies are brushing off their training and development systems to ensure that they are increasing the likelihood of keeping the best talent.

Reinforcement

The link to pay is still elusive, but the jury has returned with its verdict regarding merit pay. Today's 3 or 4 percent merit budgets are not sufficient to truly differentiate performance levels, and there is no evidence that merit budgets will increase in the near future. On the contrary, if today's labor shortage has not led to an escalation of merit pools, it is unlikely that anything will. Rather, most companies have turned in a new direction and are focusing instead on looking for ways to integrate and maximize other incentives. Thus, it is not uncommon to find companies using the final performance management summary rating as a factor in determining a full range of rewards, including variable pay and stock options grants. The result is an aligned pay-for-performance system that reinforces the organization's goals and strategies.

Process. In recent years, we have seen a significant improvement in companies' abilities to reduce the administrative burden required to deliver an effective performance management system. Technology, especially Web-based solutions, now exists to help companies streamline many of the mundane tasks associated with performance management, including:

Performance rating and scoring

Cascading goals

Notifying employees and supervisors of the need for feedback sessions

Tracking actual performance against performance measures through the use of interlocking databases that cascade data from overall organizationally balanced scorecards

Monitoring competencies and skills to enhance developmental discussions

Monitoring completion of performance appraisals and related documentation

However, managing the process is much more than exploiting technology to track administrivia. Effective companies focus upon the ability of the overall organization to create a performance improvement culture and environment—not just an annual performance cycle. Thus, companies with systems that are considered "best in class" use some variety of the following strategies:

Measure the cost of maintaining the performance management system, and continue to investigate ways to reduce overall costs without reducing the quality of the overall effort.

Measure employee reaction to the program on an ongoing basis. For example, Motorola has adopted a short survey, released electronically to its employees every six months.

Along with other major issues, the survey inquires whether or not the employee has received feedback in the last six months. Since the CEO releases the survey, it gets attention.

Integrate the overall performance planning process into the overall operating cycle in order to increase the linkage as much as possible.

Provide regular reports on the health of the performance management system.

Educate new employees on the performance management system, and highlight it in new-hire materials. Cisco, the Internet networking company, highlights their performance management system on their intranet, setting performance expectations from day one.

Regularly review outcomes of the performance management system to measure effectiveness. This includes distribution reports, which show the distribution of ratings, cut by salary level, job band, function, key positions, and high-potential rating. Such reports illustrate clearly whether some parts of the organization are high performing while others are not. In a more complex example of using data to understand performance outcomes, Pizza Hut had analyzed performance ratings against unit profitability and turnover numbers. The resulting analysis identified the need to keep unit managers in their units for longer periods of time, in order to allow employees to develop on the job and to increase unit profitability.

The key to maintaining an effective process is to stop thinking of performance management as an ineffective but necessary burden, and instead start viewing it as a powerful motivator of behavior. Reports, systems, and tools make the difference, and Web-based delivery systems can reach all managers and employees on a 24 by 7 basis.

Link to other systems. In general, performance management systems that help to create and sustain a high-performing organization are well integrated into other strategies and programs.

Thus, we are seeing companies beginning to systematically create and maintain strong linkage points among various systems, including:

Rewards programs: Using performance management summary ratings as a direct link to recommendations for merit pay, variable incentives, and stock.

Managing "out" systems: Strengthening managing out or severance programs in recognition of the fact that organizations without a high percentage of strong performers cannot expect candidates for organizational renewal to be identified through performance management.

Leadership development and succession planning: Using 360-degree input gathered through performance management to identify leadership needs and to serve as a "circuit breaker" to stop candidates with inappropriate competencies from being promoted to key positions or roles.

Annual operating cycles: Many organizations are borrowing a tactic from GE and creating an annual operating cycle that includes specific time set aside to develop performance criteria and measures, followed by goal cascading and end-of-year measurement. This approach ensures that the performance management cycle is in accordance with the overall business.

Retention systems: Employers with acute retention problems are beginning to identify those employees who are always on the cusp of receiving significant rewards, but for some reason have not done so. Such employees are at special risk of being lured away by competitors. A simple analysis of employees with strong 360-degree rating and performance measures, yet who are consistently offered average reward levels, can identify employees who are at risk.

This broad integration allows organizations to take the pressure off of performance management systems and to recognize that a variety of interlocking programs makes great business sense. And why not? We are long past the days when we viewed base salary as the only appropriate method to motivate employees. An impressive array of compensation programs and techniques have been adopted, each of which is targeted at addressing a specific issue. The programs are designed to work in harmony, but not in lockstep.

These seven factors work in harmony to create a world-class system, and make all the difference between good performance management systems and great performance management systems.

Role of Technology in Supporting Performance Management

As cited previously, technology has played a major role in helping managers to move away from the administrative burdens associated with performance management. HR departments now routinely use technology to assist in streamlining systems.

Typical technology applications include the following examples within three categories:

1. The Web. Use of the Internet and company intranets to support performance management systems, including the following:

On-line performance appraisal forms.

Administration and analysis of full-circle feedback or other types of customer input.

Creation of self-paced learning programs to help managers understand performance management systems and the like. For example, the University of California, San Diego, has placed their entire management reference guide on the Web, making it accessible to employees and managers. Their system provides comprehensive assistance with a five-phase model: job description and essential functions, standards of performance, observation and feedback, performance evaluation, and performance development plan.

Creation of individual scorecards that cascade companywide balanced scorecards. A major telecommunications company has created a report that automatically sends employees a monthly update of their individual performance against goals and objectives

2. Use of third-party vendors to assist with routine administration, including:

Administration of competency and skills databases.

Tracking completion of performance appraisals.

Technology-driven databases of performance objectives and language to provide timely and meaningful feedback are available. One Web-based vendor provides a tool that contains competencies tracked to specific job categories (managers, professional, supervisors, etc.), sample goals, blank appraisal forms that can be customized, sample rating categories, and a database of areas for improvement tied to performance deficiencies. The program is modestly priced.

3. Modules created by ERP providers to manage and track performance management. As an example, PeopleSoft's Workforce Analytics module tracks companywide performance against a balanced scorecard and calculates retention probabilities for individuals, groups, and departments, using performance criteria and output as one of the key variables.

We can assume that technology will take us in new areas in the next few years, further reducing administration and tightening the linkage with overall business strategy.

Conclusion

What's next? Ten years from now on, will anyone still care about performance management? The answer is an unqualified yes! As organizations embrace the philosophies and practices already in use in high-performing companies, performance management's importance to the organization will grow. Already we are seeing executives giving attention to performance management, as they recognize even more fully that it is the road that leads to higher levels of productivity.

Web-Based Compensation Planning

*Diane Gherson and Allen P. Jackson**

Introduction

Compensation systems were one of the first HR applications to be automated. In the 1960s, mainframe-based systems were used to track salaries for payroll and reporting purposes. In the mid-1980s, PC software automated tedious manual tasks in the HR department, such as job evaluation and corporate salary planning. As we enter the first decade of the twenty-first century, the ubiq-

*Diane Gherson is a Principal and the leader of Towers Perrin's Reward Management practice. Located in the Irvine, California, office, she specializes in developing compensation strategies and programs that create competitive advantage.

Irvine office address: Koll Center North East Tower, 2010 Main Street, Suite 1050, Irvine, CA 92614.

Allen P. Jackson is a Principal specializing in executive compensation in Towers Perrin's Stamford, Connecticut, office. In addition to consulting, he helps coordinate the Firm's changing compensation data and technology activities.

Stamford office address: One Stamford Plaza, 263 Tresser Boulevard, Stamford, Connecticut 06901-3226.

uitous corporate intranet has propelled a third revolution: line manager compensation decision tools.

Plans and Employee Population Issues

The first step is to determine what compensation plans and employee groups will be covered and which managers will use the Web for such things as planning, budgeting, and ongoing analysis and administration. Will all compensation plans be included? Will both hourly and salaried employees be covered? It clearly makes sense to deliver compensation planning and administrative tools to managers of large employee populations, but what about smaller plans that might cover only a handful of people? For example, what is to be done about executives, with their supplemental pensions, deferred compensation plans, and multiple levels of annual and long-term bonuses? And what about the complexities faced when dealing with international populations, with their housing allotments, automobile subsidies, regional and local living allowances, tax complexities, and currency volatility? The advice provided here is generally to focus on the larger group first, and then tackle the smaller, complex groups when the initial plans are under control.

Compensation Plan Components

Web-based compensation systems should be able to deliver compensation plans providing for both fixed and variable compensation as well as stock.

Fixed Compensation

Fixed compensation is the base or "fixed" pay of an employee and excludes all variable compensation, such as overtime, incentives, bonuses, and so on. It also covers any adjustments to base pay. The determination of base pay encompasses such processes as setting merit increases, defining and evaluating a position, establishing appropriate salary structures, specifying the skills, knowledge, and behaviors (competencies) required to perform a job or fill a

---

Things You Need for a Good Web-Delivered Compensation Program

Up-to-date data.   If the data in your HRIS, such as salary, department, and salary range data, are not up-to-date, the benefits of putting the data on the intranet are negated.

Who works for whom.   You must have an electronic method of assigning employees to their manager.

Security.   The application must be robust enough to prevent intrusion.

Hyperlinks.   Hyperlinks should be available to other total rewards and/or HR web pages, including externally administered programs (perhaps including stock options).

Explanations.   Definitions of key terms and explanations of eligibility should be available in a knowledge base or context-help format.

Human assistance.   Trained service center representatives should be readily available to assist manager.

Workflow.   Systems should be designed to ensure the proper routing of suggesting increases to senior management, HR, and payroll personnel and to permit collaboration by managers with respect to employees who moved within the company or worked for more than one manager during the year.

---

role, and providing appropriate adjustments based on such things as geography, inflation, and market forces.

Fixed compensation components include:

- Base pay
- Merit increases
- Across-the-board adjustments (e.g., cost of living)
- Progression/step increases
- Equity adjustments
- Promotion adjustments
- Skill premiums
- Shift differentials

- Geographic differentials
- Expatriate premiums

The "reference markers" for determining fixed pay are

- Grade/band ranges
- Market pay levels
- Competency levels
- Job evaluation points

Variable Compensation

Variable compensation is the cash portion of an employee's compensation, which is added to the fixed portion and "varies" on the basis of the achievement of certain goals or results. The purpose of variable compensation programs is to tie rewards to business goals and to align employee performance with business strategy.

Included in this category of compensation are:

- Individual, group/team, business unit, and corporate incentive programs
- Sales commissions or incentives
- Profit sharing, productivity incentives, and bonus programs
- Various forms of cash long-term programs that are incentive-based

Variable Compensation Components. The components of variable compensation are:

- Individual incentive compensation plans
- Bonuses
- Commissions
- Performance shares
- Variable merit/lump-sum incentives
- Business unit/division/corporate incentives
- Team/group incentives
- Profit sharing
- Gain sharing/productivity incentives
- Cash recognition awards

Stock

Stock is a form of reward that carries with it an equity position, or ownership, in the company. The reward can be provided through the transfer of company stock to the employee or the opportunity to receive company stock under certain conditions, such as options to purchase. Stock compensation usually takes the form of a long-term incentive that rewards recipients for increases in the company's stock price, but it also can be used as "currency" in lieu of cash to pay all or a portion of annual incentives or even salary.

Stock components include:

- Stock options
- Stock appreciation rights
- Stock grants
- Phantom stock
- Stock purchase (qualified or nonqualified)
- Restricted stock

Compensation Planning and Budgeting

Enter the Web-based total compensation planning tool. The first companies to develop these tools, not surprisingly, were the high-technology companies. Dell Computer, Oracle, Cisco Systems, and others began to publicize the results of their home-grown systems in the late 1990s. The results were staggering. At Dell, for instance, the salary planning process was reduced from eight weeks to three. Other companies quantified the impact on their transaction cost in the millions of dollars, using the cost of managers' time as a key component of the calculation.

But technology played only a small part in this revolution. Compensation decision power already had been shifting from HR to line managers with the attacks on bureaucracy, empowerment of management to manage, and depletion of corporate compensation departments in favor of generalist HR partners. Compensation programs now are more complex and customized to the individual business. Cost-of-living increases and profit sharing were fairly simple to manage centrally. But today the majority of companies pay their employees a bonus that reflects individual contribution, stock options based on individual contribution, and salary increases based on a number of factors. At high-performing companies in the United States, even hourly employees are more likely to be paid for performance than receive an across-the-board wage increase.

However, the goals and objectives for automated compensation analysis and delivery systems remain largely the same: to bring the needed information to those who must make pay decisions, and do so quickly, accurately, and in the form in which they can best use the information. Web-based systems do all of that better than any previous system.

Getting Ready—Determine the Manager's Population

Before a manager can administer the compensation plan, the population must be determined. Because it is role-based, the Web-based application must "know" who is a manager and to whom he or she directly reports. In the absence of a manager, each employee must be given a "default" manager—generally a second-line supervisor.

Each plan has eligibility rules, and an employee must be assigned to the appropriate compensation plans. Then the Human Resource Information System (HRIS), or compensation program logic, determines if an employee is covered under that plan as of a specified date. In other words, HR indicates the date for "freezing" the employee population, that is, calculating eligibility, verifying who worked for whom on that date, assigning managerial responsibility for performance management and compensation, and creating budget pools. The example table (Figure 7-1) presents data on a manager's work group, the data generally provided by the HRIS.

Getting Ready—Rating Employees

As discussed in Chapter 6, on performance management, the manager now accesses the rating that was generated during the performance management process or, if that process was not Web-enabled or the data are not in machine-readable form, enters

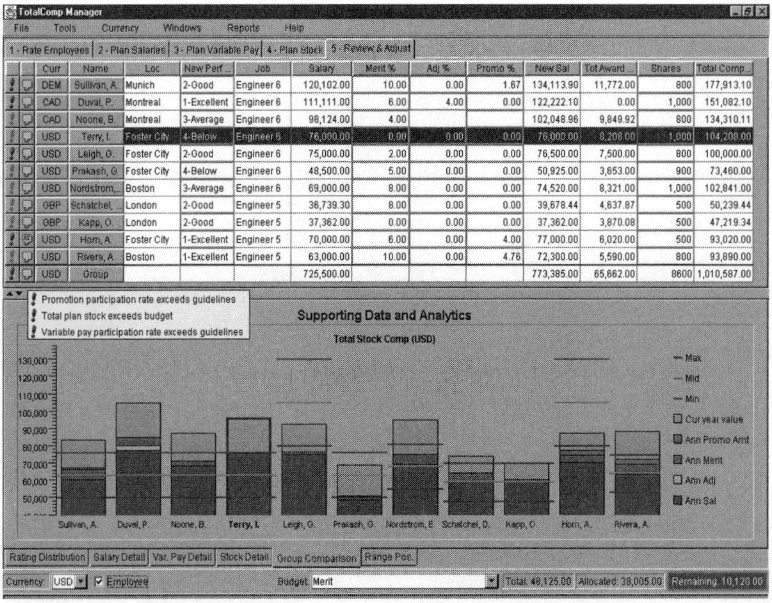

Figure 7-1 View of manager's work group.

the appropriate performance rating into the application for each employee.

The system automatically generates graphics that depict the distribution of the ratings (see Figure 7-2)—both the actual distribution for the manager's employee population and the desired distribution.

Compensation Planning—The Performance versus Position-in-Range Matrix

One of the more popular tools used by managers in the analysis and planning phase of salary administration is the performance/increase percentage matrix.

The example matrix (Figure 7-3) contains a list of performance categories and increase percentages, and highlights one employee. The guidelines in the range quartiles show the suggested percentage increases that could be given by a manager to an employee depending on the employee's position in the range. Position-in-

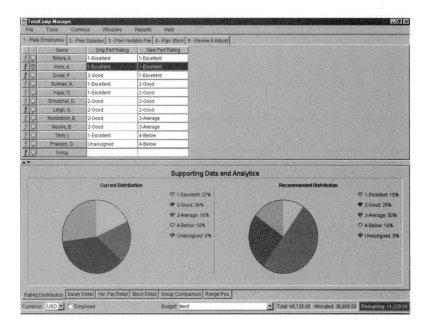

Figure 7-2 Manager's view of performance rating distributions.

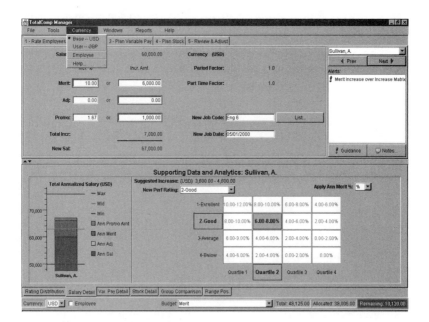

Figure 7-3 Manager's view of individual employee percentages.

range is a function of current pay versus external market benchmarks, internal jobs deemed to be of similar value to the organization, or both. Jobs can be assigned to salary ranges strictly according to market rates; on the basis of traditional evaluation methods such as point factor, classification, or slotting; or via newer, competency-based approaches. Both "narrow ranges" and "broad bands" typically have a midpoint or control point set to reflect the approximate market rate for those jobs, as well as a minimum and maximum reflecting the least and most amounts of money normally paid for those jobs in the marketplace. Armed with these data, the manager is properly prepared to plan actual compensation changes.

Planning New Base Salaries

When the performance rating versus position-in-range matrix is finalized, the manager can proceed with compensation planning. As shown in Figures 7-1 and 7-3, the manager can enter either the percentage increase provided by the matrix or an actual dollar amount.

Running totals are maintained for total compensation amounts and for the budgeted pool amount, offset by the amount the manager allocates to each individual, along with the remaining total available. The manager then plans each employee's change (or no change, as the case may be) until all of the employees are reviewed, using as many real-time updated iterations as he or she believes are necessary.

Planning New Variable Compensation

In a fashion identical to that used for base salaries, each employee who is eligible for variable compensation is now reviewed, and a suggested amount of compensation is calculated. The graphic shows the total compensation amount (in bar form) for each employee, taking into account the amount of the new annualized salary that was suggested, as well as the suggested variable amount. These amounts are added together, along with any other variable amounts that the employee is eligible for.

Planning Stock Compensation Awards

The manager can now decide on the award of any stock (usually stock options, except at the senior executive level) that is part of the total compensation package. Companies often outsource the administration of this component using either dedicated software or the financial services firms that handle option exercise and other stock transactions for the companies.

When this step is completed, managers can generate statistics for their own work group and, under certain conditions, determine where they stand in relation to other groups. In addition, reports are available showing roll-ups and grouped departmental or line-of-business statistics. Compliance reports for equal-pay and EEO purposes should also be produced for managers to review.

Approving Compensation Plans

After a manager submits a compensation plan, it is accessible to the approving manager for review and approval. The manager can both "roll up" for an aggregate view of pay-for-performance and "drill down" to examine any one individual's pay plan (see Figure 7-4). Individual plans are automatically rolled up, and compensation managers can review program status and summary data at any time. Group-level analytics provide visibility at each level in the management hierarchy before compensation actions are taken. Insightful graphs help managers accelerate the roll-up process while giving them a clear vision of the planning and budgeting of their groups.

The Next Wave—Employee Decision Tools

Web-Based Total Rewards Linkages

If the compensation plan is part of the overall total rewards program, then it should be delivered as a fully integrated program. This means that the plan should be accessible from the HR home page as a major hyperlink and should be labeled as such. The total rewards home page should provide applications for the subcomponents of the total rewards program. For instance, all the compensation plans could be grouped under the "My Finances" icon

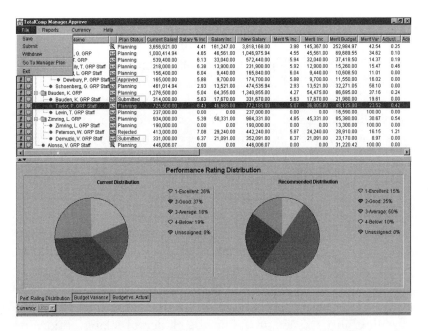

Figure 7-4 Group level view of managers' compensation submittals.

and applications. Regardless of the application's place on the site map, the compensation user should be able to navigate easily through the application to connect with the other components of the total rewards program. From the compensation pages users should at any time have access to the benefit components, the career applications, and those applications pertaining to the employee's work environment. This in turn would help ensure that the primary goal for the total rewards program is met: to communicate the overall value of an employee's experience at the company.

Although every organization's total rewards program is unique, delivering these new attributes on the Internet uses the Web's powerful presentation capabilities to the sponsoring company's advantage by linking all these components in order to promote retention, loyalty, and pride.

The corporate intranet has become an important source of employee information, replacing traditional communication methods in many companies. Employee websites give employees more control over their employment relationships, enabling them to check on company news, stock performance, benefit opportunities, career opportunities, and total compensation status. A Towers Perrin study found that higher-performing companies are more likely to share the details of their compensation programs, such as salary ranges and grades, with employees. Consequently, their employees are significantly more likely to understand how to maximize their pay. However, there is nothing inherently new about these companies' communication with employees about pay—the only difference is the medium.

The next wave of compensation systems is likely to represent a further empowerment of the employee in the employment relationship. "mypay-myway^{SM}" is just one approach to allowing employees to customize their mix of total rewards to suit their personal needs. Employees already choose from a flexible array of benefits and, in many organizations, can buy extra vacation days with forgone salary. Technology will enable companies to extend that flexibility to, say, providing the choice of taking options or cash, benefits, or salary. At that point, the Web will facilitate employee decisions, enabling the employee to run scenarios, tax analyses, or valuations in order to make annual elections for the total pay package.

On-Line Compensation Surveys and Market Data

Compensation surveys are a method of obtaining external market pay data to help companies establish wage levels and evaluate their pay practices against those of other companies. These surveys play a key role in determining the overall appropriateness of salary ranges and annual and long-term incentive targets, and can suggest the need for market adjustments in the cases of certain individuals.

The first wave of on-line compensation survey tools essentially duplicated existing "results" programs. They gave users electronic access to information they already had on paper—published survey statistics that typically remained unchanged for the year-long (or 24-month) survey cycle. The second wave of survey tools entails more truly interactive database queries, enabling users to create custom peer groups and exclude their own data from the samples. A future wave will involve companies storing information on survey job matches in their HRIS to ease subsequent years' data submission processes and to facilitate multiple submissions per year when labor markets are fiercely competitive. Yet another development will be the "data warehouse," with companies voluntarily banding together and allowing members to access each other's benchmark-position-tagged HRIS. This will be done under very strict security guidelines that bar access to individually identifiable data and comply with U.S. federal antitrust rules governing the sharing of compensation survey information. The data warehouse approach eliminates the lead times inherent in such activities as planning the survey, preparing and administering the survey instrument, and tabulating and analyzing survey data, because each participating company supplies data "as it goes." Warehouse members also will be working with more up-to-date data and will be able to perform a wider range of macro-scale, total-cost HR analyses not possible in the face of the limitations of benchmark survey data.

Compensation surveys can cover benefits or pay. Sometimes the two are dealt with in a single survey, but it is more common for them to be covered separately.

8

Technology and Employee Development

*Joseph Gibbons**

Employees as Human Capital Investors

We have moved, over the past five years, from viewing employees as assets, however valued, to a much more pointed realization about them: Employees are discretionary investors of their human capital, as shown in Figure 8-1. They are, for the most part, free to involve themselves, or not, in the organization for which they work. They can provide their best insight and energy, they can hone their skills so that their personal service to the enterprise excels, or they can hold back for whatever reason.

High on the list of contributions workers make to their enterprise are those that come from their knowledge base. A survey by

*Joseph Gibbons is a Towers Perrin consultant in the New York office where he specializes in developmental activities for the new workforce.

New York office address: 335 Madison Avenue, New York, New York 10017-4605.

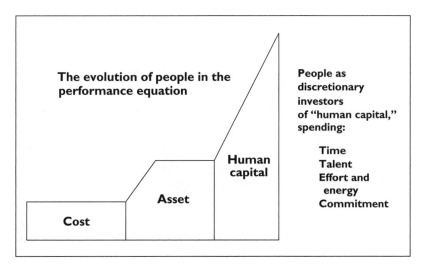

Figure 8-1

the National Center on the Educational Quality of the Workforce (see Figure 8-2) has suggested that increasing worker education results in greater productivity than increasing capital allocations or work hours.

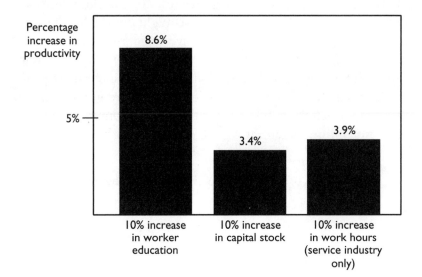

Figure 8-2

Training's Competition

When we speak of training and development, we should first look at some definitions to ensure that we are speaking of results rather than activities. Activities are visible and measurable and give us the comfort of believing that we are genuinely accomplishing something. However, they are still only activities. Results are measurable as well, but defining the activities that contribute directly to results is a tortuous path. Organizations are interested in results; they directly impact the bottom line.

- Training is an *activity.*
- Learning is a *personal result:* one person's absorption of ideas, skills, and competencies.
- Development is the *ultimate result* for employees and for the organization; it means a person moves from one level of potential contribution to a higher one.

Training, both formal and informal, in whatever mode it is delivered, is one of many important *activities* with a desirable result: workforce development to increase productivity, innovation, and competitiveness.

But there is competition for scarce resources within businesses. Other activities in which an enterprise might engage for the same bottom-line results might include investments in technology or marketing, greater expenditures in research, or a faster and more supple procurement or distribution system. Training must prove to the enterprise that it produces results. There are simply too many other activities holding out their own promise of bottom-line results if the organization will simply invest heavily in them.

The Four Contributors to Employee Development

Training

For years, classroom training was seen as the primary means of employee development. An organization decided on a course of action—perhaps introduction of a new product or an initiative to combat increasing worker compensation claims—and decided that some or all employees would take a classroom course in new product sales or safety. All employees took the same course and, hopefully, all employees gained the same knowledge.

In time, these same courses were packaged, sometimes badly, and put on corporate intranets, CDs, or videotapes to make them more widely available and less expensive to administer. More recent additions to computer-based training include better-designed programs to keep participant interest alive; use of audio and video clips; and some form of interactivity, such as testing, question-and-answer rooms, or student-instructor chat rooms.

Over the past few years, we have seen synchronous training, where employees in remote locations attend the same class at the same time and have enhanced interactivity through real-time e-mail or voice-to-voice conversations with their instructor and classmates.

Training is a useful tool for imparting knowledge and information, and, when combined with skill-building exercises, can create a knowledge-sharing experience. It has some limitations, however, as seen in Figure 8-3.

Positives	**Negatives**
• *Consistent:* Imparts the same or similar knowledge to all	• *Top-down:* Tends to be one-way communication
• *Useful:* Explains new initiatives, provides information on new policies and practices	• *Paternalistic:* Participants become students responsible for learning new information
• *Informative:* Excellent way to ensure that needed information is passed along	• *Information-only:* Little use of other learning vehicles
• *Immediate:* Opportunities usually provided for questions, challenges, explanations, and discussions	• *Individualistic:* Even with group discussions, emphasis is on the individual learning new material
• *Comfortable:* Uses the same format learned in school	• *Intellectual:* Uses a knowledge-only platform for the most part
• *Compliant:* Ensures that required knowledge to fulfill government or organization requirements is imparted	• *Collectivized:* Assumes all participants are at the same level and have the same learning needs and styles

Figure 8-3 Training: Positives and Negatives.

Most computer-based training, despite the hype given to it recently, is still training. Its goal is to impart predetermined knowledge. It uses an anytime, anywhere classroom, but is still individualistic and imparts intellectual content, with perhaps a bit of skill building and motivation thrown in. It is usually cheaper (at least for large groups being trained) and often more convenient. And when there is sufficient broadband width to pump multimedia into the wires, and up-to-date hardware on the user's end to receive it, the results can be exciting.

When the Internet or a sophisticated corporate intranet is used for distance learning, interactivity can be added, a greater range of standard courses can be accessed, and, with new developments in bandwidth, the imagination of the producers is the only limit to the types and amount of graphic material presented.

Computer-based training has radically altered the corporate training field in a number of ways (see Figure 8-4). It has:

- Conquered distance and enabled employees around the world to benefit from knowledge previously available only in selected sites
- Reduced the attendant costs of training: travel, accommodations, and class size limitations

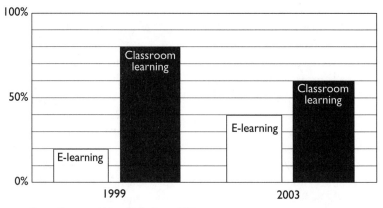

Source: Corporate University Exchange, 1999

Figure 8-4   E-learning projected market share.

- Enabled companies to purchase off-the-shelf courses at a fraction of the cost of developing them and providing stand-up trainers
- Opened entire free libraries of secondary sources to bolster course content
- Added course-specific chat rooms to replace student dialogues and bull sessions
- Opened the doors to innovation in distance learning by providing a business base for training. The flood of net-based businesses in the training field is almost overwhelming, and the consequent competition among them will spark continuously improved products
- Raised the bar for course developers by increasing demand for better graphics, real-time video and audio, and expectations of "edutainment" as part of education
- Raised the bar for instructors, since the competition for great teachers will only increase exponentially as a more sophisticated audience of learners sees the possibilities of this new distance learning.

The future of training is almost certainly Web-based, at least for those courses with wide audience appeal and "need to know" information. But these, by many estimates, comprise about 80 percent of the learning now provided by corporate training.

One note of caution. The dropout rate in distance learning is much higher than in traditional classroom instruction. There are seldom attendance sheets in distance learning. Participants feel they can learn at their own pace, so they may skip through, or drop out of, a course whose promotional material is better than its content. There is little human interaction to develop insights and feelings about the material presented, and, yes, some distance learning courses have hardly evolved from the old computer instruction manuals of the mid 1980s. Dull is deadly in the business of learning.

Aside from interesting and arresting course content and presentation, four elements are required for distance learning to work its promised wonders in corporations:

- A workforce accustomed to technology-based learning. This means that the great number of baby boomers in the present workforce, who grew up with little technology in their crowded classrooms, must adapt to a different learning style if distance learning is to succeed. Generation X and Generation Y are, for the most part, techno-savvy consumers of information and have less need for high-tech instruction.

- A recognition and reward system that validates learning in some concrete way. Whether by accreditation or degree, tangible rewards for those who have completed courses and utilized the knowledge they have learned, or a continually raised bar of knowledge that weeds out the obsolete and the intransigent, companies that wish to obtain the benefits of a distance learning curriculum must get serious about paying for knowledge winners and moving out losers.

- A high priority given to learning. Like the statement in many annual reports about "our people being our most important asset," corporate statements about the importance of learning delivered to people working 60-hour weeks lose their credibility. Employees in a company that is a real learning environment should not have to pursue company-necessary distance learning at home or on weekends. Learning should be part of the workday. See Figure 8-5. Merrill Lynch, in an April, 1999 report entitled *The Book of Knowledge*, echoed the view that knowledge workers bolster a company's bottom line—a fact that's even reflected in a company's share price.

"Those companies that have created growth by leveraging their 'off balance sheet' human capital have, in turn, seen their share prices rewarded with higher valuations."

"Given the intangible nature of human capital, it simply cannot be line-itemized on a balance sheet, as with tangible assets. We believe rising price-to-book ratios reflect, in large part, the fact that the productive assets driving growth are increasingly 'off balance sheet' assets."

—Merrill Lynch, *The Book of Knowledge*, quoted in *Fortune*, 2000

Figure 8-5

. . . The team compares companies' share prices in the old economy versus the new one.

- Some way to substitute for the group work and interactivity lost in distance learning. Communities of practice, discussed in Chapter 9, can be fine substitutes for this, as can distance teams working on real problems.

Coaching, Mentoring, and On-the-Job Training

An EDS study from 1996 (see Figure 8-6) claims that 70 percent of workplace learning is informal, that is, not predetermined by the company. As people on the job ask for advice, read an article recommended by another worker, or discuss a problem, learning takes place. When informal learning involves a more-experienced employee, we might call it "coaching" if task-related, or "mentoring" if it concerns the general increase of skills valued in this particular company. It must be emphasized that, even when companies set up formal coaching and mentoring programs for their employees, the only formal part is the program itself; the content is, and must be, informal, tied to the moment, and sought after by the employee who wants to learn.

The same EDS study divided and field-tested informal learning in four different categories:

- Pragmatic learning—a piece of knowledge or a skill necessary for the job

---

The EDS research emphasized the importance of informal learning in work teams and said that the following factors created an environment for informal learning:

- The authority to decide their own outcomes
- Clear and achievable goals
- Sufficient time and resources to meet their goals
- A climate of tolerance for diverse perspectives
- Cooperative problem solving
- Effective leadership
- A reward structure tied to meeting the team's goals
- Sufficient job security to want to continue learning

Figure 8-6 Research on workplace learning.

- Intrapersonal—an individual's skill needs for navigating the workplace, solving problems, and coping with change
- Interpersonal—cooperating and working with individuals and groups
- Cultural—understanding organizational norms and behavioral expectations

Experience tells us that all of these types of learning are vital to employee success, as shown in Figure 8-7. Yet they do not occur by turning on a computer to take a course or in a classroom. They occur because a company has fostered an environment in which it is alright to ask and learn, and there are informal rewards for those who help others master the next problem.

But where a culture of learning has already been established, interactive technology can be a great asset. While the person in the next cubicle might be the first one I approach for an answer, he might well direct me to a database or give me the e-mail address of an in-house expert halfway around the globe. As long as it is alright to ask questions, technology-delivered answers will eventually be part of the solution.

The role of a training department is more than being an imparter of knowledge in a formal setting. It must find technological ways to deliver just-in-time answers to those who need them now. The same course content that seemed so remote when taken in a classroom can, if part of a knowledge capital database,

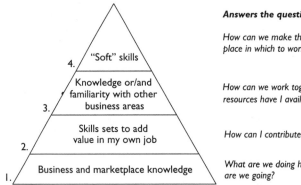

Figure 8-7 Types of learning and their impact on success.

give the immediate answer to a pressing question, settle a problem that employees could take weeks researching, or offer an insight that eventually affects the bottom line.

Whether we call it a "knowledge capital database" or "just-in-time training," technology-enhanced information, delivered when needed and in the required dosage, extends the reach of formal training and helps foster the learning environment required in a world of frantic competition.

Communities of Practice

Informal learning of the best sort takes place in communities of practice, informally organized groups sharing common tasks or concerns. There are seldom set meeting times for communities of practice; and the membership list might be a handwritten list of "go to" people, or a name shared with the advice "He has their addresses on his Palm Pilot." Members may be only tangentially connected to people in the group or may work with them every day. Communities of practice arise when shared intellectual and emotional interests drive people to discuss important work issues with each other and need newer forms of knowledge management, as referenced in the following quotation in Figure 8-8.

These arrangements are highly informal and any attempt to formalize them usually sends them underground. They act as shadow learning centers where intricate and interesting issues are discussed and insights flow. Communities of practice may include vendors and customers, people in other companies, or even, occasionally, competitors. They appear on no organizational charts but are probably the most effective and valuable learning teams in any company.

> "We cannot 'manage' knowledge the way we have managed physical materials in the past. Knowledge is messy, it is slippery, it seeks community—it has all the qualities of a self-organizing system."
>
> —Verna Allee

Figure 8-8

Communities of practice "happen" when the environment is right. When learning is valued and enough space and time are provided for people to talk over the issues they are working on, these communities seem to arise. Out of them come problem-solving techniques that have eluded the rest of the company, innovations when one person asked another, "Why not try that?" and a strong element of mutual respect and support for the work that members are doing. They are also, incidentally, the most powerful retention tool a company has for top technical talent.

Although communities of practice usually focus on the hard side of the business (how to solve an intricate technology or customer problem), they flourish when the "soft" side of work (teamwork skills, work-life balance, respect for the individual) is emphasized. A people-first environment combined with a strong business mission seems to be the most fertile soil for these communities to arise.

These communities are driven users of technology, but little is related to standard training. They seldom request training because they find their own answers through their research and contacts. What they need is access to other practice communities. And they get this access in public seminars and workshops where they can make contacts, share information, and learn where the cutting edge is in their field. Companies with the best practices make these seminars available or routinely allow groups access to internal communication technology or make conference rooms available for meetings on a "no questions asked" basis.

Organization-Wide Learning Communities

Over one-half of the *Fortune* 500 companies from 20 years ago no longer exist. A case can be made that many of these successful companies reached the limits of their learning capacity and were simply overtaken by unforeseen events. Learning and communication were top-down, warning signals heard on the front lines were ignored, and, enamored of their past, they failed to see the future rising up before them. They stopped learning right before they disappeared.

Three key requirements are needed to set the stage for growth into a learning organization:

- *Core technologies* that provide knowledge management capabilities and are open to all members of the organization and to external sources of knowledge. Databases, individual knowledge agents, and groups with specialized skills are all connected in a high-priority knowledge ecosystem driven by technology.

  For example, training courses, on-line and organized into specific relevant subjects, enable users to get quick answers to questions. Multiply the many training courses offered by the number of specific subjects they touch on, make each of those subjects short enough for quick understanding and immediately accessible to users, and you have one facet of a perhaps hundred-faceted knowledge database.

- *Critical interdependencies.* Just as the worth of an e-commerce company is based more on its audience-reach than its present profitability, an increasing number of nodes and links in a company's knowledge ecosystem increases its value exponentially. If, as is becoming more apparent, knowledge creation is wealth creation, the value of this complex, ever adaptive system called a learning organization keeps increasing with the number of contributors and users.

  Learning is an action, not a passive ingestion of knowledge. The more people and departments a company has drawing from and replenishing its knowledge base, the more the entire organization will have actions, and activities, that are more realistic, more consistent, and more successful in the marketplace.

- *Knowledge engines and agents.* These are the sources and producers of the knowledge needed to populate databases, answer questions, reformulate issues for better understanding, and set up feeds for a constant stream of usable knowledge into the process.

  A learning organization requires continual feeds of information and knowledge organized in easily accessible ways to maintain its value. All these feeds, whether individual people or purchased information, cost the company something: time, money, recognition for the effort involved. There must be some reward given to the people who populate the knowledge database and, perhaps, another kind of reward for those who use it.

In an organization-wide learning community, many of today's often-discussed employee issues become nonissues:

Need for respect and empowerment of individuals	A nonissue. Learning organizations cannot work without giving a high value to individuals and their contributions.
Developing an "ownership" mindset	Another nonissue. If knowledge is power, and individuals are patched into the entire knowledge database of an organization, they are automatically treated as if they were "owners," which of course they are.
Need for employee development and continual learning	Work becomes development in an organization-wide learning community.
Productivity improvement	As the learning organization gathers steam, problems become easier to solve and information from "market outposts" gives the entire organization a better grip on market realities.
Attraction and retention of key personnel	There is no better way to attract and keep employees motivated than to give them every opportunity to improve their skills.

A Tentative Conclusion

Information technology is the engine enabling good companies to grow better and middling companies to compete. But information technology alone will not do the trick; it is only a vehicle, a communication device. While Web-based employee development on all levels benefits mightily from information technology that erases distance, compresses time, and makes once hard-to-reach knowledge immediately available, the common wisdom is that the hard work of culture and process change must occur if the benefits of technology are to be fully realized.

But information technology acts as a fifth column within a company to quicken change and make new options available. Once installed, it runs by its own rules, which are often contrary to the rules of traditional business. New roles are created, power is distributed more widely, and expectations are raised. The instantaneousness of information demands new adaptive behaviors.

To put it simply: Information technology puts the market in control through the power of information, as shown in Figure 8-9. It renders many of the old rules obsolete:

- *There is little time for analysis.* Everything happens so quickly that informed intuition replaces analysis as the driver of business decisions.

Technology-Driven Changes

The Internet provides:

- Instant speed
- Continuous connectivity
- Disintermediation
- Choice
- Self-service

Information technology leads to new organization designs

The world is connected

The new electronically enabled marketplace demands:

- Value-added service
- Best cost
- Continuous innovation
- Cooperation between rivals

- The controlling middle in companies falls out since creativity and innovation occur on the edges where the company meets its customers
- The employee becomes all important, serving the customer directly out of a networked organization
- Rules are replaced by principles and constant communications

And diversity must be built into the employee, product, service, and customer bases

---

Figure 8-9 Technology-Driven Changes.

- *Imagined control is lost.* Market intelligence changes so rapidly that long-term planning becomes useless. Everything must be reacted to immediately, and by the person most deeply involved with the problem.
- *Blame has become useless.* In a rapidly changing business environment driven by instant information, the only wrong decision seems to be making no decision.
- *People issues move to the fore.* All other assets become secondary to attracting, retaining, developing, and deploying the right people. Only people can act on the knowledge information technology provides.
- *Free agents rule.* As discretionary investors of human capital, employees have the ultimate say in whether a company will be successful or not. They can take their hard-earned knowledge and move elsewhere if there are few chances for development.

The information revolution goes well beyond distance learning or Web-based training courses. It brings business into a new dimension where space and time are erased, where market demands are immediately met or the market moves on, where the only sensible approach to people is to treat them as discretionary investors of human capital. In this new dimension, technology-enhanced employee development is more than something nice to have—it is something that is needed in order to play.

CHAPTER

9

Implementing Web-Based Knowledge Management

Jack Borbely and Stephen J. Gould*

"Knowledge is not simply another resource with the traditional factors of production such as labor, capital and land; it is the only meaningful resource today.
—Peter Drucker, *Post Capitalist Society*

Knowledge Management is undergoing both transformation and explosive growth thanks to the advent of Web technology. Just when the effective use of an organization's collective knowledge has become the ultimate competitive advantage,

*Jack Borbely is a Principal at Towers Perrin and Director–Information Services, responsible for the Firm's collaboration, intellectual capital management, and retrieval technologies. He is located in the Valhalla, New York, office.

Valhalla, New York office address: 100 Summit Lake Drive, Valhalla, New York 10595.

Stephen J. Gould is a Principal at Towers Perrin, and a member of the Firm's global retirement leadership group. He has been leading Towers Perrin's knowledge management initiatives for the past four years, from conception to global deployment. He is located in the Boston, Massachusetts, office.

Boston office address: 500 Boylston Street, 17th Floor, Boston, Massachusetts 02116-3734.

there arrives a technology ideally suited for creating, accessing, collecting, and using knowledge. In short, the Web's ability to overcome past technological barriers has made it the foundation of any future knowledge management undertaking.

The purpose of this chapter is to identify and discuss elements of the Web that facilitate knowledge management and to share insights about implementing a successful Web-based knowledge management operation. To accomplish this, we will draw heavily on our real-world experiences at Towers Perrin.

What Is Knowledge Management?

Broadly defined, knowledge management (KM) is the capture, maintenance, and sharing of knowledge to help people do their jobs better and add value to the work of the organization. Properly instituted, KM allows practitioners to find the best research materials, supporting documents, work products, and historical data available not just within the organization, but in the world beyond as well. Knowledge management is much more than the technology that supports it and is most successful when organizers focus on several basic building elements:

Purpose: Clear line of sight between the KM strategy and an organization's goals and business strategies

Culture: Dedication to learning and the sharing of knowledge

Processes: Roles, business activities, and management practices that facilitate and sustain the building and sharing of knowledge

Connections: Environment and mechanisms that facilitate interactions among people for the creation, collaboration, and transfer of knowledge

Content: Well-organized and accessible information that is relevant, accurate, complete, and appropriate

Technology: Integrated systems and tools that enable easy capture, storage, retrieval, and sharing of knowledge

Web Technology's Connection with Knowledge Management

In the past, successful and consistent use of a firm's collective knowledge often failed because users couldn't get the full range of information when they needed it and how they needed it. There was too much extraneous matter mixed in with the good, and no one seemed to know how to wade through it all, once they had managed to find it. The Web changed all that.

Web-based KM systems can overcome the traditional and still widespread obstacles to making the collective knowledge of the organization available and useful to all individuals:

Disparate and incompatible sources of organizational knowledge are now organized by a browser, which has the power to look to the right and to the left. In addition, the "common content languages" of HTML, for format and display, and XML, for platform-independent data exchange, can provide almost unlimited access to documents created anywhere in the world.

Information overload can be mitigated by well-designed KM systems with filters that screen out all unnecessary or irrelevant matter, unless the user requests a "broader view." Tunnel vision has given way to universal access because the Internet, as a "network of networks," enables organizations to link seamlessly to the right content, regardless of where it resides—inside or outside its confines.

Questions of timeliness have disappeared because of the Web's seven-days-a-week/24-hours-a-day global accessibility. In addition, "distance learning" capabilities, the provision of synchronous as well as on-demand learning experiences, and connectivity to portable technology, such as wireless telephones, all serve to enhance Web capabilities.

Users can "have it their way" by creating customized learning portals, which can present knowledge that is personalized to the needs and preferences of the user.

Example: A Knowledge Factory Puts Its KM System on the Web

The impetus for developing a knowledge management system will differ among organizations, depending on their business needs and structure. A good example is a global consulting firm such as Towers Perrin, where there is a significant connection between effective knowledge management and meeting the needs of our stakeholders (clients, employees, and shareholders). Being a "knowledge factory" of sorts, we are highly dependent upon the continual creation, assimilation, and use of knowledge by expert consultants serving global clients.

More specifically, several of the firm's key goals and strategies have a strong knowledge/information component and dependency. These include continuously improving the quality and efficiency of work for clients and leveraging our intellectual capital across our consulting population. Our overarching principle of building relationships and producing results for our clients dictates that we place a premium on innovation, leverage, efficiency, and communication:

Innovation: *To deliver innovative and high-impact solutions to our clients.* Before the Internet, it was very difficult to provide direct-client access to the firm's intellectual capital, its people, and their individual and collective knowledge.

Leverage: *To fully leverage the firm's intellectual capital to benefit our clients, our people, and the firm.* The Web can provide worldwide, immediate access to best practices and client knowledge created anywhere in our global organization.

Efficiency: *To improve the cost-effectiveness of our work environment.* Standardizing the technology infrastructure (within and across enterprises) ensures that the right audience will benefit from the timely and efficient sharing of content. Additionally, it guarantees that the collection and use of knowledge can proceed in a consistent, orderly way.

Communication: *To provide broader access to the critical information/ resources needed to serve clients and manage information more effectively.* The Web's ability, both to provide easy links to experts and content, and to conduct real-time or synchronous learning or work sessions among geographically dispersed participants, allows a level of communication previously unimagined.

Technological Building Blocks of Web-Based KM

For organizations of all types and sizes, not just a global knowledge factory such as Towers Perrin, certain Web-based components should be included in every KM environment. These include such features as content development and publication, personalization, communities of interest, collaboration, individual learning, measurements, data integration, and knowledge generation. It will be useful to explore each of these features individually.

Content Development and Publication

The contents of a KM system can be likened to any other business "inventory," varying with the company's business and values. In recent years, hundreds of organizations of all types have created the new position of "knowledge manager," whose role is to oversee the creation, distribution, and maintenance of accessible and valued information. This role exists in direct response to the present-day reality of too much information of too little use or relevance.

Using a combination of Web-based content, filtering, publishing, and "push" features, the knowledge manager ensures that organizations collect, organize, and make available in a timely manner the collective knowledge of the organization in ways that improve competitive advantage and individual performance. Key benefits of Web technology that come into play in managing the content of KM systems emerge primarily in two areas:

Knowledge capture: The ability to integrate traditional sources such as client work, research papers, and user-maintained databases with new sources, such as on-line discussions, real-time work sessions, and on-line seminars.

Content publication: Including templates and classification schemes that permit users to search the KM database for what they need in a given situation, receive relevant information rather than a flood of broadly classified material, and have instant access to job-related knowledge.

Personalization. An effective knowledge management system also takes advantage of the Web's ability to present each user with a customized portal, a feature that vastly improves both the appeal and utility of the system for users. Personalization is the engine behind the KM system's ability to mass-customize continually, that is, quickly and accurately to provide appropriate knowledge relevant to a specific individual's work and interests. For example, a customized portal for a user in the role of a consultant at a professional services firm can provide these services:

E-mail and a full calendar of appointments linked to all relevant details

Complete client information, including the client company's mission statement and position in the marketplace, consulting needs and status of work in process by the consulting firm, and biographies and photos of key managers and decision makers

Individualized links, similar to bookmarks, to sources of knowledge regularly used in the consultant's practice, a feature that can be added "automatically," based on the user's needs

Content filters that push relevant news and information to those most likely to need or want it because of their position and current assignments, such as the results of new research on benefits, practices, or newly developed technical resources

Customized learning that responds to the user's needs and learning styles

Personalized company or organizational information, including calendar reminders of virtual and real-time meetings, educational opportunities, benefit plan options available to the individual user, or invitations to participate in user surveys on the effectiveness of the KM system

Communities of Interest

The Web's collaboration and communication tools, combined with content filters and push features, support dramatic improvements in providing up-to-date, relevant knowledge and information to communities of interest. While interest communities by definition are composed of people with a strong professional concern in a given subject or type of work, it is often not humanly possible to stay abreast of all the new internally and externally generated knowledge that may be relevant. Filters and push technology overcome the research limits of busy people. See Figures 9-1 and 9-2.

This personalization benefit from Web technology supports shared or mutual interests. These on-line features can be a critical advantage to organizations with certain environments:

> Firms in which knowledge is dynamic, and its users in the organization need to be kept aware of the latest knowledge, new business objectives, and environmental factors, such as government regulations, competitors' moves, and other matters of knowledge relevant to their work

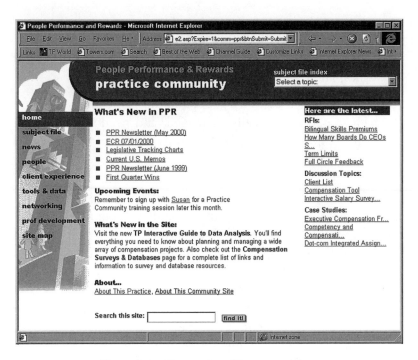

Figure 9-1 Community of Interest webshot.

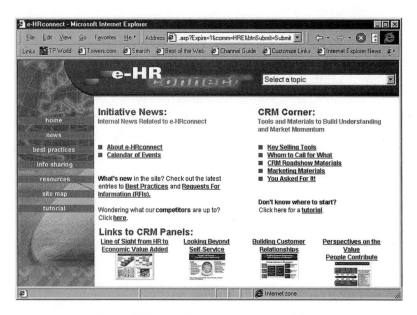

Figure 9-2 Knowledge management webshot.

Organizations in which new staff need alternative avenues for getting up-to-speed quickly on business, industry technical issues, and organizational memory

Firms in which users who make up interest communities are widely, perhaps globally, dispersed, and need new information as it becomes available, not at annual meetings or through regular mail

In Web-based knowledge management systems, serving managers and professionals with changing and evolving needs for up-to-date, useful knowledge, the Net permits the use of two types of communities of interest, each with distinct advantages enabled by Web technology:

Planned communities, whose members are identified in advance by the specific work they do, their line of business, or the areas of information they require for their work. Although an employee can self-select to become a member of a planned community of interest, the premise is that people will gravitate to on-line environments reflecting their ongoing core interests. Actuaries and compensation specialists may need different kinds of knowledge, which will be reflected in their respective on-line communities.

Extemporaneous communities, also called ad hoc interest communities, will be created and populated by staff members themselves. These are frequently organized around projects, using readily accessible and familiar Web-based collaboration and communication tools. The Web-enabled "empowerment" of individuals and groups is particularly valuable in a global professional services firm such as Towers Perrin, where the development of intellectual capital is often initiated by individual creativity and entrepreneurial behavior.

Collaboration. No capability of an intranet-based knowledge management system so defines this medium as does collaborative work and learning. The Web's ability to provide virtual meeting rooms and interactive seminars for on-line attendees represents a quantum leap forward for sharing knowledge. Individuals who can participate fully, while never leaving their homes, offices, or satellite workplaces, provide the ultimate example of overcoming the limits of time and space for busy, scattered employees.

Real-time learning experiences can be scheduled in advance by e-mail, with communications that include the agenda, participant names, and relevant background materials. Using customized KM portals, the background material can be tailored to the specific needs of the participants. "Codified" or "explicit knowledge," as it is often called, can be stored in systems. Critical consultant experience, or "implicit knowledge," can be shared through this medium.

In multimedia KM applications—still in their infancy but increasingly affordable as Web technology advances—video and audio streaming add sound and broadcast features to the on-line meeting or seminar, together with text, graphics, and interactive capabilities that permit attendees to ask questions and contribute ideas extemporaneously, just as they would if all were in the same room at the same time. Interestingly, the tool that Towers Perrin uses to enable such virtual sessions is Lotus Development Corporation's product called "Sametime."

Several features of Web technology make this medium for collaborative work and learning superior to teleconferencing or even videoconferencing.

Notes: Meeting minutes or participants' notes are easy to generate because they are recorded and saved by the system and immediately available for reference or future review.

Documentation: Files and other collateral material needed during the on-line session can be accessed instantly. Nobody needs to remember to pack all the paperwork that might be relevant for the meeting.

Classroom atmosphere: Interactive technology permits participants to ask questions electronically when the question occurs and ultimately to receive answers, but without disruption to the seminar or meeting; the moderator or leader can easily respond during the session or afterward, to all the participants or just one, as appropriate.

Equipment: Unlike videoconferencing, Web-based conferencing requires only a desktop PC.

Collaborative work made possible by a Web-based KM system is different from real-time seminars or meetings structured to convey knowledge. It is analogous to on-the-job training, in that it routinely brings together colleagues in locations throughout the world who contribute their expertise and learn from one another while the work is being performed.

Collaborative work conducted in real time has the further advantage of eliciting and communicating the tacit knowledge that is as much a goal of KM systems as is explicit information; this includes the facts and other data that systems readily document and codify. Experience-based opinions, and perspectives based on insights rather than data alone, are the kind of tacit knowledge that emerges in work sessions more often than in textbooks or other documentation.

In short, a Web-based KM system that incorporates synchronous, collaborative work and learning can be as effective as in-person meetings or seminars, and it can achieve a high level of effectiveness at a fraction of the cost involved in bringing geographically dispersed consultants to one location.

Individual learning. Knowledge and learning experiences on demand are also a critical component of an effective knowledge management system, and the Web's ubiquity, capacity, and interactivity make it an ideal tool for delivering training whenever and wherever users want it.

A Web-based KM system exploits one of the fundamental benefits of computer-based training that arises from an indisputable learning premise: People learn best at their own pace. They absorb more useful information when they can control the flow of knowledge and information, review when necessary, delve deeper into or skim course content as they wish, and otherwise customize the learning experience to fit their own preferences or abilities.

With the right technology and the Web's capacity, even a novice user can find a vast library of easily accessible courses, recorded work sessions, white papers, presentations, video clips, research results, and other learning materials that can be downloaded on demand to any location the user chooses. In a well-designed KM system, users can search by topic, level of proficiency, type of presentation, line of business, or a variety of other classifiers, simply by entering plain-language requests and clicking a menu choice.

From the company's perspective, Web-based learning libraries provide the ability to create and build competencies among employees right in the organization, without the need for transfers or travel. In competency-based performance management, the KM system can do double duty as the repository of training and development experiences needed for creating or improving specific competencies. In addition, even testing at the end of the learning experience can take place on-line.

As interactive multimedia KM systems become more widespread, presentations that simulate actual work experiences with the user as an active participant will further add to the teaching power of the Web: users will learn by doing everything from laboratory experiments to client meetings.

Measurements

Another characteristic of effective KM systems is their ability to measure their own effectiveness, which can both justify the investment of time and resources and permit continual improvements based on what has worked well, in contrast to what was less successful. Such measurements can be based on readily collected, accumulated, and correlated information provided both by the system itself and by individual users. They can include both hard data and the relatively hard-to-measure factors implicit in a system designed to help optimize the use of knowledge and human capital.

Measurements of KM effectiveness are generally of two types: measures of the aggregate impact of KM, largely quantitative and reportable as data; and the more qualitative assessments of individual users' experiences with the system. Both are crucial, especially for a professional services organization and most other organizations where knowledge and its use are critical factors of success. Sample measurements include:

Aggregate impact measurements

Time required to assemble a project team or complete a project

Number of employees at key competency levels

Time/cost savings of "distance learning" versus alternative methods

Revenue gain or expense reduction associated with heavily KM-dependent work

Before-and-after customer satisfaction surveys

Qualitative assessments. Just as important, however, are measurements based on the individual user's experiences with the KM system. Using Web-based tools, users can provide important insights into the actual use and perceived value of the system. They can identify features that have been helpful, note missing pieces, pose questions, and make suggestions for improving the system to make it more valuable. On-line surveys, questions attached to user sessions, or even virtual focus groups can automate the collection of user feedback.

Knowledge Generation

An effective KM program builds on its own success and momentum. Knowledge generation refers to knowledge that has not necessarily been collected from organizational and external sources, but has been created by both the *use* of the KM system and the *lessons* knowledge managers have learned from that use.

For example, knowledge that originates with the KM system itself can answer such questions as these:

What types of knowledge delivery formats are most effective in improving performance, considering time, cost, and performance measurements?

Which users or user communities benefit most from KM use? Which do so least, and why?

What do usage and user surveys tell us about competency gaps that should be addressed by training, development, staffing, and recruitment functions?

Which organizational units, functions, or locations seem to have a surplus of intellectual capital or an abundance of men and women with higher-level use of the KM system and competencies to match?

Which new competencies (such as the ability to learn and apply strategic planning principles presented in virtual seminars) should the company add to its competency framework and recruit for, or develop? Which individual managers and professionals in the organization contribute most to the KM system by creating and imparting new knowledge? Who are the real thought leaders?

The mechanization of a KM system on the Web permits real-time tracking of usage, measurements, and correlation with measurement data generated by other HR and business systems. In the new world of Web-based HR management technology, this can have profound and far-reaching impacts on the company's ability to improve its intellectual capital cost effectively.

Lessons Learned from Towers Perrin's Work Establishing a Knowledge Management Project

The components for building a successful knowledge management environment described in this chapter should work for many different types of organizations. However, the right approach to implementing and leveraging a successful environment can be highly specific to each organization's structure and business needs. The details will vary for each firm undertaking such a project. It might be helpful, however, to share some of the observations and experiences of the Towers Perrin team.

Organize the right KM team. We assembled a diverse group of dedicated people to serve as our core KM team. It included people from different departments and lines of business who brought expertise in communications, technology, web design, project management, knowledge management, and subject matter. This approach helped us gain broad buy-in and engagement at the outset, and combining so much varied expertise and so many perspectives clearly produced a much better result.

Maintain a line of sight to business priorities. In developing a prototype applicable to one of our lines of business, we combined the knowledge and tools needed by people to do their work with general firm-wide information. We learned that our people were not engaged or interested in initial efforts that tended to focus on general corporate information. Our experience reinforced the premise that content has to be very relevant to users and usable in the work they do.

Instill audience ownership. Our content was structured around major items of practical knowledge; communities and members were asked to contribute to the review of content, development, and quality. Building the best technical system alone will not result in a positive return on investment. For sustained benefit, the users must be sufficiently engaged to take ownership and responsibility for the community's continued use and evolution.

Listen to your audience. We tested the design and overall communication and training plan with groups of people with different skills, needs, and geographical locations, and we made adjustments based on their feedback. Users will give the best and most relevant feedback, an approach that increases buy-in and connection.

Overcome organizational inertia. We rolled out the environment in phases and immediately started leveraging the platform through virtual seminars, hot-topic discussions, and other events. Organizations often make a mistake by assuming they are done as soon as the KM system is deployed. In reality, the work has just started. If the KM activity is to take hold and really transform the work environment, the firm must establish a long-term commitment and plan. In addition to sustaining the system, the plan should include efforts to both reinforce the messages and demonstrate the value of the new KM environment. In the end, the challenge is to effect change in behavior up and down the organization, and to succeed, it is necessary to win the hearts and minds of the audience. That requires an ongoing effort.

Assess and adjust. We developed performance assessment criteria that can be tracked over time through quantitative and qualitative analysis. We have already made changes based on a better understanding of how consultants actually use the environment and how well the technology supported various collaborative efforts. We have been encouraged by consultant participation in the early stages of the rollout: Over one-half of the initially targeted community members had participated in one or two of our virtual seminars on hot practice topics. Feedback was very positive about the event's value. Our perception was that many more people were able to participate without any hand-holding, compared with earlier efforts; we considered this a very positive trend.

Essentially all members have used the site, and the numbers are growing; the average length of time working within the systems has doubled, and we believe that more time is actually spent on work and not just browsing.

Meaningful percentages of survey respondents indicate that the community has reduced the time required to complete a client assignment, improved the quality of the client deliverables, and aided in the development of new business opportunities.

Prove the concept; leverage the success. Based on our demonstrated results with the first line of business, each of our other lines of business is now working with our core team developing its own KM environment based on the common technology platform, tools, processing, and staffing models. By achieving this shared vision, we have been able to integrate our knowledge across all practice areas and to support many of our Go-To-Market initiatives, such as Mergers and Acquisitions, Total Rewards, and Human Resource Effectiveness.

Leverage the platform. The theme for next year is "leveraging the platform." First, we are extending the "community" concept to our clients, thereby creating a tighter and more tangible partnership opportunity. Second, using the past year's experience, we will continue to test new approaches, activities, and tools, and then leverage those lessons to the rest of the firm.

In addition to focusing on people, we are also enhancing and leveraging technology. There is a continual stream of new products and improvements to consider, such as video/audio streaming, distance learning and collaborative tools, electronic project rooms, and better Web integration and telephony. Demand for bandwidth is insatiable, both for people in the office and for all of our mobile users. It is important to keep the need for these tools in perspective to make sure they really do contribute to the firm's success. We recommend the use of smaller pilots to make sure the enhancements are worth the cost and effort.

Cultivate partnerships with vendors. Collaboration with our vendors is increasing and producing much better and faster results

The Challenge of Measurement

While Web technology provides the means for measuring the effectiveness of a knowledge management system (providing up-to-date data on quantitative measurements, such as hits and on-line feedback for qualitative response), the development of measurement strategy remains a major challenge for most developers and managers of KM systems. There are several central issues that need to be addressed in a measurement strategy:

- Identify places to invest additional resources and effort to add value to the system for users.
- Determine the effectiveness of the KM system in improving revenue growth and profitability.
- Ascertain which types of users (by function, responsibility level, line of business, or other category) are most and least satisfied by the system, and why.
- Decide which measurements should be tracked over time, especially in the early phases of KM system development, as awareness among users grows and enhancements are introduced.

Web technology also permits the collection of qualitative information that not only measures the growing use of the Towers Perrin system, but also provides key insights about features that work well and improvements that will provide value to users and their clients. We obtain this feedback in two ways:

- Quarterly surveys of Towers Perrin practitioners, with questions focusing on the impact of KM system use on day-to-day work, as well as the system's value in attracting new business or expanding current assignments
- Feedback buttons throughout the KM system, asking users to "rate this page" from a range of perspectives, including ease of location and need for additional links or more information

Such survey results provide Towers Perrin with key insights on possible missing pieces, improvements in technology, and practical, real-world issues in the realm of KM.

Recognizing the importance of developing and applying meaningful measurements, KM system managers at Towers Perrin developed a strategy that includes both quantitative and qualitative measurements.

(Continued)

> Interestingly, our experience has been that while the quantitative data are important, and indicate continuing growth in the use and value of the system, the qualitative information gained through user-surveys and feedback provides greater insights into ways to improve the system for individuals and user communities.

for all involved. There is great interest in knowledge management among many key application and hardware providers, and thus a willingness to work more closely with us to better understand our business needs and to implement workable solutions.

Summary

The culture, content, and process challenges of KM notwithstanding, the rapidly changing Web technology landscape is creating unprecedented opportunities for organizations seeking to make KM part of their way of doing business. All of the technological building blocks exist and are continually improving, from content management, personalization, and collaboration, through data integration and measurement. It is our prediction that virtually all organizations will be incorporating Web-based knowledge management into their business strategies before long.

PART II

Designing and Implementing Web-Based HR

10

Creating a Business Case for Your Organization's Web-Based HR Initiative

*Jennifer Lego**

MOST OF US are convinced that using Web-based tools will significantly improve the delivery of HR services to employees, managers, employment applicants, retirees, and suppliers. We intuitively know that efficiencies such as lower costs will result, due to redesigned processes and elimination of manual intervention. Further, we believe that customer satisfaction levels will improve due to faster and better completion of transactions, and new services and communication opportunities will open up. The Internet is the best conduit to come along to date. But how do we convince senior management of these facts? A business case is needed.

*Jennifer Lego is the manager of the metropolitan New York Towers Perrin Technology Solutions consulting practice, which focuses on technology and administration issues within Human Resources. She concentrates on process, strategy, and business case development.

New York office address: 335 Madison Avenue, New York, New York 10017-4605.

What Is a Business Case?

Just what is a business case, what should be included in one, and how can we make sure the business case will be accepted? These questions and many others are often asked of us during consulting assignments. This chapter will answer basic questions about a business case that will help the reader be successful in future projects where a business case is required.

Definition and Scope of an HR Web Business Case

A business case can be mystifying if you have never put one together before. Quite simply, a business case is a tool that supports planning and decision making and includes financial analysis, business benefits, and consequences related to the fundamental questions posed by the project. A Web-based HR business case can be used to address all types of questions, for example:

- Why do we need a Web-Based solution?
- Should we implement employee and/or manager self-service? And if so, when?
- Should we use our existing intranet for handling the HR transactions?
- Can we use our legacy Human Resources system as the underlying database for the Web solution, or do we need a new global Enterprise Resource Planning (ERP) system?
- Should we plan and implement a shared services group as part of the Web initiative?
- Can we go with a one-vendor HR portal strategy, or should we go with a "best-of-breed" approach?

A business case must always be built around objectives: business, financial, functional, operational, or some combination. A business case will include a project timeline, critical success factors, financial analysis including payback period, contingencies, risks, and any indicators that would signal a change in the business results of the project. By identifying contingencies, risks, and indicators that would change business results, the business case audience is reminded that contributions to the success of the business case require input and awareness in many areas. Some of these areas may be beyond the control of the company, such as new government regulations, or changes in the competitive market. Tangible and intangible issues, benefits, and risks are also typically included in a business case.

The business case author must remember that no matter how carefully the business case is thought out and presented, readers will not always draw from it the same conclusions as the author has drawn. It is important for the author to provide as much evidence as possible to support the business case objectives, to draw effective conclusions that address the subject of the case, and to identify any findings that could be misinterpreted.

Why Is a Business Case Necessary?

A good business case is normally essential to selling a major project within an organization. An exception may be a project dealing with e-business, which will be addressed later in this chapter. To help create a successful business case, you must understand what drives the success of the business, or of the business unit. It is almost impossible to propose solutions to a problem or business issue if the basic business of the company is not understood. Having an accepted business case also helps manage costs and benefits during project implementation and assists in keeping the project on track.

A business case provides continuity during the life of the project. Executives and project sponsors get promoted, move on to other projects, or leave the company. Their replacements will undoubtedly ask why the project was undertaken and how much progress has been made. A current and well-documented business case will explain the rationale for the project, outline the expected benefits and costs, and could show actual results already achieved—all of which helps secure the support of the new employee.

A business case can also be used to show how the project will achieve the intended goals, helping to answer any "naysayer's" concerns and keeping the project focused. The case should also be used to establish a benefits tracking process from the beginning of the project, so that continuous feedback can be delivered to project sponsors, and all interested parties can be made aware of the project's success.

Clearly, there can be many reasons for building a business case other than the financial justification of a project.

The Business Case Team

It is almost always better to develop a business case using more than one person; it is better to use many people working together as a team. This team could be called a core team, review committee, steering group, or something else that fits with the culture of the organization. The team usually has representation from several parts of the organization, including the IT group and users, Human Resources staff, business unit managers, senior financial managers, and other high-level executives. The team also gathers information from outside the organization to support the business case.

The team will work together for the duration of the business case development. Development could take anywhere from a few weeks to several months, depending on the amount of detail necessary in the case. A sample timeline for building a business case is shown in Figure 10-1.

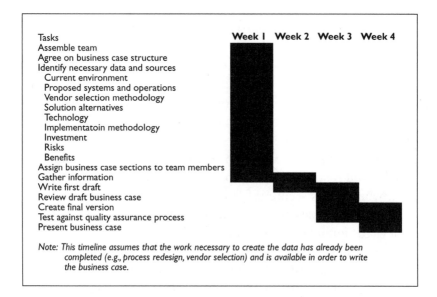

Tasks	Week 1	Week 2	Week 3	Week 4
Assemble team				
Agree on business case structure				
Identify necessary data and sources				
Current environment				
Proposed systems and operations				
Vendor selection methodology				
Solution alternatives				
Technology				
Implementatoin methodology				
Investment				
Risks				
Benefits				
Assign business case sections to team members				
Gather information				
Write first draft				
Review draft business case				
Create final version				
Test against quality assurance process				
Present business case				

Note: This timeline assumes that the work necessary to create the data has already been completed (e.g., process redesign, vendor selection) and is available in order to write the business case.

Figure 10-1 Sample timeline for business case development.

The business case team will gather the costs needed, identify possible benefits, develop the linkages with the organization's e-business goals and long-range business plans, identify people costs, and assign value to any IT contributions. Through working on the case together, the team becomes a vehicle for spreading a sense of ownership and support for the business case. The team is also important in a highly competitive or critical atmosphere, because any conflicts or questions over the business case can be worked out early and communicated widely by the working team. Finally, it may be advisable to bring any people especially critical of the intended Web-based project onto the team at the outset as a way to ensure that their concerns are being addressed and perhaps to also win them over.

What Should Be in the Business Case?

A business case should be clear, logical, objective, and thorough. The business objectives should be clearly stated and should support what the business is trying to accomplish. However the business case is designed, it must be directed toward achieving its purpose, whether that is securing budget, planning for a large technology implementation, providing decision support, or something else.

Risk factors should clearly be identified and divided into two groups:

1. Risk factors completely beyond your control (rate of inflation, competitor's actions, foreign currency exchange rates, natural disasters, acts of war, government regulations, etc.)
2. Risk factors you *can* influence or control to some degree (skill levels of professional staff, timely completion of related projects, achieving cost control goals, recruitment and hiring of key individuals, etc.)

The five most common sections or categories included in a business case are:

Introduction and overview

Assumptions

Recommendations

Business impacts

Risks and contingencies

These categories can be arranged in any order that makes sense for your particular audience.

Introduction and Overview

The "introduction and overview" is a statement of the purpose of the business case and project goal. It should be kept brief and to the point, much the same as an executive summary. Project or company history may be reviewed at this point if relevant. The overview should include an assessment of the current environment related to the project, including relevant issues, what is currently working well, and what is not working well. The desired project outcome should be outlined, including major changes that will impact technology, the organization, HR, employees, line managers, and others. It may be necessary to include a high-level statement on financials at this point, specifically, the possible investment and high-level savings related to the project, again depending on the audience.

Sample Business Case Table of Contents

- High-level business case (executive summary)
- Strategic context
- Assessment of current state
- Desired project outcome
- Assumptions
- Recommendations
- Financial analysis
- Risks and contingencies
- Implementation plan
- Supporting appendixes

Assumptions

Assumptions can be as detailed as necessary and can cover categories such as available project resources and staffing, technology, financial considerations, global solutions, processes, service quality, outsourcing, HR and organizational structure, or other areas. Examples of some assumptions that may be found in a Web technology business case are the following:

- The current HRIS (e.g., PeopleSoft, SAP, Lawson, Oracle, or other system installed in your organization) is the system of record and will be used to support the HR website.
- All legacy HR applications not part of the HRIS will migrate to it within 18 months and will use all of the HRIS system's available functionality.
- All line managers will have access to the Internet through laptop or desktop technology.
- All employees will have access to the Internet through desktop technology or kiosks.
- The HR service center will be responsible for supporting line manager and employee questions concerning HR transactions initiated through the Web or other self-service applications, e.g., Interactive Voice Response (IVR).
- The IT help desk will be responsible for supporting line manager and employee questions concerning self-service technology.

As you can see, this example is not detailed. However, this level of detail is usually sufficient in the body of a business case. More detailed supplemental information can be placed in an appendix, if needed.

Recommendations

The business case recommendations must be laid out in a logical fashion so that the audience understands why the Web-based HR solution is being developed and implemented. There should be no gaps that the audience must fill in and no major questions with regard to such items as timing, costs, roles, responsibilities, and impacts left unanswered. When presenting the recommendations, consider grouping them and possibly summarizing the benefits and opportunities presented by the business issues. Consider presenting the rationale for the Web-based initiatives, the specific recommendations, and the expected outcomes. In making the HR technology recommendations, a sample opportunity and rationale summary could be as follows:

- Maintaining separate and unique HR websites across the business units causes increased expense, duplication of work, conflicting policy issues, confusion in employees' minds, data integrity problems, and questions regarding the system of record. Therefore, a single website is needed.
- Collecting information for corporate-mandated programs such as succession planning is time- and labor-intensive, especially when done manually, and therefore a global data reporting solution is suggested.
- Self-service tools for line managers and employees, specifically IVR technology, have been used in benefits open enrollment and to obtain 401(k) account balances. Due to the limitations of IVR technology, it could not be extended to other areas. Web technology affords us the opportunity to extend to other areas.

You may want to consider organizing the opportunity and rationale summary section by, for example, technology, organization, and functional area impacted.

Next, recommendations should be listed that specifically address the opportunities identified. For example:

- Use Web technology for manager and employee self-service applications.
- Migrate the various HR legacy systems being used in the business units to a single, global HRIS platform, such as PeopleSoft, SAP, Lawson, or Oracle.
- Use the HRIS-provided workflow as the primary vehicle to redesign processes and to eliminate duplicate data validation and entry.
- Begin an Internet training program for HR staff. Increase the Web HTML and Java Script skills within HR and IT development groups.

Finally, the expected outcomes should be listed for the business case area being discussed. For example:

- Line management and business leaders will have access to management information and transactions, rather than having to rely on HR for initiation, extraction, summarization, and processing.
- Employees will be responsible for personal data changes and transactions, e.g., adding a dependent, changing a beneficiary, or applying for a new job.
- Managers will have all performance management and compensation data, as well as modeling tools, at their fingertips.
- Career development will be a more open and collaborative process for employees, as they can more easily participate in setting and tracking career goals and can self-enroll in training and learning offerings.
- Speed and quality of decisions will be improved through use of Internet tools.

Hopefully, this example of opportunity summary, recommendation, and expected outcomes shows a logical sequence for presenting the information. Keep in mind that these are only a few examples. You may be required to use a different format dictated by the culture of your organization. Also, remember that information must be presented to align with the way in which the audience processes information in your organization.

Business impacts

The business impact section identifies what the reader can expect to see at the conclusion of the project. The expected outcomes in the example above were the business impact statements for the technology area in the example project.

The overall business impact must be addressed also, and must include a financial analysis. The rigor of the financial analysis will vary from business case to business case, depending on what is required by your organization, but at a minimum, return-on-investment (ROI) and cost/benefit analysis calculations are expected.

A simple definition of ROI is the measure of the productivity of the investment in the HR Web technology project, without accounting for interest expense, inflation, opportunity costs, and so forth. ROI is the income from the project divided by the total project costs, as a simple ratio, where ROI measures the incremental gain from an action, divided by the cost of that action (e.g., an investment that costs $100 and pays back $50 has an ROI of 50 percent). Management often will set a "hurdle rate" as the percentage below which they will not invest in a project.

Cost/benefit analysis is widely used for planning, decision support, program evaluation, proposal evaluation, and other purposes. The term itself has no precise definition beyond the implication that both positive and negative impacts to the business are going to be summarized and weighed against each other over time. Some business cases will include a break-even diagram as part of the cost/benefit analysis, similar to the simple example in Figure 10-2. Management may define the "hurdle rate" as a project com-

OPERATING COSTS / SAVINGS (IN THOUSANDS OF $)		
Add:		
	Service staff	1,000
	Management and Administration	500
	Technology - Employee Service Center	300
	Technology - Web	250
	Technology - HRIS/Payroll Core Application	500
	Subtotal	2,550
Less:		
	FTE removal through reengineering	(4,500)
Add:		
	Incremental operating expenses	175
	Net annual savings	(1,775)
ONE TIME INVESTMENTS		
	Web Technology	1,000
	HRIS/Payroll upgrade	700
	Internal project labor	650
	External conversion and consulting expense	400
	Total one-time investment of capital	2,750
Estimated Return on Investment (ROI in years)		1.55
Estimated Return on Investment		65%

Figure 10-2 Sample cost/benefits information.

pletion date. If that date is too far in the future, the project will not get funded. That is, if a project cannot break even after a specified time period, such as 24 months, management will not view the investment as a sound one.

Other costs often reviewed in the business impact section of a business case include soft, or intangible, costs. These could include things such as improvements in corporate image, customer satisfaction, or employee morale. Does it contribute to an important business objective; is it large enough to matter? For nonfinancial benefits, you may want to consider the following:

- Make the impact tangible. Rather than just stating "improved employee satisfaction," describe why, for example, employees will retain ownership of their own data.
- Connect the impact with business objectives and business case results. If the business objective is to move to a new global HRIS that includes employee and line manager self-service, clearly state what the expected results are in relation to these objectives, even if a dollar amount cannot be attached to the results.
- Emphasize the anticipated financial or other business value of the objective. Even if you cannot assign a known dollar amount to the benefit, you may be able to state financial benefits in terms of increased productivity, expanded market share, improved competitive position, or some other measure.

The cost/benefit portion of the business case is the section that usually receives the greatest scrutiny. It is important to ensure that all data and benefits used in this section can be supported and defended. The author will also need to judge how much detail goes into the body of the business case and what is more appropriate for an appendix.

The final item that is usually included in this section of the business case is the project timeline. This can be high-level or quite detailed, depending on the type of project covered by the business case. The timeline shown in Figure 10-3 is an example of a high-level project timeline.

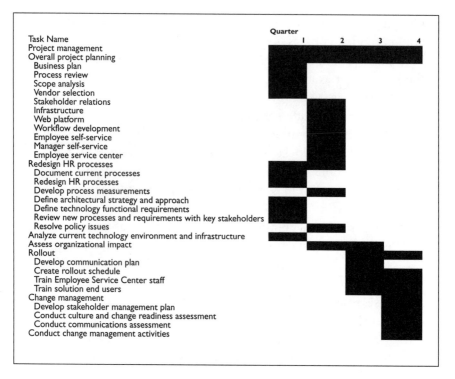

Figure 10-3 Sample project timeline.

The timeline section should, at a minimum, include when the analysis period begins and ends and a statement on whether it is synchronized with the calendar or fiscal year.

Risks and Contingencies

It is important to clearly identify any risks and contingencies related to the business case. They are usually stated so that the audience is clear about how the expected benefits could be impacted. A typical way of arranging risks and contingencies is to arrange them according to high, medium, or low threats to the project, as shown in the example.

Example of Possible Project Risks

High-risk threats

- Competing IT projects (for example, implementation of the new Financials package) could result in either the redirection of scarce IT resources or an increase in expected external consulting fees.
- If the project falls behind schedule, Business Units A and B have stated they will delay conversion to the new HRIS by 18 months, due to anticipated acquisitions.
- Limited experience with a global HRIS implementation may impact the desired project timeline.

Moderate-risk threats

- Delays in vendor product delivery may cause delays in expected savings.
- The current HR staff may feel threatened and a large portion of them may leave due to lack of understanding of probable future organizational structure.
- Growth due to acquisitions may require increased resources for IT and HR, which will delay expected cost savings.

Low-risks threats

- Project phasing may change due to geographic differences.
- Customer service quality may suffer during implementation.

Data Sources for the Business Case

A business case should clearly state the boundaries of the analysis so that the audience is comfortable that all relevant costs and benefits are included. Data will come from many sources throughout the organization, to support the scope of the case, as well as from external sources. These sources can include the following:

- The business plan
- Budget information (historical, current, or future)
- A feasibility study
- Results from a pilot project

- An outside consultant's estimate
- Vendor data
- Market data
- Industry data
- Benchmark or "best in class" information

It is not necessary to include data from all of these sources. Use only those that help build a solid business case. However, whatever the data source, ensure that it is relevant and reliable.

Selling the Business Case

Not all business cases succeed in convincing management to proceed. In fact, many fail because they have not been marketed properly to senior management, the HR or IT community, or the business units. Business cases often fail when met with skepticism or a cold shoulder from management, since they will, as a result, not be supported whole-heartedly by the organization. Business cases sometimes fail when they don't clearly fill the immediate objective such as meeting a needed time frame or expected cost reduction amount. Business cases can fail when the proposal or plan is implemented and the real costs (or benefits) turn out to be very different from the business case estimates. Three main reasons business cases fail are the following:

1. They are not based on learning and experiences gained from previous business cases for Web or HR technology projects. Often business cases promise unrealistic results. Management knows projects run late, exceed budget, and deliver less than expected.
2. The business case does not tell a sufficiently convincing story with compelling logic and facts. You have to do your homework.
3. The business case has been developed in a vacuum, without necessary input from all areas impacted by the proposed project. Business cases dealing with IT, communications, and infrastructure changes usually cut across boundaries such as organizations, management levels, functions, and

budgets. Therefore, it is necessary to draw selectively from all involved entities.

It is critical to include stakeholders in business case development. After the business case is developed, a series of meetings with key stakeholders and senior management may be needed to familiarize them with the business case and proposed project, to gain their support, and to get input on the business case prior to securing their final approval.

Specific Web Focus Required

Although this chapter has so far outlined the framework for a traditional business case, Internet-based projects have some unique considerations. Some of these are addressed in this section.

It is without doubt that the Internet has fundamentally changed many things in companies: how information is shared, how projects are conducted, how all types of transactions are completed, how employees communicate with others (internally and externally), and how IT investments are viewed. Today, organizations around the world turn to Web technology to change the way work is accomplished.

Lessons Learned

- Challenges to business cases are primarily to methodology or analysis.
- Clearly show how a proposed project supports business goals.
- Make the business case compelling, specific, and accurate.
- Use a consistent approach to business case design so that your organization can learn from previous business case exercises.
- Remember to take egos and the need for validation into account.
- Understand the constraints under which business units operate.
- Stay on top of changes in the regulatory and competitive environment in which the business operates.
- Structure the business case team to minimize the influence of any one individual, department, or business unit.
- Get input from the business units.

Because of this, many companies are discarding conventional thinking about the need for a return on investment and are focusing on how the initiatives advance their overall business strategy. A small but growing number of companies has recently begun searching for new ways to measure ROI of their e-business projects. For less strategic projects, such as those that increase the efficiency of the supply chain, traditional ROI evaluations are still being used. But the bottom line is that e-business is seen increasingly as something that must be pursued at all costs.

There are two conflicting views on the importance of an e-business business case—whether one is necessary or not. In a recent survey of 375 IT and business executives conducted by *InformationWeek* in conjunction with *Business Week*, only 17 percent of IT managers and 12 percent of business executives said their companies formally required them to demonstrate the potential payback of their e-business applications, and 28 percent of IT managers and 39 percent of business executives said their companies required no ROI evaluation whatsoever.

This portion of the chapter will examine thoughts relevant to both sides of the argument. The reader must decide what is appropriate, based on the culture and requirements of a particular organization.

Argument 1: A Business Case Is not Necessary

The basic economics of information technology are unlike those of more traditional assets. People in the IT world are finding it necessary to develop new financial strategies rather than rely on the old strategies to help prove the necessity or benefits of an IT project. The rate of technical advancement is also accelerating, and standards and architectures are changing daily. Nevertheless, the legacy-based management practices and financial strategies of both technologists and financial officers have changed little in the face of these new realities. Developing rational and viable financial strategies to accommodate technological change is an institutional imperative for effective information technology management.

It is felt that as the role of IT becomes increasingly strategic to the success of an organization, a new set of metrics must be applied to investments. This set of metrics should attempt to measure IT's ability to generate increased revenue or faster growth for the business through Web-based projects, rather than through focusing solely on non-IT investments. It is also believed that in today's environment, when a business case involving e-business becomes clearly provable, it is too late to win competitive advantage. Before the Web, IT projects were typically measured—and justified—by the cost savings or efficiencies they brought to a company. Invest money in a common HRIS for the organization, for example, and the ROI will come from lower process and administration costs over time, for the IT and HR departments. E-business is different. Goals of a Web project are often strategic and involve many areas of a company. Web project investments affect areas that are more difficult to measure, such as maintaining a competitive edge, keeping pace with competitors, and improving total revenue and customer satisfaction.

ROI, by its very nature, is based on steady-state behavior and may be difficult to apply during major industry transitions. The dot.coms really focus more on return on relationships than return on investment. The traditional cost/benefit analysis is focused on cost reduction. With e-business, the focus is aimed more at business efficiencies and new revenue channels. Also, traditional ROI doesn't always work for e-business because there may be no reliable benchmarks for similar businesses.

Most IT workers say developing Web-based applications is relatively easy, compared with broader, deeper, functional HRIS applications. But measuring their financial benefits is another story. It is not easy to calculate traditional ROI on these projects because the primary advantages of a company's Internet or intranet applications—improving employee productivity, morale, decision making, information sharing, and time to market—are difficult to quantify because they don't directly generate revenue. Many Web applications are internally focused, so determining a rate-of-return figure is challenging. A strict ROI calculation may not justify the time spent collecting and organizing supporting data. Even with these issues, IT managers say their companies often earn back the money spent on HR Web development costs in one to three years, in savings from expense reductions in widely divergent areas, from printing and postage to employee productivity.

For organizations that do not choose to conduct a formal ROI evaluation for Web technology projects, there needs to be coordination between the CEO, the CIO, and all employees and business partners that will be affected. The probable benefits and risks must be discussed in order to minimize the possibility of failure.

E-business requires businesses to work in a more short-term mode, measured in weeks or months rather than the multiple-year mode that most "brick-and-mortar" organizations are comfortable with today. Projects in the e-business environment must bring results to the bottom line immediately.

A sense of urgency—meeting or beating the competition—is forcing many companies to push ahead with Internet projects without considering strict ROI calculations. Business leaders are less concerned about a dollar return than with enhancing the company's competitive edge, creating a marketing channel, or improving customer satisfaction. Because of this, companies may choose to forgo a formal business case development for Web-based HR projects.

Argument 2: A Business Case Is Necessary

Counter to the arguments just presented are equally valid reasons for retaining the use of business case development for all Web-based HR projects.

As the e-business market matures, business leaders are insisting that funding for Web projects be justified. Many companies believe that the use of conventional ROI metrics can and should be applied to Internet projects, proving how e-business is becoming more ingrained in the business mainstream. Companies also state that they are less likely to conduct an e-business project without doing an ROI study than they were a few years ago.

It must be noted that it is easier to measure the ROI of an e-business application that cuts back-office processing costs than one that improves customer satisfaction. Whatever metrics are used in a business case for Web technology, they must be flexible enough to adapt as a company's e-business strategy evolves. Business and IT managers must demonstrate some level of return on Internet investments, and many are devising new ways to demon-

---

Criteria for Web-Based IT Investment Decisions

- Proposed project fit with the overall business strategy
- Anticipated return on investment
- Likelihood that the IT department will be able to fulfill the project requirements within the stated time period
- Ability of the business to adjust to the changes the new system will demand
- Regulatory or other mandated requirements

---

strate the value of Web projects. Some companies look at each part of the business the project impacts, using value metrics within those parts. Companies also are viewing websites as separate businesses with their own profit-and-loss statements.

Conventional ROI metrics—for example, comparing the estimated cost of using an electronic form versus using a paper form, and calculating how long it will take to recoup the IT investment—can be used to determine e-business investments. Some other topics that should be addressed in an HR Internet business case are the following:

- How the initiative targets and helps customers (employees, managers, etc.) with improved service quality
- How it leverages, or helps reuse, existing IT infrastructure and resources
- How it helps position the company to be the first to market a particular service to attract, retain, and develop intellectual capital
- How it fits strategically with other business, IT, and HR organization initiatives

If some or most of the above items are within your scope, then a business case for Web-based projects may make sense for your organization. If a case is completed, you will probably find it necessary to use all of the sections outlined in the beginning of the chapter.

A Framework for Transforming Your HR Function

*Brian D. Beatty**

 THE TOTAL TRANSFORMATION of Human Resources (HR) as a function has become both a business necessity and a strategic, value-adding opportunity. This transformation, which calls for a paradigm shift that will change an HR department from a functionally fragmented, administrative cost center to a value-adding, integrated organization aligned with corporate business strategies, will not happen incrementally in most cases, but will require an overall framework, such as the one described in this chapter.

The transformation of HR can, and should, be based on more than technology that makes the work more "efficient," cutting costs or speeding delivery of products and services to HR cus-

*Brian D. Beatty is a Managing Consultant in the Chicago office of Towers Perrin. He specializes in the transformation, redesign, and reorganization of the HR function, especially in the use of technology to bring about needed change.

Chicago office address: 200 West Madison Street, Suite 3100, Chicago, Illinois 60606-3414.

tomers in the organization. The enabling technology of the Internet and other new and emerging technologies provide the tools needed for HR transformation, but in themselves cannot make HR the strategic partner it should be in organizations dependent on human capital for their success.

Instead, the true transformation of HR requires analysis and identification of opportunities for improvement in five interrelated areas that are the "success drivers" of effective HR, including the *people* in HR and their competencies; *processes* used to deliver HR products and services; the *culture* of the HR organization; its *structure*; and the *technology* used. This integrated, or "holistic," approach is guided by the organization's business rationale for having employees, now and in the future, and adds value to the organization for reasons that include:

- The availability of the right people to do the work of the organization at levels that provide competitive advantage
- Enterprisewide alignment of individual goals and work objectives with strategic business goals
- The reduction of risk factors associated with inadequate competencies, noncompliance, or poor morale
- Cost savings in doing the work of a transformed HR department, which move directly to the company's bottom line

For most organizations undertaking this critical HR transformation process, the approach recommended here ensures that no important issues are left unexamined, that all opportunities for improvement have been identified, and that the final design of a transformed HR department truly adds value to the organization.

Today's HR: The Need for Transformation

In undertaking this approach, a useful start is an understanding of the issues that usually need to be "overcome" in HR transformation, the historical and still prevalent issues limiting the ability of HR to think and act strategically. These issues, which have shaped the culture, people, processes, structure, and technology of HR, help provide an understanding of the current state of affairs in most HR departments—"how we got this way," and what needs to be changed to transform HR.

HR's Culture: Reactive, Supportive, but not Strategic

The cultural issues that have historically limited the human resource function's ability to think and act strategically (which continue to pervade many HR departments despite huge gains made in the "status" of HR's role as a strategic business partner) stem from HR's long history as a reactive, almost "defensive" function in the organization. Never recognized as a profit center or potential source of revenue (except by cost cutters who achieved short-term gains through downsizing or other reductions in force), both the old personnel department and today's HR department have been essentially "order takers" for the more strategically oriented functions that bring results to the bottom line. For example,

- Manufacturing people faced with quality control problems see a need for more and better training of production workers, and go to HR for new training programs.
- New government regulations require improved record keeping, policy development, and distribution. HR must respond with collection and analysis of new kinds of data on applicants and employees, and other measures to ensure compliance with employment law.
- Unwanted turnover is decimating the company's technical human resources, as young engineers seem to be treating the company as a "training ground" for better jobs. As a result, HR's compensation managers are asked for a more attractive pay package to stem the tide.
- Finance personnel who planned the new merger have projected a 20 percent reduction in total employment by the end of the year, and give the job of "streamlining" the new organization to the HR department.

Historically, these and similar business requirements, and the measures taken to address new needs, have been identified, and their remedies set in motion, outside the HR function. As "order takers," HR people have been presented with business requirements and asked to provide solutions, usually within parameters determined in advance by non-HR strategic planners. The results can be disastrous, in their creation of an HR department culture that is essentially reactive, for the real needs of the business.

For example, those first- and second-year engineers who are leaving for "better jobs" may not be leaving for better pay, regardless of what they say to company people in exit interviews. The real problem is that they see little or no opportunity for advancement; or feel they are working with outdated technology; or simply have no confidence in top management's ability to lead the company. Higher pay would help, but the "best and brightest" engineers (with the best job offers) would still leave for companies that seem to have what they want from an employer.

The point here is that the HR function can, and should, be proactive, both in identifying the business requirements that call for new or improved HR programs, and in developing the strategies that will most effectively address these requirements. It should be the HR department that tells the manufacturing department that inadequate training is causing quality problems, and what kinds of training or recruitment programs are needed; tells the merger planners which workers will be redundant in light of the new business plan; tells what to do about turnover; and so on. Further, in its new role as a strategic business partner, the HR function needs to shed its historic self-perception as a "support" function that responds to, rather than anticipates, a business's demand for personnel.

In some organizations, that is already happening, with HR vice presidents among the top officials shaping corporate strategies in their companies. For most companies, however, the cultural "sea change" required to transform the HR department will require more than just a "seat at the table" of top management, and, in addition to the *culture*, will include changes in the kinds of *people* performing HR work, *process* issues, the *technology* used, and the *structure* of the HR function. As shown in Figure 11-1, all five of these "HR success drivers" are included in the overall HR transformation process.

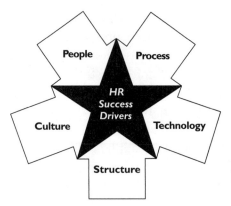

Figure 11-1 The need to transform HR. Such dramatic change requires a holistic approach to transformation.

People Issues: New Competencies Required

The transformation of HR needed to make this function a strategic partner and key contributor to the success of the organization must also address "people" issues that have historically plagued the function. The competencies of HR staffers, as well as the leadership attributes of HR directors and managers, have been shaped by past position requirements that no longer apply in most modern organizations and can only obscure the "vision" needed to develop new HR competencies.

Historically, HR staffing requirements have been a "moving target" influenced by new and changing regulatory requirements; the need for "specialists" in a growing range of HR functions from Equal Employment Opportunity (EEO) compliance to pension planning; the needs and values of a changing workforce; and technological change, which has affected both the HR function and most other work in the organization. As the overall HR function has grown and diversified, the need for specialists and technically competent staffers has grown apace. Today's new and emerging technology is already helping change that, but new "core competencies" and developmental goals are needed in most organizations to truly transform HR.

As shown in Figure 11-2, the most important of these competencies is the ability to think and act strategically as a partner

New HR Competencies

Strategic Priority	HR Competencies Required	
Partner with business unit management to develop business strategy	○ Knowledge of business and market dynamics ○ Organization change expertise	○ Strategic problem solver/influencer ○ Valued business advisor/member of leadership team
Leverage technology to maximize HR's effectiveness	○ Knowledge of core HRIS functionality and power of state-of-the-art technologies	○ Ability to translate HR needs into IS specification ○ Aggressive vendor management
Develop workforce talent to build organization capabilities	○ Learning and development needs analysis ○ Learning and development design and sourcing	○ Capability measurement
Anticipate and forecast staffing needs and influence future sources of employment	○ Forecasting on key job family requirements based on future capabilities	○ Relationship building with traditional and non-traditional sources of employment

Figure 11-2 New processes, technologies, and roles require new competencies for the HR staff and enhanced people programs to support those competencies.

with business managers in the development of business-based HR strategies. To do this, an essential requirement is knowledge of the business and its current and changing requirements; a "vision" of HR staffing requirements, which has often been obscured by the need to develop and administer benefits programs; a succession plan; or a more efficient Human Resources system.

The ability to think and act strategically, in a context defined by the business needs of the organization, is more than just a "leadership competency" that should be possessed by the HR vice president or his or her senior staffers. Knowledge of the business and its changing needs should shape planning and decision making at all levels of the HR department, in all its functions. Even the smallest change in the company's benefits plan—say, the addition of new mutual fund options for retirement planning—should be made for reasons that relate to business-based HR strategies, not because "others are doing it" or because the actuaries find it attractive.

True integration of the HR function—the "Holy Grail" that continues to elude most multifunctional Human Resources organizations—comes when all functions and staffers have the same, correct understanding of the business needs of the organization, and what these requirements mean in terms of current and future needs for people and their competencies.

As is true for all other programs and goals of the "transformed" HR department, HR development and forecasting must proceed from a strategic, business-based understanding of organizational needs, which requires a top-down transformation of HR-staffers into business managers.

Structure: Fiefdoms, Unclear Roles, "Locus" Issues

Structural issues, that is, how the HR department is organized to do its work, have also been an historic impediment to the function's ability to act strategically. As the old personnel department expanded and diversified (from a "hiring and firing" function to one responsible for a dozen or more specialized functions, from recruiting to retirement planning), each specialization has tended to become a feudalistic "fiefdom" of its own, with narrow objectives and little or no conceptual integration with other HR fiefdoms. These specialized functions (created in part by new regulatory requirements, but also a predictable outcome of the increasing complexity of benefits, compensation, training, development, succession planning, staffing, job design, and other HR disciplines) have had their own requirements for specialized knowledge and expertise, and usually their own "mission" as a business activity.

Another structural issue that has historically prevented HR from bringing "one voice" to the strategic planning table has been the ongoing debate about the proper "locus" of HR responsibilities and roles. Is it essentially a centralized staff function, or one best performed by line managers, and business unit staffers? Which parts of each HR activity (such as recruitment and applicant tracking) are better left at the headquarters level, and which should be left to field managers or operational people? Unclear roles and overlapping responsibilities are endemic in HR, especially in diverse, sprawling, and increasingly global organizations.

Process Issues: Why HR Is so "Ripe" for Reengineering

In part because of structural fragmentation, in part because of traditionally "reactive" culture in HR that has led to ad hoc solutions to immediate priorities rather than business-based strategic planning, and abetted by stand-alone PC systems and application-specific processing, the typical HR department by the end of the twentieth century had become a "process quagmire," a reengineering expert's dream come true. Virtually every process in a functionally robust HR organization—from the hiring of a new employee through promotions and training, to termination and retirement—involved redundant tasks, duplicative record keeping, and unnecessary activities created because they "seemed like a good idea at the time" and were made possible by rapidly advancing HR payroll and benefits technology.

Technology: Hard to Design, Harder to Integrate

The basic subject matter of a Human Resources system—people—consists of the most unpredictably volatile, diverse, and hard-to-quantify "content" anyone ever tried to put in a computerized information system. Infinitely variable in their attributes, continually changing as individuals, and growing or diminishing in value as corporate assets according to individual motivation and personal circumstances as much as anything else, people and data about people represent the greatest challenge ever faced by developers of corporate information systems.

For too many organizations, the way out of this dilemma has been the design and development of HR systems that focus primarily on events and transactions; the automation of administrative activities involved in hiring, paying, training, and moving people; and keeping records to ensure compliance with regulatory requirements and to keep track of head count.

The transformation of the HR department for organizations, where technology's main purpose is to automate administrative functions, will need to include a new mission for HR systems, one that goes beyond the automation of existing processes and transactional record keeping to help create and manage the skills, knowledge, and other attributes of employees that "matter most" to the organization and its success. Human Resources competencies, from leadership talents to technical skills, are the most important attributes of people in the organization, and an HR system that ignores or gives short shrift to competencies is of little help in transforming HR.

Because of HR technology's historic role as an "automater" of existing processes (and its more recent role as the "enabler" of business process reengineering that makes the same processes more efficient), the first need for organizations taking on this new HR systems mission will be to refocus the goals of the HR system's organization. Using intranets and other new technology, the work of HR systems that is transaction-based can be effectively "distributed" to others, including employees, managers, and outsourcing providers. Then the HR systems organization can focus on the challenges of creating and implementing technology that supports HR competency, development, and management, including:

- Strategic development of competency frameworks—different in every organization—that identify the specific attributes of people needed by the organization to succeed, now and in the years ahead
- Measurements of competencies that "make sense" from the company's business perspective—what is really needed, at what level of proficiency, and how it is determined
- Training and development programs delivered and managed by HR systems technology, each designed to meet strategic objectives, in "tailored" formats when appropriate, and closely monitored and measured for results
- The conceptual and systematic integration of all HR activities affecting or affected by competencies, from recruitment and staffing through assessment, development, succession planning, and competency-based pay

Holistic Approach to HR Transformation

The business reasons for having employees (whether they are regular employees, contingent workers, contractors, or even people working for an outsourcing firm) provide the essential framework for developing a "holistic" approach to transforming HR. This approach, illustrated in Figure 11-3, permits a step-by-step analysis, development, and implementation process for HR, that is

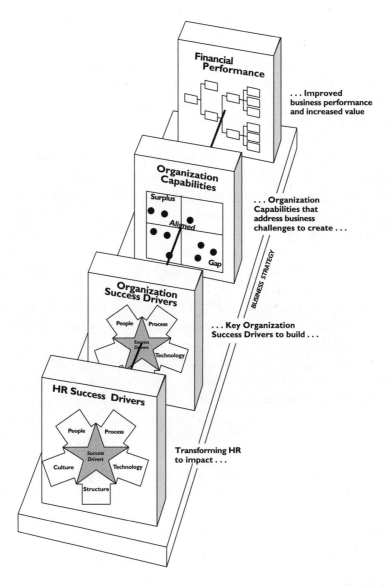

Figure 11-3 A holistic approach to transforming HR's success drivers will yield the maximum return.

guided by the same overall "business rationale" for having employees. The "steps" in this process may overlap, or be conducted simultaneously, and there may be some returning to previous steps when new data emerges, priorities change, new technology becomes available, or simply when a dedicated project team of business-oriented HR and IT people hits on a "better idea" for improving the HR function.

Because all projects need an overall mission at the outset, the first step in HR transformation is usually to articulate, communicate, and gain acceptance for the "change agenda," what it is that drives the need for change, and the overall goal of the process. This can be as brief as saying, "To make HR a strategic partner in creating a competitive advantage for the organization through its people," or it can be a laundry list of issues that seem to be the reasons why HR is ineffective.

In most cases, because HR in the past has not been a strategic player with a unified, change-oriented view of its own operations and all activities, a generalized agenda that "no one can argue with" is usually the best way to start. The next step, the conduct of fact finding and opportunities for improvement, is at the heart of the HR-transformation process, and typically requires a broad and deep "constituency" of participants, providers of data and insights, transformation "champions" who lend support, and the usual share of people who resist change of any kind. Subsequently, a new strategy for the HR function will be articulated, and an integrated solution designed and delivered.

Fact-Based Analysis Builds Business Case

The fact-finding process necessary to initiate a successful transformation of HR is ideally enterprisewide, in-depth, and customer-focused. As shown in Figure 11-4, it includes analysis of the internal HR organization as it exists; a needs analysis that identifies specific requirements of HR's customers; a cost-to-value analysis of existing HR products and services; and external analysis that includes best-practices research as well as trend analyses. In each area, the HR-transformation project team is always looking for

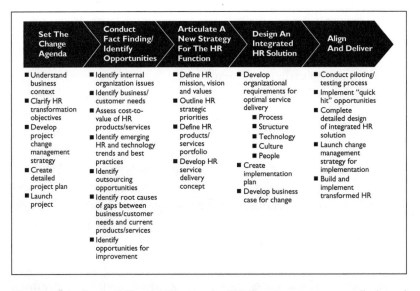

Figure 11-4 Successfully transforming the HR function requires a well-planned approach.

opportunities for improvement, as well as the "facts" of the current state of affairs, a perspective that helps integrate fact finding with other steps in HR transformation.

Internal Organization Analysis

A comprehensive review of the existing HR function includes analyses of all five areas identified as "success drivers" for HR-transformation:

- *Culture* of HR, including perceptions of the function's role, understanding of strategic business goals, values, how they view HR's customers, and policies and working conditions affecting these and other cultural issues
- *People* staffing the function or responsible for HR activities, their current competencies, developmental needs and programs in place, and how performance is measured and rewarded

- *Structural issues,* including the roles and responsibilities of those now performing HR activities throughout the organization, which can include not only staff and line HR people, but also managers and employees themselves.
- *Processes* now in place for HR product/service development and delivery, what it takes to hire a new employee, enroll someone in a training program, conduct a performance appraisal, and so on
- *Technology* currently used, or "in the works," for HR use, including both enterprisewide and application-specific systems, with particular emphasis on information retrieval systems, often a weak point for organizations in need of HR-transformation

In each of these areas, fact-finding analysis and the preliminary identification of opportunities for improvement can and should be further categorized by both specific HR functions, such as recruitment and training, and the "market segment" of HR products or services in the organization. In the holistic approach recommended here, these specific targets of analysis—such as line managers' roles in staffing and recruitment—will have been identified in the agenda-setting stage of HR transformation and are further refined in the HR customers' needs analysis part of fact finding.

Business and Customer Needs Analysis

In this critical area of fact finding, the objective is to identify what HR-customers need from the function, as created by the business needs of the organization. The illustrative chart in Figure 11-5 shows an example of an outcome of this type of analysis, which identifies the strategic business priorities for HR, ranked in terms of their importance to the company's ability to compete and how well the company currently performs compared with their competitors.

This approach to identifying HR's business priorities ensures that they are aligned with overall business strategy, and points the way to key "gaps" between what is needed by HR's customers and

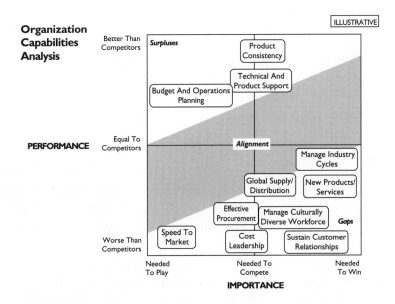

Figure 11-5 Business/customer needs analyses identify strategic business priorities for HR.

what they now get in products and services. In the illustrated example, for instance, further analysis of the "Speed to Market" program may reveal fragmented responsibilities for getting products to market promptly, with weak links between research-and-development and marketing. The HR function's business priorities might include team-building programs that help research-and-development and marketing people begin working together to achieve this goal, such as the development of team-based measurements and rewards. Because the overall process of HR transformation is holistic and driven by the same business goals, fact finding is not limited to the identification of existing issues, but also includes identification of opportunities for new or improved HR programs that address these issues.

Ideally, especially in large or complex organizations with a range of HR customers with varying needs, the business and customer needs analysis is conducted within a framework that uses a "segmentation scheme" to reflect these different needs for products and services. Without losing sight of the overall business priorities that integrate the transformation process, analysis should be able to separate the requirements of line managers from those of staffing professionals at the headquarters, or the needs of staffing professionals from benefits managers. This same segmentation of HR's customers is used in the cost-to-value analysis of HR products and services.

Cost-to-Value Analyses

In this all-important part of building the business case for HR transformation, the "hard" data of HR department resource allocation is compared with customer surveys that assess both the importance of each activity and its effectiveness as currently performed in the organization. The outcome of these analyses is illustrated in Figure 11-6, by a resource-allocation-gap analysis.

Fact-finding example. Analysis identifies improvement opportunities.

A fast-food restaurant company with over $4 billion in U.S. sales was experiencing declining growth in profitability in the late 1990s, in part because of the high cost of turnover among employees in the tight labor market of the time. Recognizing the need to transform HR to control turnover, the company undertook a fact-finding analysis that included:

- Interviews with 160 HR customers and 160 HR providers in nine regions
- Written surveys and assessments from an additional 142 individuals
- Focus groups with representatives of 10 regional as well as corporate HR offices
- The collection of work charts and other documentation from all HR functions
- Research into best practices in the company and industry through on-site visits and literature review

Among the opportunities for improvement that emerged, and were later incorporated into the design of a transformed function,

Total HR Time By Product/Service Area

- Staffing 2.6%
- Supporting Acquisition 10.2%
- Compensation 14.7%
- Strategic HR Planning 9.2%
- Benefits 14.0%
- Career And Individual Development 16.3%
- Labor Relations 14.3%
- Employee Relations 6.5%
- Training And Educating 12.1%

Resource Allocation/Gap Analysis

$ PER FTE SERVED (000's): $400, 300, 200, 100, 0

Bars: Strategic HR, Support Acquisitions, Compensation, Labor Relations, Employee Relations, Career Development, Benefits, Training And Educating, Staffing

EFFECTIVENESS (Least — Most) / IMPORTANCE (Least — Most)

HR Product/Service Budget Costs

Description Expense Line	Total (Per Ledger)	Staffing The Organization	Training And Educating Company People	Total (Ties To Budget)
Temporary Labor	100.0	0.0	0.0	100.0
System Charges	2,000.0	200.0	600.0	2,000.0
External Training	600.0	0.0	600.0	600.0
Relocation Services	1,100.0	1,100.0	0.0	1,100.0
Total	3,800.0	1,300.0	1,200.0	3,800.0

Customer Survey Results

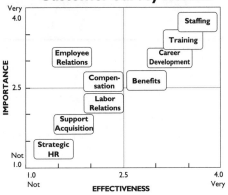

IMPORTANCE: Very 4.0 — 2.5 — Not 1.0
EFFECTIVENESS: 1.0 Not — 2.5 — 4.0 Very

Staffing, Training, Employee Relations, Career Development, Compensation, Benefits, Labor Relations, Support Acquisition, Strategic HR

Figure 11-6 Cost-to-value analyses identify potential resource allocation imbalances and customer service gaps.

were tools to help store managers diagnose retention issues, enhanced career management processes, staffing models to identify new labor pools, and solutions for common retention-issues.

The main components of this process are analyses that focus on:

- Each HR activity, such as staffing or training, to identify how many people are performing the activity, how much time they spend on it, what percent of their time is spent on administrative versus strategic or customer-service activities, and how much time they spend on non-HR work
- Cost analysis of HR, by business unit, division, country, or other parameters; HR labor costs compared with budgeted expenses; and the costs of specific HR products and services
- Customer surveys of the users of HR products and services, which identify the relative importance of each activity in helping the business unit execute business strategy, how effective HR is in providing what they need, and perceived gaps between importance and effectiveness

External Analyses

Not only does no organization operate in a vacuum, isolated from external events such as new legislation or trends affecting labor markets, but in today's technological and business environment there's a strong "positive" side to research that looks outside the company for ways to successfully implement HR transformation. New and emerging technology has already "transformed" some leading-edge HR departments, or specific functions within them, and "best practice" applications of new approaches in HR management can often suggest important opportunities for improvement (if aligned with the company's strategic business needs).

As shown in Figure 11-7, external analyses can be conducted in all five of the areas that drive HR success. In each area, both the overall "emerging trends" and "best practices" examples relevant to the organization can be identified, assessed for their "fit" in resolving gaps or requirements to achieve business-based

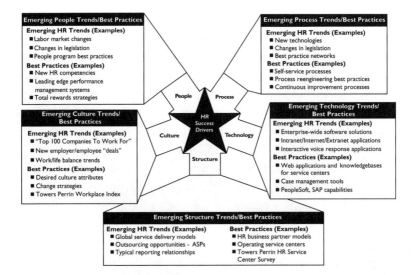

Figure 11-7 External analyses foster innovative solutions to current issues.

HR transformation, and considered for inclusion in the new HR function.

The overall trends are important because they provide a context for best-practice examples: for example, the growth and diversification of outsourcing opportunities, a trend affecting a growing number of HR functions, means many things to many different organizations and should not be narrowly defined by best-practice examples, no matter how many are included in the analysis.

Bringing It Together in Operational Design

Once HR business priorities have been identified, as well as "gaps" between current resource allocation and the critical issues that matter most to the organization, the HR transformation process moves from strategy formulation to operational design. In this stage of the process, all of the "opportunities for improvement" identified in earlier analyses are brought together, weighed for importance as changes that address strategic business needs, and incorporated in an integrated plan for HR transformation. As a picture emerges of an operational reality, including new "deliverables" in each of the five areas analyzed in this holistic approach, specific improvements that will have the most impact on the organization's business needs for human resources will come into focus. While the overall effort to change will probably affect all areas of HR—leveraging technology, clarifying roles and responsibilities, integrating related functions, and eliminating non-value-adding work—analyses conducted up to this point will have identified the business-based priorities for HR transformation and suggested improvements or new activities for each of the "success drivers" of HR.

For example, if a critical business priority for the HR function is management development and retention, the design of an operational plan for transforming HR would probably include specific activities to achieve these changes in the following areas:

- *Culture.* New measurements and rewards related to the organization's success in developing and retaining key managers would be established, and HR would participate more aggressively in business planning affecting department/ retention programs and budgets.
- *People.* New competencies developed or recruited in HR would include expertise in management department, program department and implementation, analytical skills that help identify retention and turnover factors, and a strategic understanding of the importance of management retention.
- *Structure.* The roles and responsibilities of all participants in management development—from recruiters and trainers to department heads and managers themselves—would be more clearly defined and structured, with terms created where appropriate to address development/retention issues.
- *Process.* Streamlined processes for enrolling in management development activities, development of a range of appropriate formats that address both the company's and individuals' needs, and improved linkages between management devel-

opment and rewards-promotion programs would integrate development with individual growth and career aspirations.

- *Technology.* Included here is leveraging of existing technology and possibly new systems to integrate development programs and policies with staffing, succession planning, recruitment, HR planning and competency-based assessment and rewards, as well as the use of on-line training and development materials accessible to all managers, where appropriate as a delivery mechanism. To help with retention, consider the possible use of Web- or IVR-based attitude surveys to identify issues contributing to high turnover among managers, and extranet and intranet "portals" that provide discounted products and services, such as retirement planning and investment advice.

Process improvement example. Simplified, Web-based hiring for health care.

A newly formed company, created by the merger of three regional health care organizations, had as its primary strategic goal to become number one in market share in its geographic area, but was having trouble hiring quality people in a strong economy. Low unemployment and increased competition were showing the flaws of existing hiring processes, which were slow, unnecessarily limited in scope, unappreciated by managers, and often ineffective in hiring the right people. Analyses of the processes being used led to:

- Use of Web-based technology to post current and future job openings, outsourcing resume collection, and initial screening
- A vastly simplified application form and reduction in the number of visits by applicants
- Development of technology permitting managers to access applicant files, make salary quotes within their budgets and job offers themselves, and post their own job openings immediately
- Redesign of the orientation process to eliminate excessive time spent on compliance and record-keeping issues

Implementation of Transformed Function

The actual implementation of a transformed HR department, one that contributes to strategic business goals and adds value to the organization through more effective utilization of people and technology, typically requires a comprehensive implementation plan, such as the one partly shown in Figure 11-8. Such a plan and schedule identifies the responsibilities of those responsible for HR transformation, provides time frames for specific activities and deliverables, and provides an overall view and management tool for senior management responsible for resource allocation.

In the "real world" of HR transformation, of course, many of the specific activities in the implementation plan will have been under way for some time, identified as process improvements, or introduced with new technology earlier in the analysis. The comprehensive implementation plan integrates the totality of the change effort, and ensures its alignment with the strategic business needs that initiated the process of adding value to the HR function.

Further, it should be added that "implementation never ends" in certain respects, as new business requirements, better processes, new technology, and other inevitable changes provide new challenges and opportunities. By the end of the transformation process, however, the HR function is in a position to be newly responsive to change.

> Its *culture* is shaped by strategic business perspectives and a "proactive" approach to shaping the workforce of tomorrow.
>
> Its *people* have new competencies that include a better understanding of the business and its changing requirements.
>
> Its *structure* is shaped by broad business needs rather than isolated functional specialties, and responsibilities for responding to change are clearly defined.
>
> *Processes* have been questioned, sometimes eliminated, and streamlined to be more effective, creating new ways of looking at no-longer-sacrosanct processes.

Key Implementation Activities/Steps	Resp.	1997				1998			
		Q1	Q2	Q3	Q4	Q1	Q2	Q3	Q4
Finalize Detailed Implementation Plan And Establish Infrastructure	Implementation Manager								
Finalize And Implement Change Management Strategy For Implementation	Change Management Team								
Pilot /Test Key Elements Of New Model	Implementation Team								
Identify elements to test (e.g.,service center concept, new technology, business partner role)									
Conduct piloting process									
Incorporate learnings into full roll-out	Service Center Team								
Build Service Center Operations									
Redesign delivery processes for all affected processes/services									
Set target performance measures for year l									
Implement partnering process with customers									
Build facilities/install equipment	Technology Team								
Implement New Technology									
Develop client server applications									
Develop intranet applications									
Purchase and install enabling technologies									
Build system interfaces									
Design Shared Consulting Services	Implementation Team								
Redefine HR Business Partner Role	Implementation Team								
Staff New Organization	Staffing Team								
Create detailed role profiles and competency requirements									
Develop staffing process to fill open positions									
Assess current HR staff on new competencies									
Implement training plan to build new competencies									
Conduct staffing process									
Training	Change Management Team								
Design core curriculum for ongoing HR staff development									
Communication	Change Management Team								
Design and develop communication materials for service center launch									
Distribute communication materials for launch									

Figure 11-8 Implementation of the integrated HR solution requires a comprehensive implementation plan.

171

New *technology* has eliminated much of the administrative work, time spent on transactions, and other non-value-adding activities that in the past left HR with no time to think and act strategically or to explore new technology for HR as it emerges.

12

Planning Your HR Technology Strategy and Web Architecture

Lori G. Lanzelotti, Alfred J. Walker, and J. Alec Wilder*

Introduction

So what should our technology strategy be to help Human Resources (HR) accomplish its goals? Is it our strategy to be an entirely Web-based HR delivery? Or should we have a mixture of solutions, some Web-based, some call center–based, and some using voice response? And an even better question might be how

*Lori G. Lanzelotti is a consultant in the Philadelphia office of Towers Perrin. She specializes in the development and implementation of Web-Based HR applications.

Philadelphia Centre Square office address: Centre Square, 1500 Market Street, Philadelphia, Pennsylvania 19102.

Alfred J. Walker is a Senior Fellow in the Towers Perrin Parsippany, New Jersey, office. He specializes in the use of technology to improve the effectiveness and efficiency of the HR function.

Parsippany office address: Morris Corporate Center II, Building F, One Upper Pond Road, Parsippany, New Jersey 07054-1050.

J. Alec Wilder is the practice leader for eHRcommerce at Towers Perrin. He specializes in bringing e-commerce techniques and applications to HR processes, and is located in the Philadelphia office.

Philadelphia–Centre Square office address: Centre Square, 1500 Market Street, Philadelphia, Pennsylvania 19102.

to decide where to begin in determining our HR technology and service delivery strategy.

At the outset, it is important to understand that the delivery of HR services through the Web and Web-enabled technology combines the efforts of many separate activities, people, technologies, and organizations, and has undergone some significant changes with the introduction of technology as one of the primary delivery vehicles. Where there were once only two channels open to us to deliver HR plans (the HR staff member and written procedures), we now have Web-based self-service options, traditional HR systems, IVR, and perhaps a service center.

HR Technology Strategy: Purpose and Influences

First, why even have an HR technology strategic plan, and what is the purpose of such a strategic plan, anyway? Is it another bureaucratic document that demands a great deal of work to put together, but in reality, sits on your shelf collecting dust? Or can it be a highly useful instrument that helps guide future HR technology investment for your company? We must ensure it is the latter.

The primary purpose of an HR technology strategic plan is to build a realistic model and framework of the technology and supporting infrastructure that HR will need to meet future business requirements, and a workable plan to get there. The strategies in the plan are all aimed at increasing the effectiveness of the HR programs, processes, and service delivery by shortening cycle times, increasing customer service levels, reducing costs, and adding new service capability.

Avoid These Mistakes

Examining the history of technology planning efforts and studies of previous strategies, we see that there has been a checkered past. Too often we have underestimated the difficulty of installing technology solutions, while at the same time overestimating their expected capabilities, performance, and usefulness to the end user. We continue to hope that, in the future, commercial HR technology will finally deliver us from the drudgery of day-to-day HR administration, freeing us to become the business partners we wish to be. Most of the HR technologists preparing the plans are optimists at heart, and unfortunately often buy too readily and too fully into vendor sales enthusiasm. In doing so, the planners set forth a bright future, often based upon beliefs and assumptions that are inaccurate, and setting expectations that cannot easily be met. The HR user community, too, often underestimates the work required to change underlying processes, as well as their own behaviors. And this does no one any service.

Influences

Therefore, to make a plan realistic, we must recognize that there are a number of factors at play here influencing HR technology strategies, and that the plan is not as simple as adopting vendor products, even if that vendor is a global player. HR technology concerns one of the most complex sets of issues found in companies today, and these issues must be considered when developing a comprehensive delivery strategy. These include the following, and are also depicted in Figure 12-1 below:

- Overall business needs
- Major HR strategies, goals, and objectives

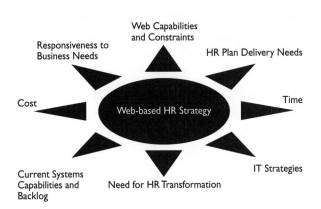

Figure 12-1   Some Web-based HR technology strategy influences.

- IT strategies, given that there is such a fast-moving field of technology, where advances are made every day, and new products can render existing ones obsolete in a matter of months; ability to support certain platforms; existing ERP and legacy systems

- HR transformation goals, the need to drive HR staff to a level of greater value to the business, and the need to redesign HR processes

- Recognition that there is a limited IT budget, and that it requires a constant reprioritization of projects

- Overworked HR and IT staffs, with uneven skill sets

- Business changes, such as new product releases, reorganizations, and mergers, and acquisitions that occasion HR technology maintenance

- The understanding that HR system purchases and implementation efforts are slow and expensive, and during that time, user needs are often not satisfied

- Overlapping solutions by other products, where several products may be able to offer solutions to a problem

- Hundreds of federal, state, and local regulatory and compliance requirements that must be met

- A growing list of user needs and demands for new applications, due to a wide array of HR, benefits, and payroll plans, and programs, ranging from staffing systems to pension calculators, almost all of which need to be delivered with technology, and whose Web expectations are being set by commercial sites

- Different customers to deliver services to, for example, employees, managers, applicants for employment, and retirees

These influences, many of which are external and beyond our control, must be managed in such a way as to minimize their potentially negative impact on service delivery. Since what direction to take is not always clear in the face of so many conflicting demands, a carefully constructed strategic technology plan, factoring in these issues, becomes a necessity.

Business Proposition Questions

Developing the strategic plan must center on the following business questions:

1. What are the various HR products and services that are to be delivered? Each of the functional areas of HR has a series of HR programs and plans, with underlying process steps and transactions that need to be considered for delivery through the Web or other technology

2. To whom will they be delivered? What is the target audience for each of the HR plans? Are the plans different for hourly and salaried employees? Does each plant or division have the same plan? What about senior management? Applicants? Retirees? Expatriates?

3. How will they be delivered? Will the primary delivery vehicle be the Web? Or will it be via IVR? Some transactions and events plans are still best handled on a face-to-face basis. How will these be handled?

4. When are they to be delivered? What are the timings involved with each HR plan, transaction, or process?

5. Who is responsible for the product design and content? Who is the plan and/or process owner for each product and service?

6. Who is responsible for delivery and support? Who is on point for delivery? The HRT group? IT?

7. What is the cost of supply, support, and delivery? How do we cost the service? By unit-costing methods? By transaction? On a per-employee basis?

8. How will we maintain quality in the delivery channels? What measures are to be used in which processes to ensure timely and accurate service delivery?

Content of the Strategic Technology Plan

The final plan, while different for each organization, should at least contain the following components:

- Put forth a *vision* of how HR services will be delivered in the future, at least the next several years.
- Outline a *framework* for HR technology development; *investment amounts* for software, people, hardware upgrades, etc.; and application *priorities* over the next several fiscal years.
- Establish enterprisewide information and technology *platforms* for HR.
- Describe the objectives and *charter* of the HR Technology (HRT) group or groups.
- Make specific recommendations for *choosing* among conflicting technology solutions, e.g., when to use the Web, when to use the call center, etc.
- Recommend how to establish and sequence introduction of *technology upgrades and new releases.*
- Outline how to launch and *manage* HR technology projects.
- Set forth the suggested *organizational structure* and roles for the HR, Benefits, Payroll, and IT staffs.
- Establish data accuracy and measurement *standards* for key HR data and processes.
- Describe *global* jurisdictional and reporting requirements.
- Publish *confidentiality, security, and privacy policies.*

The strategic plan is meant to be a living document and should be updated at least semiannually, unless there are reasons to do so more frequently.

Four Steps to Setting Your Strategy

Step 1—Determine Your Goal: Create a Vision of the Future Delivery Model

A strategy is not the goal, but a means of getting there. Therefore, we need to agree on what is the ultimate goal. The goal, and the strategy for getting there, should represent a consensus of senior management in the HR and IT functions, with concurrence from the primary business managers.

A highly successful method for gaining consensus on this issue is to develop a sample depiction of the future state and have the users and management react to it. Presenting it visually in a focus group session, or in individual interviews, will draw out opinions and thoughts that will help coalesce their thinking about the preferred delivery methods. The following is a sample of such a delivery model.

A potential vision and model for HR service delivery— High-tech as well as high-touch. Figure 12-2 is a graphical depiction of how transactional and informative HR services could be delivered through technology to various user constituencies. It presents a picture of both technology and personal HR service delivery. All of the HR roles and services are not intended to be supplanted with technology. Rather, there is a distinction made in the model between the HR work delivered to the various businesses through the HR generalists and business-related HR staff, and that delivered with technology. The individual face-to-face advice and counsel role is still preserved in this model, and in fact

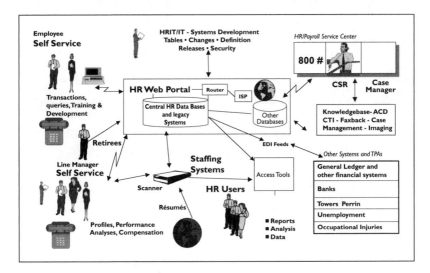

Figure 12-2 Possible HR service delivery model.

enhanced. Taking the day-to-day transaction and administrative work from the HR generalist and moving it to the Web, or a service center, provides the HR staff more time for their primary role of HR as business partner and consultant.

At the center of the model is the interaction of employees and managers with technology through the HR portal, an employee-focused view. This portal utilizes the employee self-service initiatives that will be the gateway through which the transactions that involve access to the main ERP or HR system, such as Oracle, Lawson, PeopleSoft, or SAP, and other major systems, will occur. The intent here is to take the burden of the administrative work and some specialized work away from the business HR staff and move it to technology and/or into a service center where efficiencies of scale and greater consistency in delivery can be gained.

Essential to this model is that the HR leadership group must work in close contact with senior business management to help ensure that HR plans, programs and the delivery of services are aligned with overall business objectives.

Also prominent in the delivery model is the proposed HR service center, which will handle day-to-day inquiries from employees regarding HR, payroll, and benefits. The service center will also be used to handle management inquiries, as companies move more into the "manager workstation" concept, enabling managers to become more self-reliant by using technology directly to handle more transactions themselves.

Some questions and challenges to your choice of a goal. Remembering that the HR technology and service delivery strategy will all be directed toward achieving the goal, it is vital to ensure that the goal is the proper one. Some challenges or "tests" about the choice are required before settling on the final model. Examples of such questions follow.

Does the model support enterprisewide talent identification and retention? The workforce challenges facing organizations will have a dramatic impact on their success in the next few years. Items such as finding and developing the proper talent, retaining intellectual capital, building organizational capabilities, increasing employee productivity and commitment, strengthening managerial talent, and developing appropriate total rewards structures are high on the HR agenda for most companies.

Does it help with HR transformation? The complexities of the business environment, with the effects of competition, emphasis on marketing, and growth of the workforce on a global basis, have created a situation where management in most companies has realized that HR services cannot be delivered, or managed, in the traditional manner. Nor can "silos" exist where there are companywide programs to administer. There are too many employees, in too many organizations, using too many products, who need constant interaction with each other, to manage them all separately. Since competition and economic reality are changing the way HR business will be conducted in the future, a new model for HR service delivery is called for.

Does it provide for a new and efficient delivery method? The complexities of conducting businesses on a more uniform basis are bringing many new HR delivery problems to the surface. New HR programs, such as leadership development, succession planning, total compensation, and core competency development, will require a more cohesive delivery capability than before. In addition, there is the need to supply normal HR services, such as benefits, transfers, staffing, and payroll, in a much more efficient and consolidated manner. Employing self-service drives down costs.

Will it enable more consistent plan delivery? Most companies today have become quite complex, with a mixture of products, customers, and geography directing the supply of normal HR services. Decentralized business operations sometimes cause certain differences in the HR program design and delivery, the approach they use with employees, and processes. These differences have created administrative strains and anomalies in many HR plans and programs. The challenge in the future is to efficiently design and deliver integrated HR programs that can be implemented across different business units in a more cohesive manner. Building a more streamlined, uniform delivery methodology is a high priority.

Will it help businesses with new product launches, employee-training, and new competencies? Business pressures and new product introduction normally require cross-organizational and geographical coordination with respect to manufacturing, sales, and marketing programs, as well as new support methods, such as the supply of needed materials and customer communications. The demands on sales training in multiple products and systems will increase, and any new work procedures and operations must be highly efficient and operate at a low cost. The support, training, and knowledge about these new products, and the new compensation and commission arrangements that may be needed, must all be available to the HR staff, management team, and the employees on an instantaneous basis. Management, therefore, will require a much greater amount of information regarding their workforce and organizations than is available today.

Does it help with enterprisewide HR plan coordination? A major challenge facing HR is how to coordinate and connect business needs with the HR products and services, which will be provided on an enterprisewide basis. The HR organization of the future will need the ability to act more on a companywide basis than today, while still having the capability and sensitivity to respond to local business issues and needs. The Web-enabled model provides that solution, since it can accommodate language and currency differences, and help span cultural barriers.

Once the goal and model have been agreed on, the work of selecting the best strategies to achieve that goal can begin.

Step 2—Select the Strategies

Develop underlying concepts driving the plan. Underlying HR technology strategies are several other relevant technological and service-related concepts that the strategy should consider, since they frame the final service delivery. These include

- **24/7/365**—Providing manager and employee access to systems and information with the ability to work on HR technology applications with anyone, anytime, anywhere
- Supporting **distance and just-in-time learning** to facilitate knowledge and skill building for employees
- Utilizing **workflow** automation to eliminate routine, redundant, manual, paper transaction processing

- **Streamlining processes,** eliminating non-value-adding handling of paper, reducing or eliminating an excessive number of approval signatures and redundant non-value-adding steps in the process
- Implementing solutions that increase manager and employee **self-sufficiency** (e.g., interactive voice response, intranet-Web applications, fax-back, Lotus Notes databases)
- Capturing and building the organization's **intellectual capital** and making it easily accessible by others, reducing or eliminating lost "business knowledge"
- Helping to reduce unwanted turnover
- Increasing the employee learning curve for **new skills** and for new product introductions, which will ultimately result in maintaining high customer satisfaction

Determine the preferred delivery methods. Each HR process, transaction, and event needs to be analyzed, and a choice made as to the preferred method of delivery to the customer. For example, a name change or choice of a new primary care physician would be rather difficult using the telephone, due to the lack of some characters on the phone keypad and its slowness. But these would be easy on the Web. On the other hand, accessing one's account balance for one's 401(k) plan is easy on the phone, perhaps even easier than on the Web. But the Web would be better for delivering the entire total reward event cluster to which the account inquiry might belong. So choices have to be made to ascertain what the "bundles of delivery," or processes, would use as their primary delivery vehicle. Further, the choices have to accommodate the different customers and audiences. Retirees would most likely not have access to the company LAN, but they are on the Web, so their choices might be more limited than those of employees, but still be acceptable.

In the process of choosing the delivery method for each process, a fallback method must also be selected to handle groupings of people who do not have easy access to the Web, such as shop floor employees, certain disabled employees, and retail store employees.

Establish a framework to determine application priorities and rollout. With limited resources, time, and budget, application prioritization must have an appropriate methodology. By aligning solutions to business objectives, management is able to determine which applications are those with the highest impact and therefore those that may deserve favorable treatment in the plan. Selection of which applications to deliver, and when, is a key strategy component.

An example of such a prioritization would reveal the impact of HR applications on HR goals (H = high impact, etc.):

Sample Key HR Technology Goals and Priorities	Expand HRIS System	Extend HR Service Center	Build HR Web Portal
Build flexible organizational designs for speed, flexibility, and innovation	H	L	L
Support business new product launches	M	L	H
Support new performance management and reward systems	H	M	H
Streamline HR processes to increase satisfaction and quality and reduce costs	M	H	H
Provide meaningful information to management for better decision making	H	M	H
Create best-in-class HR organization	L	H	M

Other possible priorities to consider include:

Reduce overall cost of delivery.

Improve efficiencies and speed of response to customers.

Build on the technology investment; obtain ROI.

Integrate HR and technology solutions.

Improve or expand HR functional capabilities.

Improve customer (i.e., employees and managers) service satisfaction levels.

Deliver enterprisewide solutions.

Go with a one-vendor strategy or best of breed? The proliferation of system solutions normally requires a plan that covers numerous technologies. The technologies used to deliver HR services over the next several years will likely include Web-based solutions, traditional computer-based systems, both stand-alone and networked PCs, multimedia solutions, resume reading and handling methodologies, optical scanning, imaging, and voice recognition systems. So, if this is your situation, this is not a one-technology or one-vendor strategy.

For an HR service center, the same applies. Here, technology may well include unified networks encompassing case management systems, voice networks, a knowledge base, and call-patching capabilities, among others. And in the future, more expert-based applications and multimedia products will be available.

The delivery-and-technology aspect of the model is the access to key business data, primarily employee and/or organizational information, anywhere, anytime, and with embedded workflow capability by authorized personnel, permitting work to be delivered more efficiently and from a distance. Manager and employee self-sufficiency is a necessary component of the model. The technology model must also support the information relationships contained in the HR business model, and it relies upon the acceptance of all stakeholders and customers of HR.

List your assumptions. Because of the complexities of business and a growing workforce, it is impossible to fully understand and have access to all user needs, requirements, and environmental impacts when developing strategy and project plans. In our rapidly changing, highly competitive business environment, business processes and strategies change within 6–18 months, with mergers and acquisitions very likely. The effort, cost, and time necessary to collect all relevant information in one location is not feasible, cost-effective, or timely. It is for this reason that the future HR model, and the technologies and HRT organization needed to support it, continually receives input from HR, IT, and line management. Further, assumptions are therefore used to provide the framework for building a project plan and strategy in a more responsive manner.

Possible assumptions checklist. Developing a strategic plan must build upon a number of assumptions regarding the business in the future. For example, will it be sufficiently profitable to implement the plan? Can we assume no mergers or acquisitions? What about continued management and user support? The following is a checklist of possible assumptions to help you.

- All suppliers of data are responsible for properly updating their respective data elements.
- Major processes will be redesigned for speed and will be workflow-enabled.
- Not all HR processes or programs will require information on employees, plans, programs, and organizations to be maintained in a central HRIS system, website, or data mart; for example, medical data will be stored separately.
- Changes will occur in the next year or two, which will require altering HR technology implementation priorities; therefore HR objectives and HR technology strategies will have to be reassessed.
- HR staff will be identified and committed to the project.
- There will be qualified, trained HRT resources identified, for each major process and application, to interface with the users and to manage the implementation work.
- HR staff from all units, as well as management, will support the strategies.
- The HR service center will be enhanced to handle most HR transactions in a single unit. The center will also act as a single point of contact with employees for Web support, and for handling queries regarding their plans and HR programs.
- Sufficient funds will be available to carry out at least the first phases of the strategies in an acceptable manner.
- Reporting relationship data will be maintained in the database.

Step 3—Determine the Web-Based Architecture and Infrastructure

Establish guiding technology principles up front. In order to set the framework for service delivery architecture, and roles and responsibilities, it is desirable to set forth some guiding principles to which all parties would agree. These principles might include the following:

- Make sure that development work adheres to the IT project management methodology.
- Standardize certain technologies and platforms to reduce cost, increase knowledge of features, and enhance support and maintenance.
- Utilize economies of scale, and move similar work together to take advantage of IT competencies and skill sets, technology investments, and better management of processes that they support.
- Develop standard definitions and meanings for data elements.
- Develop uniform and consistent methods of presenting key HR data, which provide "intelligence" rather than just raw data, in order to improve and expedite decision making, and enhance understanding of the data.
- Move data responsibility and data entry to the source (i.e., employees, managers, applicants, and so on) to improve accuracy, integrity, consistency, and timeliness of data.
- Collect, and provide access to, detailed data that allow users to define their own data requirements rather than just summary statistics.
- Ensure that the data collected and maintained in the HRIS system, legacy systems, and data mart have sufficient integrity and accuracy levels to permit management to rely upon it.
- Ensure that the data supplying the website (HRIS or data mart) are maintained and updated on a timely, frequent basis to the desired level of accuracy.
- Maintain the proper privacy, security, and access levels for the information.

Selecting the Web deployment strategy. The Web delivery environment for HR services will be even more complex in the future than today, with 40 or more Web-based applications to maintain. A key strategic decision will have to be made as to whether the Web delivery will be delivered with in-house staff or moved to an external service provider.

Setting the architectural framework. The Web-based HR service delivery architectural framework should be designed to be robust, scalable, flexible, and secure. In addition, it should allow accessibility for a number of HR customers, from any point on the globe, at any time, and allow for integration of a number of both open-end and closed-end legacy databases. These conditions demand a complex integrated network of applications, processes, databases, and servers, composed of internally maintained systems, as well as external vendors and hosts.

The core of the Web-based architecture should consider a model, along the lines of Figure 12-3, which depicts the contents of a three-tiered approach.

The first tier (Client-Side) represents the technology that would be evident to the employee, manager, or HR user—the client—and would be maintained on a desktop computer or kiosk. Here, the customer interface technology would contain the presentation graphics, or GUI components, along with a browser, to access the Web and to present a common look and feel. This layer would also permit the user to activate a channel to an external website or go directly into the corporate site. In addition, the desktop would contain the normal office suite of applications, such as a word processor, spreadsheet application, and access to the local LAN.

The middle tier (Server-Side) contains the Internet servers, application servers, all the presentation and business logic, HR processes, system calculations, and core HR systems, such as SAP or PeopleSoft, as well as supporting logic and content carriers, such as knowledge bases. In addition, Active Server Pages (ASP) handle the HTML formatting tags, and Component Objects (or COM Objects) are all contained here. These components execute transactions and move the data from the databases to the customer,

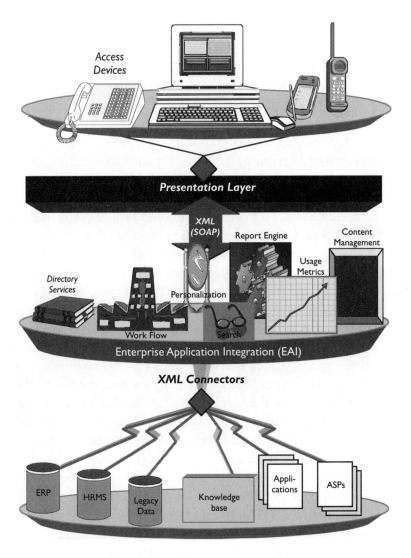

Figure 12-3 Three-tiered architecture.

within the established editing and workflow rules. This tier also handles queries dealing with multimedia components, IVR, and access to or from a call center.

The third tier (Enterprise Information) houses the data in a database server, and can access certain native HR systems, or store the data in a data mart, or data warehouse, for access, reporting, and analysis.

Choosing platforms. Selection of Web hardware and software platforms should be covered in the plan. Specific choices should be made by the IT organization, within the context of their IT standards, but should include as much open integration as possible in all areas. The plan should include the acceptability of such items as the server hardware (examples: Microsoft's NT Server and LINUX or Sun Servers; standard e-mail systems, such as Lotus Notes or Microsoft Exchange; network architecture; desktops; and any Internet and telecommunications protocols).

Software platforms, too, must be within IT standards and should cover the use of: HTML Access and Java Applets; security firewalls, sign-on levels, and authentication; use of Active X, Java, or VB Script; workflow technologies; call-center technologies; and development toolkits. Security interfaces with the directory server should use the Lightweight Directory Access Protocol (LDAP) to authenticate end users and manage their system access privileges.

As with other technologies, the selection of the Web platform and middleware software should be heavily influenced by service delivery requirements. If the service delivery requires real-time updates, then the technologies supporting an "ask, receive, verify" model are needed. If the service delivery does not require real-time update capability, then technologies supporting a "publish, subscribe" (less complex) model can be considered.

Costs, capabilities, security, and appropriateness are all important in the choice of platforms, but just as important is strategic direction and conformance to the overall vision of HR transformation principles. The combined effect of process redesign, new technology deployment, shared services, and outsourcing will increase the desired speed of service delivery and the level of customer satisfaction. Platforms and architecture that promote these goals should be given high priority.

Site map. A site map should be drawn to plan out the Web design and flow for users, since there could be disagreement as to where the specific content should reside. The map should be driven by usage and event processes, and not necessarily by organizational responsibility. For example, the Web page that handles name changes could also handle beneficiary changes, although

---

Web Design Considerations: Seven R's

Your HR Web design should be:

Realistic—People can use it, believe in its credibility, and ask for it.

Relevant—The information is meaningful to "me and my work."

Reachable—People can find it and have the time to use it.

Reliable—The site works; the server is dependable and frequently updated.

Risky—The site dares to be a different, positive experience.

Real connected—The site connects people, database information, and other sites.

Razzle-dazzle—It has few words, quick screens, and easy-to-understand graphics.

---

functionally, the name change today may be handled by the HR Records group, while the beneficiary may be handled by the Benefits department. Let the natural process flow, geared to the customer, drive the design. And keep in mind the general rule: The fewer the clicks to reach the desired page, the better.

Step 4—Determining Proper Organizational Roles and Responsibilities to Make the Strategic Plan Happen

Need for user input in setting the plan. In the past, it was primarily the technologists (i.e., programmers) who developed most HR technology, plans, and strategies. User involvement was minimal, and the planning documents, as referenced above, never came close to matching what actually happened. As a result, the technology that was delivered, the sequence in which it was delivered, and the priorities of the developers may not have been exactly what the user wanted or thought was going to happen, due to poor or nonexistent interaction between the parties. Expectations of both sides should be better managed, since the user needs change, due to changing business needs, or regulatory requirements, and the plan will quickly become out-of-date. Keeping users involved during the business year is key.

User involvement also needed in technology development and Web sequencing. Also critical in any plan is the requirement to involve users in development and installation of technology projects. Today, in implementing an application (whether an internally developed website, a purchased HRIS-Payroll software package such as PeopleSoft, or a call center), the focus is on rapidly delivering solutions that meet customer needs.

It is the responsibility of the users to ensure that, prior to any Web development or process redesign, there is a service delivery sequence mapped out for every major HR event. For example, for the annual performance appraisal, does one first go to the Web, HR staff, service center, or another path, such as using voice response?

This translates into greater involvement of subject matter experts (SMEs). Some users in HR, payroll staff, line managers, and others may find this interaction time-consuming and confusing, but it is vital to the success of the projects. It is understood that, as systems are being developed, HR and the other organizations must continue delivering services while dedicating a significant amount of time to an implementation project. However, if qualified resources are not available, the lack of good subject matter experts becomes a serious threat to the success of the project, and we again will develop applications that do not meet customer expectations.

Not only does the strategic plan need to be realistic about SME availability; it must also address their desire to participate, since their roles may well change in the new delivery model.

Strategic plan impact on HR staff. For some of the current HR staff, the work will remain mostly the same as it was before the introduction of technology, particularly if it involves dealing with sensitive issues. Most HR staff, though, will find that their work has been altered in some fashion—for example, shifted to the HR service center. In addition, through process redesign and automation, many of the processes that they had been involved with will have been streamlined.

Most high-volume processes will be Web-enabled, with workflow and self-service introduced. For example, employees will now handle some routine matters themselves through the website, and by connecting to an HR system directly or to an operational data store (ODS) or data mart fed by the HR database. Another alternative is the local HR staff member who pulls up a computer screen, clicks on the appropriate icon, and reviews those transactions that are passed on to him or her for approval, instead of handling a paper-based, administrative transaction. The work is automatically forwarded to the appropriate manager or HR unit, when the generalist is finished, depending on the particular workflow desired by the process owner.

Other changes to the work will take place as well. With the growth of hosting, outsourcing, and the introduction of shared services units, it becomes necessary to reexamine supplier activities that could be managed centrally, a function perhaps now handled by a number of HR specialists.

In the future, there will be an increased emphasis placed on interpersonal skills, consulting skills, "pure" HR functional knowledge, business savvy, and technology. Certainly these changes demand new competencies for the HR staff to fulfill their new roles. This will be easy for some staff and perhaps impossible for others.

Joint IT-HR technology development. Because of the complexities and workloads, development and support of various HR technologies and systems becomes a shared responsibility. The HR technology organizations and IT groups must act as partners on assignments, and determine where in each application the lines of responsibility will be drawn. Normally, the HRT group supports the applications (user needs, definitions, changes, cost benefits, user testing, training) and the IT organization supports the infrastructure upon which the enterprise applications are dependent (e.g., networks, workstation configurations, intranets, enterprise systems, security, and firewalls). However, this can change from application to application, depending on staff expertise and resource constraints. Each, though, is dependent on the other for support and requirements.

Change management role. Communication with the various constituencies, regarding the objectives, costs, benefits, output, and so on, of a new systems application is critical. New technology solutions can be extremely helpful, but may also signal change, new tasks, and new competencies for some users. In addition, with the new HR model, there is an expectation and assumption that certain technology solutions (e.g., the HR website) will be utilized by each employee in every business unit, making the need for communication surrounding a process even more important than before.

Managing the introduction of these new technology applications, therefore, is one of the most difficult aspects of any project, and the strategic plan should address this point. It requires expertise in change management and communications—competencies not always in great abundance in IT or HRT organizations. The higher the expectations, the higher the risk to successful implementation if they are not met; the lower the expectations, the more difficult it may be to obtain support, and a business case, for change. Balance must be sought and a proper level of communications regarding each new implementation carefully planned.

Summary

A strategic HR technology plan is a composite document aimed at presenting the methods of achieving the HR service delivery goal that management desires. It is a mixture of practical, technical, and organizational plans and initiatives, tying the company, vendors, and the employees together in an integrated fashion to ensure that they are able to receive needed information, anytime, anyplace, and able to act upon it in a better and faster manner.

13

Workflow Software
A Key Driver Behind HR Self-Service

John G. Kelly*

Introduction

Workflow is one of the most important software categories to evolve since relational database and object-oriented design, and is needed for most employee and manager transactions that require approval or are directed to more than one destination. Although it continues to evolve and change as standards develop, it holds great value for the Human Resources (HR) function, because work processes are often long, complex, and shared by many different individuals. It is especially important for manager-initiated activities, since they often involve secondary approvals.

*John G. Kelly is a consultant in the Boston office of Towers Perrin. He assists clients in all phases of the use of technology to improve HR operations and service delivery including self-service, Web design, and HR systems.

Boston office address: 500 Boylston Street, 17th Floor, Boston, Massachusetts 02116-3734.

Workflow Definition

Many products, including Web-based solutions, e-mail, group-ware, and imaging systems, are often characterized as "workflow solutions." However, e-mail, groupware, and imaging systems are primarily "passive" types of systems, in that they perform activities only with human intervention. In contrast, Web-based and client/server-based systems are active: They control hand-offs from one enabler to another.

Workflow consists of three basic elements:

- Rules that govern the process
- Information being routed
- Process metrics used to report on the process

Since workflow systems are relatively new, there are no precise standards on what a workflow system is and what it is not. Vendors are rushing in to fill this void, defining workflow according to their own unique capabilities, which unfortunately confuses the issue. However, a simple definition of workflow software is software that automates the flow of information, documents, and work processes through a company. The focus is on how work normally moves through an organization—i.e., the process—instead of the specific information.

Components and Characteristics of a Workflow System

Characteristics of a Workflow System

Workflow systems are made up of four elements: tasks, people, tools, and data.

- **Tasks.** Tasks are the different activities that must be completed to achieve a business goal.
- **People.** Tasks are performed in a specific order by specific individual or automated agents (which assume the roles of people), based on business conditions and rules.
- **Tools.** Tasks within a workflow application are performed by tools, such as business applications (the Web-based or

client/server HR system) or personal productivity tools, e.g., applications, spreadsheets, or word processors.

- **Data.** There are two types of data contained in a workflow system application: relevant data and process-relevant data. Data could include a document or message created by a system, word processor, or spreadsheet, containing an image, alphanumeric strings, or voice, video and/or database data.

The R's and P's of Workflow Systems

Another way to decompose a workflow system is into a series of elements referred to as the R's and P's of workflow.

- **Routes.** Workflow systems specify the flow of any data object (document, forms, data, applications, and so on). These objects are then sent down any number of different sequential routes and then reconciled into a single route at a specified point. Objects should be transmittable in either a broadcast mode or any other sequence described by the user. The navigation needs to be specified, according to the rules of the process.
- **Rules.** The ability to define rules, which is a valuable function for users, is an advanced feature of workflow systems. Rules define what information is to be routed and to whom. This is sometimes referred to as "conditional routing" and "exception handling," such that, if a salary increase is over 10 percent, the transaction must be routed through HR. Rule definitions are often accomplished through a scripting language or other programming activities. Some systems have user-defined rules engines that allow users to write complex rules through the use of screens and parameters. Setting up the rules and the exception handling are often the most difficult aspects of any workflow system.
- **Roles.** It is important to define roles independently of specific people or processes filling that role. As people move in and out of an organization, or change roles (jobs), it is important to reassign new individuals to specific roles without changing the people at the task level. This is important, since

a single employee may be involved in multiple workflow steps.

- **Processes.** The established processes that run businesses are as varied as the people who implement them. Often, processes are not designed, but rather emerge from common usage. (The terms *process redesign* or *reengineering* may in fact be misnomers, since seldom are the processes engineered in the first place.) Processes can, and often do, span applications and functional areas. For example, when an employee is hired:
  - ◆ HR must be notified to enroll the individual for benefits.
  - ◆ Payroll must enter them in the payroll system.
  - ◆ The security area must issue identification cards.
  - ◆ IT assigns a computer and user ID.
  - ◆ Purchasing must be notified to order supplies and equipment.
  - ◆ The office space and facilities group assigns telephones, issues keys to the office, and so forth.
- **Policies.** Policies are *formal written statements* as to how certain processes are handled. In many cases, companies should have formal polices, but in fact do not. Policies may include information on vacation and benefits, performance management policies, or steps to handle a sexual harassment claim.
- **Practices.** Practices are *what actually happens* in organizations. Practices can be considered those acts of "breaking the rules" that enable processes to work. For example, "Every salary increase must go through Human Resources, unless it is for an employee in R&D, where Jack will authorize it." Too often in designing workflow systems, "policies" are rigorously followed when more attention should be given to "practices."

Components of Workflow Systems

Automated workflow systems commonly consist of three components. These components do not need to come from the same vendor.

- **Deployment environment.** Users must have a way of getting their job assignments, accessing the necessary productivity tools, and doing their work. An example of one workflow deployment environment that could be deployed separate from a builder or engine would be Lotus Notes or Microsoft Exchange. Some workflow implementations do not use a single deployment environment, but rather track the work as it flows among Web or desktop applications. Application Program Interfaces (APIs) are provided to infuse workflow techniques into Web-based solutions, e-mail, and other application tools.
- **Builder.** The workflow application needs to be created (that is, designed or built). Workflow builders come in many types, from complex scripting languages to graphical mapping and flowcharting tools. These are aimed at different users, from skilled developers to average business users. A workflow builder, such as Oracle Workflow, defines the rules, routes, and roles of the process, as well as identifying the data, information, or objects worked on.
- **Management engine.** A workflow application must offer an underlying engine that ensures the data is being flowed to the right person (or process) in the right order, depending on the specific business conditions that exist at that point in time. The engine also tracks the location of each instance in the process.

Enterprise Workflow Defined

A typical corporate enterprise workflow system consists of multiple departments and geographies, with a diverse range of needs, all tied to a common set of business objectives. These departments and locations need to share common databases, development tools, and processing resources particular to any workflow system. Workflow systems also need to be tied into existing legacy applications.

The real advantage of organization-wide workflow comes from an organization's ability to synchronize the process that exists, as well as from its ability to adapt to new processes as they are introduced.

Enterprise-based workflow applications are getting increased attention. Development of workflow standards, continued movement to open systems, along with the growth of the Internet, are increasing the number of companies looking to implement enterprise workflow solutions.

Workflow versus Workgroup

One common source of confusion in workflow is the difference between "workgroup" and "workflow." This confusion has been somewhat exacerbated by vendors misrepresenting their "groupware" products as "workflow" products. In many cases, the "workgroup" products provide a platform for workflow, but do not provide the process knowledge critical to a workflow product.

In the case of workgroup products, information is shared between individuals, but there is no routing or process flow.

Workgroup products let workgroups or individuals transfer and share information with one another (the key ingredient: information). (See Figure 13-1.)

In a workflow application, the process knowledge that applies to the information is also managed, transferred, and routed. (See Figure 13-2.)

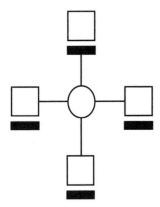

Figure 13-1 Information passing within a workgroup.

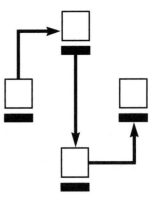

Figure 13-2 Information passing via workflow.

Basic Workflow Functions and Components

Workflow software is becoming more powerful, and the associated features expected of a robust workflow solution have increased over the last several years. Workflow systems provide extensive capabilities, such as routing, document capture, queuing, application launching, forms management, tracking, administration, designing, Web and e-mail, and external communications.

Routing

Routing is one key element of any workflow system. It determines who is the next person (or action) in the workflow process. There are three fundamental types of workflow routing:

- Automatic—allows no options because the next step is predetermined
- Conditional—allows users to choose from different routing options to determine which is the most appropriate
- Rules-based—uses a methodology where the system determines the next step in the routing process based on information that has been defined in the workflow rules

There are several routing features that ensure the information retains usability and integrity.

- *Exception handling.* This provides users and system processes with an option whenever an unusual situation is encountered.
- *Parallel routing.* This allows users or tasks to handle the same data concurrently.
- *Database agents.* These permit users to be alerted when conditions require them to take action.
- *Pending and rendezvous.* This feature allows transactions to be suspended while they wait for important data, and automatically awakened when the matching data is received.
- *User overrides.* These allow users to change the routing in some circumstances.

- *Prioritization.* This allows personnel to handle the highest-priority transaction first. Priority can be determined by user input, transaction type, aging rules, or transaction deadline.

Document Capture

Documents or objects, such as images, must be captured before they can be routed. Normally, this process occurs by one of several means:

- Scanning
- Faxing
- User attachment
- Other automated interfaces (kiosks, Internet, and so on)

This process usually provides for some preliminary form of indexing and routing information for subsequent workflow activities. Imaging systems have become less expensive over the last 10 years. They have historically been used for high-volume storage activities, such as claims processing and customer records. The decrease in imaging system costs, along with the associated hardware, has made these applications extremely attractive for the Human Resources function.

Queues

Queues contain "work in process" transactions that can be accessed by select users. They are like electronic in-baskets, except they are frequently shared by many users. This allows management to monitor and control the status of the workflow by viewing the contents of the queue.

Transaction Launching/Image Viewing

Usually, each workflow step has an application associated with it. It could be a specific application like an Excel spreadsheet, or a legacy application. These applications need to be launched as part of the step. A "document viewer" application, which provides a user with a screen image of a document, is one type of application that may be launched. An application can be immediately launched when initiating the next step in the process and can send or receive any information required.

Forms Management

Forms management is another key workflow component. Forms that were once part of a paper process are automated and used to guide the electronic workflow or transfer of information into applications. The forms contain intelligence that support data validation, routing, and the transfer of data to applications without rekeying. Forms can be stored in a repository and retrieved based on a variety of search criteria. Contents of existing forms can be queried as well.

Tracking, Monitoring, and Document Control (Metrics)

Processing transaction histories provides important information for status reporting, productivity reporting, and audit trails. This information is very important for validating the need for a workflow system.

Workflow Administration and Work Lists

Workflow administration components normally supported by workflow systems include: user profiles, queue assignments, queue management, backlog analysis, productivity-reporting, workload-balancing, and productivity statistics.

Workflow Creation Tools (Designer)

One of the most visible components of a workflow system is the graphical user development environment, which can be used by developers or, in some cases, by end users to create workflow applications by manipulating icons that represent tasks, users, processes, and routing objects. Figure 13-3 shows an example from Oracle.

Workflow systems can extend beyond the workgroup to interface with the outside world. The simplest examples are fax and e-mail. E-mails and faxes can be sent, even if the same workflow tools are not present at the receiving location.

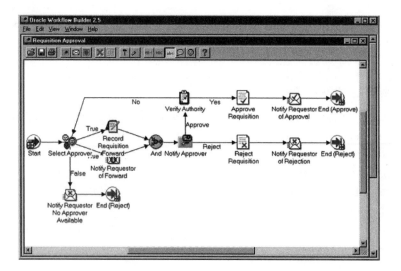

Figure 13-3 Sample of Oracle's workflow application.

Web and E-mail

Many workflow systems utilize Web-enabled and standard e-mail engines for their transport process. Such systems are natural choices for workflow applications, because the "store and forward" nature of Web and e-mail is well suited to the way people work. People transact business from an ever-changing list of priorities and the internal logic that can be built in.

Types of Workflow

Workflow systems, like most software, can be categorized in several different ways. One common way of categorizing workflow systems is how the workflow system utilizes e-mail.

Workflow systems can be deployed in three different architectural models: message-based (e-mail–based), host-based (shared database), and Web-based and client/server–based models.

Message-Based Workflow

Workflow systems can be built solely around the mail structure found in an organization. This message-centric approach is appropriate for document routing applications, such as expense requisition or purchase order approval. In messaged-based workflow, functionality resides in and is executed by the client, with only messaging functions occurring on the server.

The key elements of the execution environment (routes, roles, and rules) are all executed by one or more client processes. Data, rules for processing the document, and the document itself reside in the user's in-box. Processing rules may travel with the document or may be maintained in the user's mail application.

Message-Based Workflow

👍

The familiar paper, or mail, metaphor is preserved.

Training is often minimized.

An incremental approach to beginning workflow is allowed.

Small-scale situations are treated effectively.

Departments often serve as basis.

Support exists for multiple operating systems and multiple client platforms.

Remote users can be supported.

Work can still proceed if central workflow engine is "down."

👎

Message-centric tools are more difficult to manage because they tend to live on the client rather than on the server (as a form moves from person 'A' to person 'B' to person 'C', person 'A' is in the dark as to the form's progress).

Other users cannot access them, until changes are sent back to the server.

Workflow rules can become very complex to manage, since the rules tend to reside in multiple locations. Any change to the process needs to be propagated to dozens or potentially hundreds of applications.

The status of a piece of work is difficult to determine, beyond knowing it is sitting in someone's in-box.

The document in route is unavailable to anyone other than the current mail recipient, for systems that route documents.

Process-related "management" information, which helps users make business decisions, cannot be collected. (Example: Newly hired employees, whose applications are collected from the Internet, are determined to be 45 percent more successful than other applicants. This information might be missed utilizing an e-mail-only model.)

Host-Based Workflow

Host-based workflow processing, as with the message-based model, is done on the client. However, documents are not moved around via the e-mail system. In some cases, users may be notified via e-mail that they have a workflow task at hand. Documents are stored in a shared database on the network. Documents (at least in read-only version) are always available for viewing.

Rules and roles may be stored separately from documents in the same or different database, or they may be contained within the client software, or attached to the documents themselves.

Host-Based Workflow

👍	👎
Process-centric tools are easier to manage because they tend to live on the server rather than on the client.	Databases are terrible at "waking people up to take action."
	Training is often more extensive.
High-volume, mission-critical applications are better suited for it.	A broad commitment to a workflow approach is often required.
Changes can be accessed immediately by anyone connected to the server.	Most systems currently require a single operating system and platform within the organization to run.
Enterprises often serve as the basis.	Remote users are difficult to support.
Large scale situations can be effectively treated.	Users need to have access to the database. Databases that support replication (such as Lotus Notes) do not have this limitation. However, even with replication, there is no guarantee that users will access the latest version of the data.
Workflow rules tends to be simpler to manage, since the rules tend to reside in a single location in a single database.	
Continual access to documents is provided.	Work can grind to a halt if the server goes down.
Historical workflow information can be retained simply.	

Web- and Client/Server–Based Workflow

Web- and client/server–based workflow extends the message-based model by storing and executing the rules on the server. The server runs processes or agents that determine the next step in the workflow. The server can also monitor the workflow status and notify participants of an upcoming or overdue task. Server-based workflow applications can also integrate with other data sources and applications.

Client/Server–Based Workflow

👍	👎
Same advantages as the host-based model	Same disadvantages as the host-based model
Can integrate with the e-mail system	

Workflow Considerations

While workflow has clear value, in many cases it is not effective. There are a number of pitfalls in implementing workflow systems. It takes care, planning, and, occasionally, some luck to implement a workflow system successfully.

Reasons Workflow Projects Fail

Some workflow projects fail. There are a number of reasons for these failures, and, in many cases, there are solutions to the problems, as outlined below.

Reason #1 Not All Processes Can Be Automated

☹ **Problem**	☺ **Solution**
Complex processes with thousands of possible outcomes, determined by dozens of variables depending on specific needs, are not good candidates for workflow systems. You must program all the possible role	Avoid automating processes that rely on randomness and variability. Keep humans responsible for the major decision points in the process. Use the workflow system to move data from one point to the next. This approach

actions and exceptions that occur within the workflow process. Even if you could program all the possible permutations, maintaining the system would be difficult and costly.

takes advantage of two strengths of workflow: communication speed and automated record keeping.

Reason #2 Subjective Events Define Your Workflow

☹ **Problem**

Steps that rely on subjective analysis, evaluation, and human intervention cannot be handled effectively by workflow systems. "If you can't quantify it, you probably can't program it." Today's workflow engines cannot handle ad hoc decisions requiring "fuzzy logic."

☺ **Solution**

Quantify and convert business rules into the format that your workflow engine expects. Reduce the process map, or flowchart, to quantifiable business rules during the design or prototyping process.

Reason #3 System Performance Degrades over Time

☹ **Problem**

Workflow systems normally work fine over the first few weeks, or months. As the process ages and matures over time, slight variations creep in, so there are more process exception-handling procedures (most often outside the system). Exception handling normally requires two to three times the normal cycle time.

☺ **Solution**

Monitor the workflow process continuously and change the program as the process changes. System performance and effectiveness correlates directly with the frequency and quality of the program maintenance done. Examine audit trails and event logs, transaction monitors and capacity alerts.

Reason #4 New Tasks Corrupt Existing Designs

☹ **Problem**

A change in the workflow can often take effect only after you have completed all the work in progress and cleared the work queues.

☺ **Solution**

Build and maintain complex works with object-oriented workflow (OOW) tools, which make it easier to do so. Steps applications allow you to

Object-oriented workflows (OOWs) are complex development environments and have few standards. Approaches vary widely from vendor to vendor. This limits the interoperability among tool sets.

develop object libraries around common workflow process elements, such as approvals, routing, data validation, and security. You embed the task or workflow data with the processing rules. OOW gives you standard OOP features such as inheritance, encapsulation, and reusability. Since data travels with the code, each workflow's instance is separate and independent.

Reason #5 *Workflow Systems Are Not Heterogeneous*

☹ **Problem**

Few workflow engines can currently operate on multiple-server platforms or support multiple-client OSEs.

☺ **Solution**

Select a workflow tool that can operate within a variable environment. If you are relying on a particular feature, such as cc:Mail integration, make sure that feature is available for *every* client you might use (e.g., OLE 2.0 is not available on a Mac client).

Reason #6 *Workflow Systems Are Not Scalable*

☹ **Problem**

Most workflow product vendors design engines to maintain constant control over each workflow instance in process. These engines do not share workflows or exchange business rules with other engines. In most cases, business rules must be stored on one server, so all events can be tracked and monitored centrally. This architecture limits the ability of workflow systems to support large enterprise processes. It may also restrict workflow to a workgroup or a department.

☺ **Solution**

Choose a workflow system moving toward distributed workflow engines and workflow engines that can link to internal and external networks, such as the Internet. Java may allow workflow applications to be platform-independent.

Web workflow engines might also be able to interact with each other to exchange business rules, works-in-progress, and information about workflow resources.

Human Resources Issues

The Human Resources function is an area rich in workflow opportunities. Companies are looking to reduce overhead and replace headcount with technology-based solutions wherever appropriate. Workflow opportunities will often come as a result of reengineering activities.

Business Process Reengineering

When embarking on a workflow project, it is important not to mindlessly "pave the cow paths." "Paving the cow paths" refers to the practice of mirroring an existing nonautomated process with a technological solution. While this is not necessarily bad, you should always consider whether an existing process represents the most effective way to handle an existing business need.

Workflow and Event Processing

Often these "work processes" fall into the areas of certain "life events" that affect the employee's relationship with the employer. Some of these events (processes) could include:

- Application or requisition (hiring)
- Promotion
- Termination
- Retirement
- Birth of a child
- Separation or divorce
- Death of spouse
- Change in spouse's job status

While this is not an exhaustive list, the prevalence of life events clearly presents the opportunity to utilize workflow systems to standardize certain Human Resources processes. These activities often cut across several departments, as well as involving a number of different areas within the HR function.

By developing workflow processes that span the breadth of these activities, the events can be handled more efficiently with higher-quality results.

Employee Self-Service

Another HR area ripe for exploitation by workflow is the area of employee self-service. By allowing the employee to become an integral part of the workflow process, data entry errors can be minimized and cycle time greatly reduced. With the Web, the number of companies using the Internet as a workflow enabler will clearly increase. In order to effectively exploit the Internet, companies will also need to deploy internal workflow systems to monitor and manage workflow activities.

Human Resources Workflow across the Enterprise

The Human Resources area is one of a number of functional areas supported by most businesses. Areas such as manufacturing, research and development, finance, and so on, also have workflow requirements. In many cases, these areas need to interact. A company that has one flavor of workflow with its human resource system and another bundled with its manufacturing package has to worry about passing workflow between two unlike packages. Lots of companies will purchase applications with workflow already embedded. That will work fine, until they try to integrate them across the enterprise.

Summary

Workflow systems are growing in popularity and all signs indicate that HR will be one of the next areas for extensive workflow implementations. While no complete workflow standards exist, we are moving toward industry standards that will provide critical features, such as interoperability between workflow vendors and standard workflow application interfaces.

It is very important to be cautious when implementing a workflow solution. There are a number of pitfalls, if inappropriate workflow tools are used, or if the tools are applied incorrectly. Many HRMS vendors are rushing to market workflow functionality with their product offerings, and we need to integrate their capabilities and supply a cohesive solution to the customers.

14

HR Service Centers
The Human Element
Behind the Technology

Joseph Bender*

Web Influence

Although many believe that the Web will soon eliminate the need for an HR service center, it has become clear that some human support will still be needed to address complex issues and to assist users as they navigate through a Web transaction. Questions inevitably arise regarding terminology, how to process a change, or an interpretation of policies. Also, employees and managers often want to be reassured that what they are doing is correct, and even though there are automated support tools, such as knowledge bases, they still may turn to people for that clarification and support.

*Joseph Bender is a consultant in the Parsippany, New Jersey, office. He specializes in HR administration and technology with a particular emphasis on developing and implementing new and improved HR service delivery solutions for clients.

Parsippany office address: Morris Corporate Center II, Building F, One Upper Pond Road, Parsippany, New Jersey 07054-1050.

What Is an HR Service Center?

An HR service center can be described as a centralized group of HR staff, focused on delivering a range of HR services, in other than a face-to-face mode. Such service centers are technology-enabled to help gain efficiencies. And the scope of services can extend to almost all HR plans and programs, depending on management desires.

Since the mid 1990s, most large companies in the United States have radically changed their approach to delivering HR services. They have typically accomplished this by either establishing an internal HR service center or by shifting HR activities to an outsourced service provider. Although this chapter focuses on establishing an internal center, there are many themes and topics that are relevant to an outsourced service delivery model.

What Are the Key Characteristics of an HR Service Center?

Centralization of service delivery is a primary aspect. Prior to establishing a center, companies typically relied on HR generalists delivering most HR services face-to-face at local sites or business units. By contrast, a centralized center removes this local role and relies on phone contact with customers (i.e., employees, managers) to answer questions and resolve issues. Beyond calls, many centers also have centralized data input of HR, payroll, and benefit transactions. Such centralization can be physical or virtual, depending on the telecommunications arrangements.

Leveraged technology in this centralized environment is another hallmark of an HR service center. This typically includes use of telephony (e.g., IVR, ACD), as well as other customer service representative (CSR) support tools (e.g., case management system, knowledge base). In many ways, it is the availability and use of these technologies that have enabled these HR centers to be viable. They are critical to the delivery of centralized services of high quality and cost-effectiveness. These technologies are discussed in more depth later in the chapter.

Service Center Organization Models

There are generally two types of HR service centers that companies have established, as defined by the customers they support. *Employee* service centers primarily focus on supporting the needs of employees (typically in the benefits and payroll areas). This is the area that most companies roll out first when they begin implementing an HR shared-services organization. This is also the primary area of focus in this chapter. Where HR and payroll transactions are in the scope of services delivered, line managers are also center customers, relying on the center to support these transactions.

A shared service center where a primary customer is the *line* manager is typically the next organization model to emerge. Commonly referred to as *centers of excellence* (COEs), these have been set up in companies where many HR services were previously delivered at the business unit level. This more centralized sharing of resources across business units not only achieves greater efficiencies, but can also offer deeper expertise and service quality to their customers through more centralized specialization.

Areas typically included in the scope of these COEs are staffing, training, compensation, and so on. There has been some experimentation with supporting employee relation activities on a more centralized basis in the COEs, but this is in an early stage of development. The issues related to supporting manager needs are generally not as transactional in nature as is typically the case for supporting employees. Rather, there is a greater emphasis on the consultative activities performed by these groups, and the associated organization alignment, charge-back methods, and so on. There is generally a much greater need to understand business unit differences in order to support them effectively.

Future Trends

Introduction of the Web enables the whole paradigm of HR service delivery via a center to shift dramatically. *Self-service* by employees and managers, for both information and transactions, will dramatically impact the staffing levels of most HR centers in the next few years. Not only is customer demand driving this trend, but HR management also continues to expect lower costs from the center; this is the primary vehicle available for delivering both.

Moving HR information to a shared HR knowledge base that is directly accessible by customers enables them to answer their own inquiries and thereby reduce CSR staffing levels. Further, direct customer (that is, employee or manager) *access* to their personal HR data (or that of their direct reports) greatly reduces the need for paper-based employee profiles circulating throughout the company. With employees and managers directly *updating* HR, benefits, and payroll data, the need for centralized data entry staff in the centers is dramatically reduced. This topic is addressed in more detail later in this chapter.

Rationale for Establishing an HR Service Center

There are three primary reasons why companies establish HR service centers, but the emphasis on which is most critical varies from company to company.

Reducing HR costs is a common driver. This is generally achieved by delivering HR services on a more centralized basis, thereby achieving economies of scale and shifting administrative work to a center where less expensive resources can perform the same activities. The first HR centers were established in the early 1990s as an outcome of significant HR reengineering initiatives that had a primary emphasis on reducing HR costs. Figure 14-1 shows the relative importance of the key drivers to establish a center.

Allowing a company to *transform HR* is another key rationale for a company to establish shared services. Most companies are trying to change the role of HR generalists to become more strategic business partners. Fundamental to reaching this strategic goal is the need to remove the administrative activities often constituting a significant portion of their work activities. Centralizing these administrative activities in an HR center allows this to occur.

Finally, *improving service quality* is another key objective for many companies. When services are delivered on a decentralized basis, the level of knowledge at any location can be quite variable, and, as a result, the answers given to customer questions are not

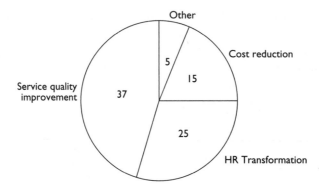

Figure 14-1 Reasons supplied by 82 companies as their primary driver to establish center.

always correct or consistent. A centralized center enables HR to train their staff in a consistent manner and to thus deliver the same answers to all customers.

Planning a Center's Scope of Services

There are many activities which companies undertake in the preliminary stages of developing an HR service center. One of the most critical is to *define the scope of activities* that should be supported by the center. Most centers that support employees as the primary customer are initially established to support benefits activities (health and welfare, pension, and so on). Many also support inquiries related to HR policies.

Data input of HR transactions and other payroll activities is often included in the scope for many centers, as they evolve over time. For many centers, keying HR transactions is often a natural extension of a centralized HRIS data entry function. As companies try to remove the administrative duties of HR generalists, the centralized input of transactions becomes critical.

Keying transactions that impact both HR and payroll systems leads many centers to include aspects of payroll in their scope of supported services. However, there is a continuum of payroll activities, and the different models that a center supports can vary significantly. Figure 14-2 lists key payroll/HR transaction activities,

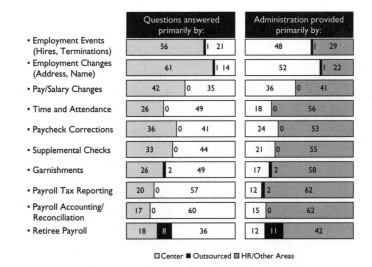

	Questions answered primarily by:			Administration provided primarily by:		
• Employment Events (Hires, Terminations)	56	1	21	48	1	29
• Employment Changes (Address, Name)	61	1	14	52	1	22
• Pay/Salary Changes	42	0	35	36	0	41
• Time and Attendance	26	0	49	18	0	56
• Paycheck Corrections	36	0	41	24	0	53
• Supplemental Checks	33	0	44	21	0	55
• Garnishments	26	2	49	17	2	58
• Payroll Tax Reporting	20	0	57	12	2	62
• Payroll Accounting/ Reconciliation	17	0	60	15	0	62
• Retiree Payroll	18	8	36	12	11	42

☐ Center ■ Outsourced ☐ HR/Other Areas

Figure 14-2   Survey respondents listing of key payroll/HR transaction activities.

and the prevalance of each activity in the center from an inquiry support role as well as an administrative role.

A key determinant as to whether a center truly supports payroll is the ability to answer paycheck questions and to make corrections when there are errors. Following along the continuum, the most complete definition of a center including payroll in its scope occurs when the center also processes garnishments, issues the paychecks, balances payroll, reports payroll taxes, and so on. As expected, many HR centers may support the transactional aspects of payroll, but do not include specific paycheck questions or actually run the payroll. Thus, there is no simple answer to the question as to whether centers support payroll in their scope of services.

Business Case

Another critical start-up activity for many HR centers is to *develop a business case* to justify the investments needed to start a center. This may be performed with varying levels of detail and rigor, depending on the company culture or management style. The key steps in preparing a business case typically involve defining current decentralized baseline costs (staff counts and HR budgets), and then projecting the staffing and budget costs for delivering the same scope of services on a centralized basis.

These ongoing savings are then balanced against the level of infrastructure and technology investments required at start-up. This payback analysis, or ROI, is the heart of the financial aspects of a business case. Beyond a purely economic assessment, many companies consider the potential for improving service quality, and enabling the transformation of HR, in the business case, as previously discussed.

As part of this business case analysis, a company may also consider the viability and cost of *outsourcing* some or all of the proposed activities under consideration within the scope of the proposed center. This is often a key start-up decision for many HR centers: whether to build an in-house HR center, or to outsource all or part of it.

The market for outsourcing HR activities evolved substantially in the 1990s, as many HR consulting firms and money management firms began to offer a broader range of outsourced HR services to clients. Of course, most companies do outsource various *components* of their HR activities (medical claims, spending accounts, 401(k), COBRA, and so on). The outsourcing market that emerged in the latter half of the 1990s began to encompass a broad outsourcing of all benefits-related activities. Today, the outsourcing market is expanding to include a fuller outsourcing of many more HR activities. At the extreme, some companies (e.g., BP Amoco) are now considering outsourcing the entire HR function. However, it is expected that this model will take many years to develop and establish itself as truly viable.

Organization and Staffing

Another key decision made at the start-up of an HR center is to determine the organization and staff model that best meets customer needs, and yet is cost-effective. Many centers begin with one model and continually experiment and refine it as the centers continue in operation and issues surface.

Although there are many operational jobs or roles defined in an HR center, the three most common are customer service representative (CSR), specialist, and transaction processor. For the most part, smaller centers will, by necessity, develop a more generalist model, with most staff performing all three of these roles as part of their jobs. The luxury of specialization is often not viable when there are only a handful of staff in the center.

In the larger centers, there is typically more specialization of these roles. Balancing the pros and cons of a more generalized or specialized model is an ongoing challenge for most centers. As part of this decision process, there are two key staffing issues impacting these models with which larger centers wrestle. First, the amount of time that CSRs are expected to be on the phone is a key decision. Most CSRs prefer to spend a higher percentage of their time performing off-phone work, but this must be balanced with the need to efficiently service customers, often requiring more phone time in the mix. Figure 14-3 shows how widely the "time on phone" can vary for different HR centers.

Second, during the time that CSRs are performing off-phone work, they typically assist with transaction processing, administration, research, and so on. Figure 14-4 illustrates an overall profile of how a typical CSR spends his/her time in an HR center. A number of challenges generally arise in moving to a more generalized "universal rep" staffing model, requiring multiple roles:

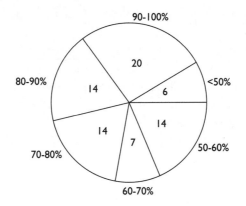

Figure 14-3 Percentage of day CSRs scheduled to answer calls.

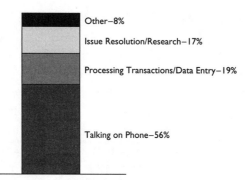

Figure 14-4 CSR time spent by activity.

- The ability to perform multiple specialized roles effectively may be a challenge for some staff; for example, accurate data entry skills may conflict with customer service skills.
- The ability to effectively balance the priorities and time scheduling of each role—deciding which role takes precedence—is a challenge for many staff.

Service Center Technologies

There are a number of technologies that most centers view as critical to an effective operation. First of all, the core HR, benefits, and payroll systems, which the center relies upon for customer data, are critical. If the functionality or data quality of these core applications is weak, it is very difficult to provide quality customer service.

Beyond these core HR applications, there are key technologies unique to a service center environment. Figure 14-5 lists the key service center technologies and their general usage levels; their relative importance to the center staff is also illustrated. Although there is not uniform agreement, most centers view the automated call distributor (ACD) and case management technologies as the most essential.

The ACD is a tool that routes incoming calls to available CSRs and tracks metrics on call-waiting, abandonment, and so on. This is a critical tool for management in monitoring the timeliness of service quality. More sophisticated products enable automatic

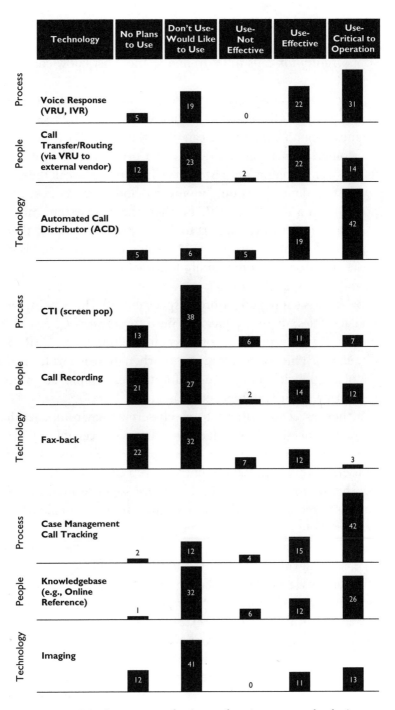

Figure 14-5 Survey respondent's use of service center technologies.

routing of calls based on the specialized skills of a CSR. This can enable a more effective balancing of workloads while maximizing the opportunity for calls to be routed to the most knowledgeable individuals.

Case management systems are also generally considered to be essential, primarily for ensuring a quality of service. By recording case notes about a call, a CSR can view the call history and save the customer from repeating details of a prior call. Also, it prevents "answer shopping" by customers who repeatedly call the center with the same question, hoping to find a more favorable response from a different CSR. Further, the case system can be used as an administrative support tool for CSRs, by enabling them to track needed follow-up actions. Management also depends on the case system to monitor timely follow-up, to review call patterns and trends, and so on.

For centers supporting a broad spectrum of HR, benefit, and payroll activities, there is typically a need for a *knowledge base* that contains HR policy, plan, and process information that a CSR can readily access. This is even more critical when there is a wide diversity in plans, policies, and processes for different employee groups (e.g., salaried, hourly, union, retiree).

Further, as centers move to a self-service environment, the need for an effective knowledge base, directly accessible by customers, becomes more critical. Historically, CSRs were the primary users of this information, but the Web enables customers to access this information as well. The more sophisticated tools in the marketplace are data-driven, enabling more personalized information about a specific employee (e.g., hourly retiree policies versus salaried active policies). This is an area undergoing much change, as companies wrestle with the right blend of content organization and style for each audience accessing it.

In a highly paper-intensive center, the need for an *imaging* system is also critical. This enables CSRs to readily access all documents received into the center, as well as those mailed from the center. This leads to a high level of customer satisfaction, since the CSR can immediately address issues on the first call. Due to the high cost of these systems, however, imaging systems are generally employed only in very large scale centers. As self-service is deployed more widely in the coming years, it is anticipated that many paper forms and documents will be eliminated, and the need for imaging will diminish.

Measures and Service Quality

Most centers view metrics as a critical component for any service center; without the ability to measure, it is difficult to monitor and control the quality of service delivered by a center. Most centers rely on the statistics automatically provided by their ACD system as a primary set of metrics.

Average speed to answer (ASA)—that is, the average length of time a customer waits before getting a CSR to answer the call— is one of the most common metrics used. Figure 14-6 shows the wide range of targets set for ASA, as well as actual results. The call abandonment rate—that is, the percentage of customers who hang up while waiting for a CSR to answer—is another critical metric. Call volumes are also tracked by the ACD, and they enable the center to track average calls per CSR, average call length, and so on. These are all critical indices for center management, and defined targets for each of these are generally included in service-level agreements with customers.

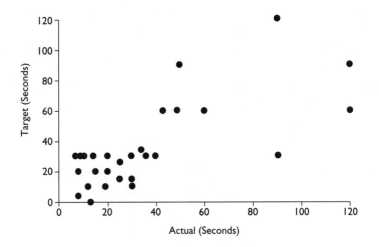

Figure 14-6 Average speed to answer. Most target 20 to 30 seconds. Twenty respondent companies in this study stated they meet their target.

The *case management system* is another critical source of information for most centers. Management can rely on it to monitor key issues and trends. Further, it is a key tool employed by supervisors to gauge whether cases are being worked, and closed, in a timely manner. Many centers also rely on it to track timely input of documents, as well as to assess whether cases were resolved correctly.

To gauge service quality and accuracy, HR centers have two additional tools available to them. Monitoring calls (either "live" or based on recorded calls) is critical for ensuring that a CSR is providing the right information in a customer-friendly manner. Based on this call monitoring, the supervisor can coach CSRs on improving their skills.

A broader measure of service quality is derived from periodic surveys of customers who have contacted the center within a recent period of time. These are typically paper-based or Web-based surveys sent to a random sample of customers identified from the case management system. Other approaches rely on a "voice mail" survey after a sampling of calls. This is a key rating that most centers monitor carefully for assessing their overall performance.

Where Next?

As self-service is implemented over time and gradually reduces both the transactions that are input by the center, as well as the more basic calls, the role of the center staff will become more specialized; more complex questions and exceptions remain over time. Although it will take some time to arrive at this state, it is clear that the number of CSRs and administrative staff will be substantially reduced.

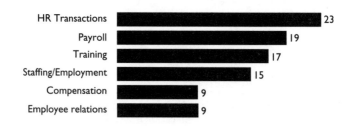

Figure 14-7 Future scope of services planned by respondents.

Many centers are also considering expanding the scope of services offered to their customers. Figure 14-7 indicates the areas where most centers plan to expand their services in the future. As discussed earlier, many centers began with a focus primarily on benefits, but intended to expand their services over time. Survey results indicate that the two most likely areas of expansion are HR transactions and staffing or employment. The next most likely areas of expansion are payroll and training registration.

Clearly, many of these areas for future scope expansion will be affected by self-service; in fact, many question whether it makes sense to further centralize activities if self-service changes the need to do so. For the most part, HR centers were formed on a centralized basis to achieve economies of scale and yield better service. But, with self-service, transactions will be fully decentralized—not back to local HR, but to the very source: employees and managers. Ironically, in many ways, technology is now pushing HR centers full circle back into a highly decentralized environment!

CHAPTER

How to Implement an HR Service Center

The Technologies and Staff Needed

*Stephen C. Brescia and April E. Hartness**

EARLIER CHAPTERS in this book have discussed why the HR service center is important and how it works; this chapter covers implementation issues, such as the technologies that are needed, as well as physical layout and staffing considerations in establishing such a center. It also discusses how an HR service center can become a shared service center, and what the differences between the two are.

---

*Stephen C. Brescia is a consultant in the Voorhees, New Jersey, office. He specializes in the use of technology in the evaluation, development, and implementation of HR service centers.

Voorhees, New Jersey, office address: 4 Echelon Plaza, 201 Laurel Road, Voorhees, New Jersey 08043.

April E. Hartness is a Principal in the Towers Perrin Atlanta office. She specializes in the design and implementation of HR Service Centers, and is the global practice leader for HR Administration and Technology consulting.

Atlanta office address: One Atlanta Plaza, 950 East Paces Ferry Road, Atlanta, Georgia 30326-1119.

Human Resources Shared Service Centers: What They Are

An HR shared service center is a centralized location where customer transactions and customer inquiries are handled. While there are many service delivery models in existence today, the model that has evolved as "best practice" is one that features an HR shared service center composed of two components: a center of excellence and a service center. The major distinction between these two components is the identity of the primary customer. For the center of excellence, the primary customer is the line manager and/or local HR staff; for the service center, the primary customer is the employee.

HR shared service centers are typically staffed by generalists and specialists, and are supported by a suite of new and specialized technologies. Phone calls, e-mails, or on-line inquiries that cannot be handled by automated telephony scripts are forwarded to customers service representatives for assistance. These representatives are typically generalists who have broad knowledge of an organization's policies and programs, and are often referred to as *tier 1 support*. Depending on the particular subject matter, 65–90 percent of all inquiries to the center can be handled by tier 1 support. This is desirable because tier 1 staff are typically lower-cost than tier 2 staff. When the inquiry requires research or a deeper level of subject matter expertise, the customer service representative will forward the inquiry electronically to a specialist for resolution. These specialist are known as *tier 2 support staff*. Tier 2 support staff have expertise in a particular functional area—recruiting and staffing, benefits, payroll, and so on. Most of the center-of-excellence staff will have HR functional expertise.

The benefit centers of the early 1990s were more appropriately termed *call centers* in contrast to true shared service centers. While record keeping, fulfillment, and mailing activities were being performed to support administration of benefits, the major focus of the center was answering employee questions. The service centers of today still answer phone calls, but self-service through the Web is changing the focus of work from answering phone calls to fuller HR service delivery and business strategy alignment. HR shared service centers provide support for managers and employees, regarding plans and policies, with respect to compensation, payroll, benefits, training, and job postings, and look to add performance management and staffing to these service offerings.

As centers have grown in sophistication, so have challenges to implementation. Successful implementation of an HR shared service center is dependent upon many factors, not just people, process, and technology. Issues such as center location, the facility and supporting infrastructure, the service delivery model, recruiting and retention, training, measurements, and thorough testing can play a major role in the success or failure of a service center.

Throughout this chapter we will take a more in-depth look at how each of these components affects implementation of an HR shared service center.

Site Selection, Facility Planning, and Infrastructure

Site Selection

Selecting the ideal site for a service center is a critical decision that impacts a variety of issues, such as employee recruitment, accessibility of the facility via mass or personal transportation, and local amenities (e.g., post office, eating establishments). In some instances, the site of the service center is predetermined based on political, economic, or social considerations. If the site has not been predetermined, several factors need to be considered.

Determining the classification of a potential site is the first factor for consideration. A *class A* building is generally regarded as a site that is less than 7 years old and has open and available space for the people, furnishings, and technology of the service center. It should also include a minimum expansion capacity of 20 percent. For example, if the current service center headcount is 100, the space should be able to accommodate 120 people. A *class B* building is generally regarded as a site that is 7–15 years old. It must still have all of the space requirements associated with the class A site to be considered a viable site for the service center. Any building below the status of class B should be removed from consideration immediately. Buildings below class B status may present considerable challenges, especially in the areas of required repairs and support for the technology infrastructure, i.e., inside wiring, heating, ventilation, and air conditioning (HVAC). In either case, the site needs to provide a minimum of 100 square feet per employee. This includes common area space, such as restrooms, conference rooms, and copy rooms.

After the potential site's classification has been determined, there are other considerations regarding the site. It needs to be located in an economically viable location with a skilled labor pool to attract quality staff to your service center.

The site needs to be easily accessible via mass transportation (e.g., airplanes, trains, and buses), as well as personal transportation. The site needs to have ample, secure parking for employees and visitors. In addition to these factors, the site needs to be located in an environmentally advantageous location. If it is located in an area that experiences adverse weather conditions (e.g., flooding, blizzards), the potential for service outages increases. If it is consistently closed due to these conditions, customers will see it as unreliable, unsuccessful, and maybe even unnecessary.

Finally, the potential site needs to include certain amenities, or at least be located near these amenities. Employees will benefit from a location that has, or is close to, post offices, shopping centers, gas stations, and restaurants.

Facility Planning

Once the site has been chosen, the configuration and furnishings of the site need to be reviewed. Will the service center have an "open plan" with nothing but cubicles? Will it have some offices? What about the computer data center?

Consider the floor plan in Figure 15-1. This sample floor plan is designed to meet the specific needs of the service center staff. The first thing to notice is that this is primarily an "open plan" configuration with variously sized and shaped cubicles for workgroups. Workspaces for the first-tier generalists and their team leaders are designed with 4-foot dividing walls to improve the "line of sight" for both managers and generalists. This improves the managers' ability to visually monitor employees, and it helps to build a stronger team environment between leaders and generalists. Second-tier specialists are separated from the generalists and

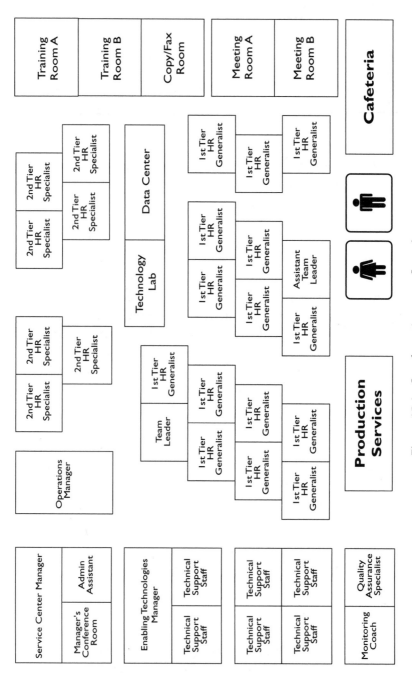
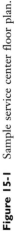

Figure 15-1 Sample service center floor plan.

normally have higher (6-foot) walls to provide more privacy for conference calls or meetings with other employees. This diagram also includes some very important features sometimes overlooked when building a service center, such as training rooms, copy rooms, and cafeteria.

One of the specialty rooms in the service center is the data center. This room houses all of the critical technological systems (Web servers, database servers, the PBX), and it has special needs compared with the remainder of the floor. Three important considerations for this room are the environmental controls, the wiring design, and physical security.

Computers do not function effectively in extreme weather conditions, so the temperature in the data center needs to be controlled between 65° and 75° F. In addition, these systems need to be wired and cabled to receive power from the public energy grid and provide networking services to service center technologies, such as desktops, telephones, and lighting fixtures.

Other important components of the facility are not shown in this diagram but are equally important. An example is the addition of sound-absorbing ceiling tiles. These tiles reduce noise, which can disturb telephone calls or meetings in progress.

Service Center Enabling Technologies

Once the business plan and site selection have been approved and completed, it is time to concentrate on the technologies needed to make the operation of the service center efficient and successful. Technologies discussed in this section have been categorized as *required* for the success of the service center, while others are categorized as *recommended* or *nice to have*.

Technology	Category
Toll-free services	Required
PBX/ACD	Required
IVR	Recommended
CTI	Recommended
Case management	Required
Knowledge base	Recommended
Imaging	Nice to have
Call recording	Recommended

These categorizations are fluid and change based on specific requirements and services offered by the service center. In addition, self-service activities, Web-based or otherwise, will continue to impact the enabling technologies within the service center.

Private Branch Exchange (PBX) and Automatic Call Distribution (ACD)

Historically, the primary customer access method for a service center has been the telephone or telephone-enabled technologies. Customers are increasingly using other technologies (e.g., the Internet, e-mail) as their preferred methods of access (see Figure 15-2). So until recently, private branch exchange (PBX) and automatic call distribution (ACD) were the "heart" of the service center. The PBX "is a private telephone switching system, usually located on a customer's premises with an attendant console. It is connected to a common group of lines from a [telephone company] to provide service to a number of individual phones [i.e., extensions]" (*Newton Telecom Dictionary*, 16th ed., p. 675). The ACD can be integrated into the PBX, or it can be a separate com-

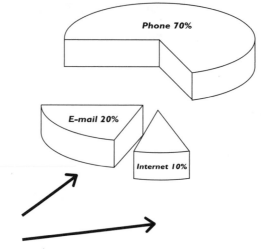

Figure 15-2 Customer interaction by channel.

ponent. It is designed to evenly route incoming calls to available service center representatives.

PBX and ACD systems can be configured in a wide range of sizes and can contain many service center features and modules. Consequently, the cost of these systems varies widely as well. "Service center class" PBXs usually have an ACD module package integrated into the system. In general, a PBX costs approximately $1500–$2000 per user, for a minimum of 100 users. This includes the ACD package, telephones, a standard reporting package, as well as the wiring needed for the system. If the service center is implementing an enabling technology, such as an interactive voice response (IVR) system or computer telephony integration (CTI), additional costs will be incurred for software supporting links to that technology. This software costs about $200,000 to $400,000 per technology. These costs will decrease over the next few years due to the integration of voice and data technologies, such as communications servers performing PBX functions through a data communications server and voice communication over data lines (VOIP).

Interactive Voice Response (IVR)

Interactive voice response (IVR) is the self-service precursor of Web self-service. Simply stated, it is a device that uses touch-tones to receive input from a user's telephone, performs a preprogrammed procedure, and provides information to the user, or asks the user for information by means of a synthesized voice. An IVR is linked to the PBX-ACD for the purpose of providing a connection for the touch-tones and potentially routing the caller to a service center representative. An IVR may also be linked to databases for the purpose of information look-ups or calculations.

The main advantage of IVR for the service center is that callers who are requesting routine information (for example, account balances, vacation days, forms) can be serviced without assistance from a service center representative. This frees the representative to address callers who have more detailed questions (for example, "I am getting married and need to change my medical coverage. What do I need to do?")

The major disadvantage for callers using IVR occurs when they are required to enter large or complex amounts of information, such as names and addresses, with their telephone keypad. To combat this disadvantage, many service centers are using speech, voice, and natural language recognition technology to perform transactions. Callers can forgo the keypad in favor of speaking directly to the IVR. High-end natural language technology even allows the caller to ask the IVR questions, be understood by the IVR, and be provided with an appropriate response.

For example, if the caller needs to schedule a meeting, the caller could call the IVR and make the appointment. The transaction may proceed as follows.

> *Caller:* I need a conference room for a meeting tomorrow between 8:00 A.M. and noon.
>
> *IVR:* OK. How many people are attending the meeting?
>
> *Caller:* Four people.
>
> *IVR:* OK. Do you need any special equipment?
>
> *Caller:* Yes, I need a PC-projector and a conference phone.
>
> *IVR:* OK. Please wait while I check for conference room availability. . . . I have reserved conference room 10A from 8:00 A.M. until noon, tomorrow, May 19th, for four people with a PC-projector and a conference phone. Is there anything else I can help you with today?
>
> *Caller:* No, thank you. That's it for today.
>
> *IVR:* Thank you.

In a Web self-service environment, the IVR can be integrated with the Web via the *click-to-call* technology discussed in a later section of this chapter. So if the IVR has information that is not available via the Web, or is even prohibited because of security reasons from being published on the Web, the user can still have access to this information through the Web.

This example represents a "high-end" offering of IVR technology. In these cases, customization and integration can lead to greater development and implementation costs. High-end solutions aside, IVR costs are broken into two components: hardware-software and script development. The cost of the hardware-software depends upon the number of system ports. A 96-port system costs between $300,000 and $400,000. This system allows for 96 simultaneous connections. The cost of script development depends on the specific applications and integration needed for the service center, and could approach twice the cost of the hardware, or more.

Computer Telephony Integration (CTI)

Computer telephony integration (CTI) is a relatively new technology solution to the service center environment and is closely linked to PBX-ACD and IVR. CTI means adding computer intelligence to the making, receiving, or managing of telephone calls. Most people think of CTI as *screen-pop* technology. Screen-pop is a solution that provides user data to the service center representative based on automatic or manual inputs from the user. For example, the caller may be prompted by the IVR to provide an Employee Identification Number (EIN) and personal identification number (PIN) before the call is routed to the representative. When the caller enters this information (via keypad or voice input), CTI does a database lookup to identify the caller, and then sends that information to the next available representative's computer screen, along with connecting the caller to the representative's telephone. Depending on the computer program being used (e.g., case management), the representative could receive the caller's name, EIN, PIN, title, dependent information, or any other information that CTI has pulled from the database. CTI allows the representative to have knowledge in advance about the caller so the call can be serviced more effectively and efficiently.

CTI also can provide advanced service center solutions. These solutions will be discussed in more detail in later sections of this chapter. The cost of these advanced CTI solutions is directly related to the complexity required by the service center. While there is an initial cost for hardware and software (e.g., servers and "middleware"), the larger costs for CTI are incurred in development. The cost for screen-pop technology can be between $200,000 and $300,000. As in the case of PBX-ACD options, integration in other enabling technologies can be between $200,000 and $400,000 per technology, or more. The major cost determinant is the specific requirements of the service center.

Case Management

The case management system is potentially the most important enabling technology used in the service center. It is a software solution that records interactions between the service center representative and the client-employee. It occurs primarily via the telephone today, but it is expanding toward other methods of contact, such as the Web and e-mail. Historically, case management systems were primarily designed and used in the information technology help-desk environment. Its functionality was usually configured for first-tier technicians with a *frequently asked questions* knowledge base and few links to back-end systems. This configuration continues to work well for help desks today, but the needs of an HR-Benefits service center are significantly different from those of the help desk.

HR-Benefits service centers rely heavily on case management systems as a medium for tracking the complete interaction between employee and representative. HR-Benefits case management systems usually require links to back-end systems for query and transactions (for example, HRIS and knowledge bases), workflow engines that push and pull work from one group to another (e.g., payroll and pension), and robust reporting modules that provide detailed summaries of representatives, groups, and the overall HR-Benefits environment. These systems continue to evolve to meet the needs of self-service environments and can act as the initial employee point of contact with HR through the use of a *case management portal.*

A case management portal is a place where all employee inputs (phone, fax, e-mail, Web, and so on) can be aggregated into one place (see Figure 15-3). This portal provides several advantages.

1. It creates a *universal queue* of employee inputs that can be routed to multiple destinations (e.g., service center repre-

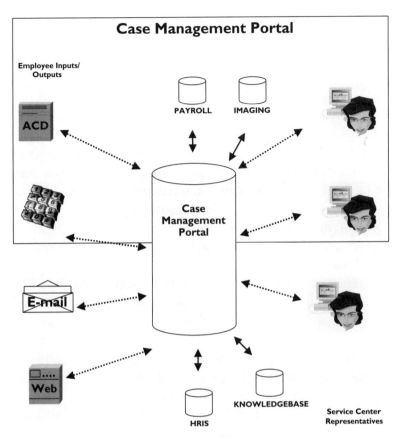

Figure 15-3 Case management portal.

sentatives) according to the business rules defined by the service center. For example, if Web chats have a higher priority than e-mail inquiries, they can be routed to representatives before an e-mail inquiry.

2. It allows employees to access authorized information from the knowledge base, case management, or a back-end system.

3. It allows the service center manager to leverage representative resources across multiple functions. Representatives can be trained to take a mix of employee inputs.

4. It creates an integrated desktop for representatives that provides one interface to access all the systems they use to complete their work.

5. It provides the service center manager integrated reporting across all employee inputs, systems, and representatives. In conjunction with a workforce management package, it aids the manager in scheduling employee shifts, as well as providing valuable information for future budgeting and staffing requests.

In this example, the case management portal is able to receive employee-entered information, such as PIN, social security number (SSN), or a previous case number; perform a look-up in one or more database; and provide this information via CTI to the representative's desktop. In a Web self-service environment, the employee could view any authorized information from the portal or its back-end systems.

Portals are a relatively new case management solution. Most vendors are currently working on developing interfaces to back-end systems, so there is still a great deal of customization to complete their portals. Portals aside, the cost of an HR-centric case management system ranges from approximately $350,000 to $550,000. This includes licenses for the software, basic CTI (screen-pop) functionality, and basic customization of data fields, escalation procedures, and standard reports. Costs for customization, such as integration with other technologies and portals, greatly depend upon the requirements of the service center.

Knowledge Base

Knowledge within the service center has traditionally existed inside binders, training documents, or the minds of the staff. Unfortunately, this has led to some difficulties in service delivery within the center. Representatives who lack the knowledge or experience to answer some employee questions either have provided inaccurate answers or were unable to provide an answer. On the other hand, employees who were unhappy with an answer, even an accurate one, "shopped" the representatives for their desired answer. These difficulties resulted in additional (unnecessary) calls to the center, disagreements between employees and service center staff, and even a lack of confidence in the service center from other employees in the company.

Modern knowledge bases have been developed to combat the inaccuracies and inefficiencies created by mixed messages from the service center. A knowledge base is "software in which application specific information is programmed in the form of rules." (Newton, Harry. *Newton's Telecom Dictionary*, 16th Expanded and Updated Edition, pp. 480–481). These rules are then applied to solve a specific question or inquiry. Knowledge bases have three audiences within a company: the employee population, the service center representatives, and the company managers. Employees can use the knowledge base to get answers for a specific topic without intervention from the service center representative, and they also can use the knowledge base to get more education on those topics (e.g., time and attendance policy). Service center representatives can use the knowledge base for finding answers to employee questions quickly and accurately, as well as for educating themselves on individual topics. Finally, managers can access the knowledge base to review specific policies and processes. For example, one of the manager's employees may be applying for family medical leave. The manager can review the procedures that must be followed to complete the applicable forms.

Employee view. Knowledge bases can also be configured to perform employee transactions. The employee who is applying for family medical leave can find out the amount of time she is eligible for, fill out an on-line form, and have a notification requesting the leave sent to her manager (see Figure 15-4).

Manager's view. The manager, from her workstation (see Figure 15-5), can review the request, approve it, and send it to the Human Resources department for any additional transaction that needs to occur. In conjunction with a workflow system, the employee would receive an e-mail notifying her that her request has been approved and confirmed, and that updated leave and return dates have been posted.

Service Representative's view. In the event that the employee needs additional assistance, she would contact the service center. Normally, the service representative has access to a greater amount of information than the employee and manager. Through the use

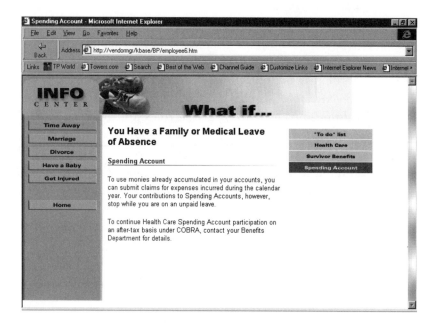

Figure 15-4 Employee view of leave of absence policy.

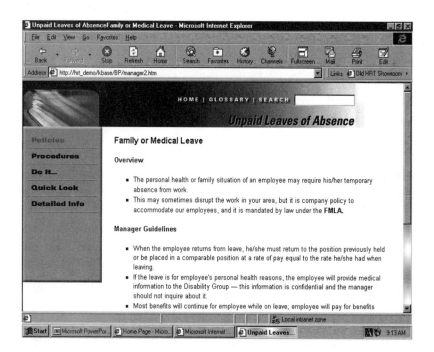

Figure 15-5 Manager's view of leave of absence policy.

of CTI, the representative would be able to determine the identity of the employee, and possibly even the knowledge base page she was looking at when she contacted the service center. (*Note:* This capability requires integration among the knowledge base, the CTI server, the Web server, the case management system, and potentially the PBX-ACD.) The service center representative would provide additional information by accessing the same knowledge base that is available to the employee and manager (see Figure 15-6).

If the knowledge base is Web-enabled, as shown in the previous three figures, employees, service center representatives, and managers can access the system via the company intranet, or even the Internet if the appropriate security measures have been taken by the company.

Normally, knowledge base configuration is closely tailored to the requirements of the service center. Each center has a certain culture, or "feel," that needs to be reflected in the design of the knowledge base, especially if it is used in a self-service solution.

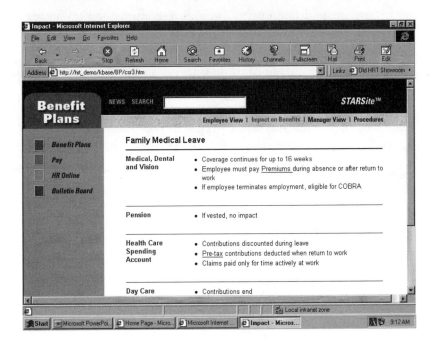

Figure 15-6 Service representative's view.

This has a direct impact on the cost range, which is usually between $500,000 and $1,200,000. This includes all the hardware, software, licensing, and customization; however, the cost of labor (e.g., people to write the content for the knowledge base) is not included in this estimate. Some service centers already have HR-related documents in electronic form, so they should expect to see lower content costs than for centers that have their information on paper or in the employees' minds.

Imaging

Imaging is another service center enabling technology used by representatives and, potentially, employees. Imaging is the process of taking a hardcopy image (e.g., form or picture) and digitizing it for viewing or storage. Software programs, such as optical character recognition (OCR) technology, can manipulate these stored images. Scanners are used to convert the text to digital, and OCR is then applied to this image to produce a text file. (Keep in mind that OCR technology is not 100 percent accurate, so proofreading of any imaged document is highly recommended.) The text file can be used to input information into databases or another back-end system.

The major advantage of using imaging in the service center is that it saves physical space from being used for paper files. In addition, imaged documents can be integrated with the case management system, so that the service representative has access to employee documents without leaving his seat to search paper files. This reduces interaction time with the employee and makes the representative more efficient.

The imaging system can also be a resource for self-service. Employees can access forms or documents from the imaging system via the self-service capabilities of the Web or knowledge base. For example, say an employee is viewing the requirements for making an address change through the Web-enabled knowledge base and discovers that she must fill out a form and return it to the Human Resources department. Through a button on the knowledge base screen, the employee can view the form and either download it or fill it out on the screen. Once the employee has completed the form, she can send it to Human Resources through the Web, fax, e-mail, or standard mail, according to the policies established by HR.

The primary cost of an imaging system is the amount of space required to hold these digitized images. These images are usually held in files on servers specifically configured for imaging. In addition, imaging systems require users to have software licenses. These licenses make up the secondary cost of this system. Scanners, which actually perform the digitization of images, make up the final cost for the imaging system. Together, these three components cost between $700,000 and $1,000,000. Please note that the labor used to scan and manage these images is not included in this cost. As with the other enabling technologies, overall costs for an imaging system vary with the amount of customization and integration required by the service center.

Call Recording

Call recording is another technology that strives to ensure accuracy in the service center. A call-recording system's primary function is to record the audio portion of interaction between the service center representative and the employee. Increasingly, the call-recording system is becoming a device that attempts to record the entire (both voice and data) interaction between the representative and employee. These interaction recorders not only record the audio from the telephone, but also record the keystrokes and screen movements on the service representative's workstation. This recording may even include representative interaction with back-end systems, such as the knowledge base or HRIS. When all of this information is combined, it gives a complete record of the interaction between the employee and the representative.

Some advantages of the call-recording system are self-evident, such as an accurate record of the representative-employee interaction; however, these systems can provide other advantages for the service center. Service center managers use the system to chart the progress of their representatives. Managers can access the recorded files and use them to complete evaluations or suggest training for the representative. Trainers can use the recordings to teach new representatives how to deal with difficult callers, or illustrate the types of calls the representative will be receiving. These recordings can be used to resolve discrepancies and conflicts between employees and representatives.

Recording systems, compared with the other technologies discussed in this chapter, are relatively straightforward. Their costs include both hardware and software. Hardware consists of the recording ports, wiring, servers, and PCs used to access the system. The recording-system's software manages connections to the representatives' desktops while providing an interface for the manager or monitoring coach to access recording files, schedule recording times, and perform changes on the system. The cost for all of these components combined is approximately $150,000 to $250,000.

Enabling technologies are at the heart of the efficiency and success of the service center. New service centers may not be able to implement all of these technologies at one time due to time limits or expense. Those centers should concentrate on the required technologies, and work toward the recommended and nice-to-have technologies over time. More established centers may be in a better position (financially or logistically) to add the recommended or nice-to-have technologies. One thing is certain: As these technologies become more and more integrated with the Web and with one another, employees, managers, and service center staff will reap the benefits of information that is readily available, accurate, and strategically valuable.

Computer Simulation Modeling and Service Delivery

One of the most difficult tasks associated with implementing an HR service center is to determine the service delivery model. "Should we have one center or multiple centers?" "What is the right number of staff?" "What is the right mix of generalists versus specialists?" These are some of the critical questions that need to be answered. These questions are complicated enough in their own right, but another set of variables must be considered that have a direct impact on these decisions. These variables include the complexity of the business processes, variability in the volume of work, staffing and scheduling issues, the use of technology, and the performance metrics that must be met.

Sophisticated computer simulation modeling software can be used to manipulate these variables and run simulations that will help provide the answers for which we are looking. Software is based on queuing theory, which has long been used for optimization in the manufacturing environment. The model basically allows us to simulate the interaction of three key variables in HR service delivery: work, resources, and performance.

For example (see Figure 15-7), if one service delivery model has two service centers with specialized customer service groups responding to inquiries, it is possible to model cross training and combine the groups, reduce staff, and determine the effect on service levels.

Another example of the usefulness of this tool is in process analysis (see Figure 15-8). Using the tool, we can identify the

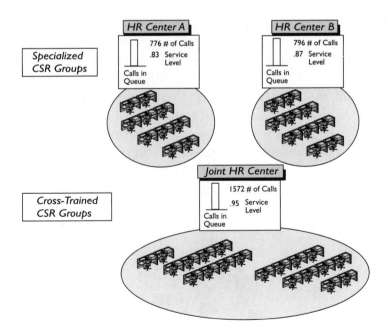

Figure 15-7 Using computer simulation to optimize service delivery options. The simulation shows that cross-training staff reduces staffing requirements, but it may incur additional training costs.

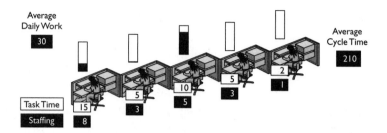

Figure 15-8 Using computer simulation in process analysis (I). Staffing based on traditional methods results in a bottleneck in Step 3 and runaway cycle times.

source of a bottleneck in a process and determine the optimal staffing required to eliminate the bottleneck (see Figure 15-9).

Computer simulation modeling provides the greatest benefit when trying to optimize an existing HR service center. In order for the software model to be effective, parameters must be set requiring detailed knowledge and statistics around operational issues, such as how long a customer service representative spends off-line for a particular process; how much time a representative spends on-line for a particular process; what the expected work volume is for each type of process, and so on. Answers to these questions are often only known once the center has been operational and good measurements and statistics have been gathered. Like so many other pieces of HR technology, the information provided by the model is only as good as the data that goes into it. While computer simulation modeling is an extremely useful tool,

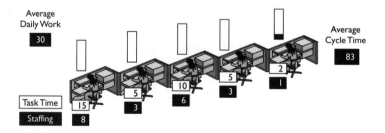

Figure 15-9 Using computer simulation in process analysis (II). Optimal staffing of Step 3 eliminates the bottleneck and significantly reduces cycle time.

there is, unfortunately, still some art to determining the appropriate service delivery model.

Requirements Definition

A *requirements definition* is a set of documentation that defines the functional requirements for technology in the service center. In more simplistic terms, it details what the technology must do in order to meet the needs of the service center. A good requirements definition is written in such a way that it serves multiple purposes.

The document can be used as a discussion guide with the non-technical managerial service center staff, to make sure there is a common understanding of what the technology will and will not do. Once the staff is in agreement, final sign-off can be given. Documentation is also used to provide detail to the information technology staff as to what implementation and support will be needed from them. Documentation can also be incorporated into any *request for proposals* (RFPs) that are needed to acquire third-party hardware and software. Once the technology is selected, the requirements definition serves as the basis for creating programming specifications unique to each piece of hardware or software. Finally, documentation can be used as a basis for developing a thorough test plan for implementing the technology.

Many organizations do not take the time up front to create a detailed requirements definition. It is easy to lose sight of what each piece of technology is supposed to do, and how the pieces integrate to support service delivery, without it. Needless to say, organizations that bypass or minimize this step generally have difficult implementations, and often end up with technology that does not meet their needs.

Training

One of the most critical factors affecting the quality of service delivery within a service center is effective staff training. The demand for effective and cost-efficient training is increasing. Major factors driving the increased demand include the following:

- An increase in the number of HR services being supported
- High rates of staff turnover
- The move toward manager self-service and employee self-service through the Web
- The use of complex technology on the desktop
- Career development and retention issues

To complicate matters, while training needs are increasing, service centers are under greater financial pressures to reduce the cost of providing services.

All of these factors have combined to force organizations to rethink the way training is delivered. Classroom study was the predominant means of training delivery in the early call center environment. The major issues with classroom training include the following:

It is predominantly lecture-based, which is not the most effective means of learning.

It is costly from the perspective of both time and people resources.

It is inefficient for training small numbers of replacement new hires.

It is expert-driven; if there is no expert, there is no class.

It is disruptive to the work, because it takes staff off the job.

It is ineffective at addressing individual learning needs; there is one course for all.

Today, organizations are moving toward an integrated approach (see Figure 15-10) to training that combines on-the-job training, independent study, and the traditional classroom setting. The key is to use each of the three approaches where it is most effective.

Classroom Training

Classroom training is most appropriate for teaching baseline knowledge and fostering learner interaction. It is also ideal when

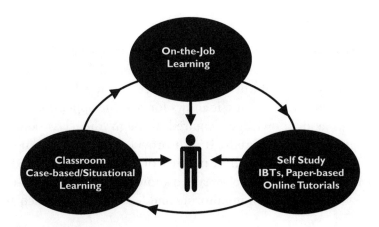

Figure 15-10 Learning strategy. A well thought out learning strategy is one that integrates synchronous and asynchronous approaches.

there is a need for culture building, for sharing functional knowledge, or for visual connection with the learner and a controlled environment. Typical courses that may be most conducive to classroom training are orientations, customer service skills, team building, technology training, and telephone techniques. The classroom environment uses a number of techniques that are effective for developing and reinforcing skills in these areas, such as facilitated sessions, games and simulations, video-audio feedback, and lectures.

Independent Study

Independent study is effective for reinforcing and learning baseline knowledge, and also allows learners to select what they need, set their own schedule with 24-hour/7-day-a-week access, proceed at their own pace, and so on. Areas suited to independent study are basic overview, terminology, basic systems training, and plan or policy changes. The independent study approach uses a number of techniques that are effective for developing and reinforcing skills in these areas, such as tutorials, on-line documents, recorded presentations, and computer-based and Internet-based training.

On-the-Job Training

By far the most effective training approach is on-the-job training (OJT). Learning and development studies have shown that approximately 80 percent of learning takes place on the job. On-the-job training is effective because it allows for real-life application of all the skills and knowledge acquired through the classroom or through independent study. It also provides just-in-time knowledge and skills for the job. A number of methods can be used to deliver OJT, including Web-enabled knowledge bases, one-on-one desk-side coaching, call monitoring and feedback, and "lunch and learns."

Recruiting and Retention

As organizations move from a call center model to a service center model, there is a need to revise the recruitment and retention strategy for service center staff. Quite simply, the strategies that worked for the call center may not be effective for a service center environment. Effective strategies must be developed because high turnover is a significant issue for service centers. Large service centers, which are doing a good job in this area, may experience 14 to 20 percent turnover rates. However, it is not unusual to see turnover rates of 25 to 35 percent or higher. Most organizations have found that the old call center recruiting strategy is not effective, for the following reasons:

It fails to account for a more complex service center environment.

It focuses on personal attributes as opposed to skills and knowledge.

It emphasizes "rule-bound" staff management that does not support individual initiative.

It socializes compensation with little differentiation for high performers.

It rewards advancement through "off-the-phone" positions.

The "right" strategy will depend upon the service delivery model implemented, but in general the following differences are found in moving toward a more full service center.

Call Center	Service Center
Minimal differentiation in calls or services	Significant differentiation in services, calls, and customer
Interchangeable staff	Specialized staff
Limited formal training	Extensive formal and on-the-job training
Leverage of technology	Leverage of intellectual capital

For an organization to be successful in its recruiting and retention efforts, it will need to define hiring requirements, define a comprehensive recruiting strategy, develop a selection process, review learning and development objectives, define performance metrics, define its "deal" with the employee, and successfully implement the strategy.

Define Your Hiring Requirements

Recruits should have a college-level education, or experience. Relevant knowledge is a plus. Higher education levels are desirable, because service center staff must be able to analyze and solve integrated problems, and demonstrate a continual drive to learn. These skills will be critical to their success, as new policies, programs, services, and technologies are introduced.

Define a Comprehensive Recruiting Strategy

A recruiting strategy should center around those approaches that will attract, and appeal to, college-educated recruits. Specialized and general Internet sites should be developed. Research shows that many of today's "generation Xers" conduct 100 percent of their job searches on the Internet. Campus recruiting and advertisements in leading journals and papers produce results, as does the strategic use of employment agencies. Of course, employee referrals are one of the most cost-effective means of recruiting.

Develop a Selection Process

In the service center environment, organizations are looking for employees who want to stay with the organization for the long run. Therefore, more emphasis is being put on screening and evaluating potential candidates. There is now a heavy emphasis on the use of customized testing for required skills and multiple, diverse interviews. Also, with the objective of trying to identify the longer-term hire, there is a greater balance of candidate screening activities and career marketing opportunities being explored with desirable candidates.

Review Learning and Development Objectives

Learning and development objectives in the new service center should support the objective of retaining staff for the long run. Extensive orientation should include departmental vision, values, and overall business strategy. Formal training places a heavy emphasis on developing knowledge with content. Organizations should keep in mind, depending on the service delivery model implemented, that newly hired employees may not be fully functional for many months.

Define Performance Expectations and "The Deal"

Candidates should have a clear and thorough understanding of what their performance measurements will be, as well as their rewards. A strong emphasis should be placed on metrics that support the quality of services delivered and solve customer problems. Teamwork, in contrast to individual performance, may also be a critical requirement. As in all jobs, there should be an expectation of a wide variation in individual performance, which should be rewarded accordingly; better performers get more rewards. To successfully retain the best candidates, it will be critical to define a career path that the candidate can see and understand, and that they regard as positive. This may be accomplished by moving the employee through various levels of supervisory roles, as well as by movement into other functional areas. It should also be possible to move good performers into positions in the organization outside the service center, such as in-the-field HR, training and development, marketing, or sales.

Successful Implementation

Some keys to successful implementation are to make sure that supervision of staff is mentor-focused, and that there is a team orientation to relationships. Both of these efforts will support problem solving and an orientation to quality, and maintain a focus on employee development. Above all, there must be an aggressive differentiation of staff, based on performance.

Challenges and Concerns

Integrated Service Delivery with Multiple Outsourced Delivery Providers

In the early 1990s, when organizations began reengineering the HR function, one of the first services to be outsourced was benefits administration—in particular, health and welfare plans, and then defined-benefit and defined-contribution plans. Initially, organizations placed all outsourced benefits administration with one service provider. The theory was that there would be efficiencies and economies of scale allowing leverage. Over time, though, this trend changed toward one of selecting outsourced providers that were the best of the breed. It is fairly common today for organizations to be serviced by multiple outsourced service providers. The challenge created by this trend is to integrate service delivery with employees, so that it appears seamless to the customer.

As of the time of this writing, there are no perfect solutions that could be described as "best practice." In fact, most organizations are just beginning to attempt to address this thorny issue, and various solutions are being proposed. One of the options being considered suggests developing a service center that sits on top of the multiple centers, whose role is to handle customer service integration, or to have one of the incumbent providers play this role. The integrating service center could then provide different levels of integration varying in complexity. For instance, at the simplest level, the center could provide information that crosses all centers, but does not require changes to any of the provider's back-end systems. In this example, a Web-accessible knowledge base could be used that directs employees as to what to do and when. Or live agents could walk employees through various processes, such as a new hire, change of address, or retirement.

More meaningful integration would involve actual transactions being accepted and written across multiple vendor systems. The employee would then be provided feedback regarding further options resulting from cross-plan or cross-vendor system implications. Of course, these transactions would all be based on programmed business rules. A simple example here would be a change of address, which may result in eligibility for a less-expensive medical plan, which in turn results in extra flex credits, which can be either rolled over into the employee's savings plan or taken as taxable income.

While initiating transactions across multiple service providers clearly provides the greatest benefit, it also represents a significant challenge. The challenge is that this would require all service providers to make changes, and rather significant changes, to their back-end systems. Compounding this problem is the fact that most of these providers are direct competitors. Web- and browser-based applications will make a solution more feasible; however, they will not provide an answer in and of themselves. To be sure, the marketplace will continue to demand a solution to the problem of effective integration across multiple outsourced service centers.

Change Management

When implementing an HR shared service center, organizations should not underestimate the significant change management issues that need to be addressed. We know from experience that line managers will be resistant to change, and will attempt to keep staff, in order to do business as usual at their business unit. A comprehensive change management strategy (see Figure 15-11) is crit-

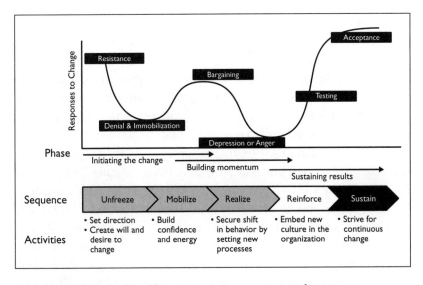

Figure 15-11   Change management strategy and sequence.

ical to successful implementation and ongoing effectiveness of the service center. A service center cannot measure up to service-level agreements if processes are not being followed as designed. While this chapter is not intended to be a comprehensive study on change management, it is helpful to look at some fundamental concepts in change management. Organizations and people tend to respond to change in the same fundamental ways.

There are three main phases to focus on in change management:

Initiating the change

Building momentum throughout the organization for the change

Sustaining the results

When a change has been initiated, people may not see the need for that change. You will often hear that they would rather just talk to a real person—and preferably a local one. It is important to help people understand the reason for change and to educate and support them in the value of new processes and new tools. During the momentum-building phase, people tend to feel overwhelmed by all the changes, and may say that they just do not have time to learn and use self-service or other tools. Here it is important to help people understand that change is a natural part of business and to point out the early successes that have already been realized. Above all, respect should be shown for people's concerns and attitudes. Organizations can learn how to effect a smoother roll-out from studying people's resistance. As change diffuses through the organization, people feel the need to transfer knowledge across organizational boundaries and build upon each other's success. At this stage, you can sustain results by extensively communicating about initiatives and work-in-progress, and by encouraging a networking among employees to share ideas and best practices. Successful change programs follow a few key principles:

- Follow a defined sequence.
- Win emotional and intellectual support.
- Model and reinforce the new way of working.
- Create experiences that shape future behavior.
- Work with resistance.
- Release talent, creativity, and ingenuity.

Change management is required for successful implementation of an HR shared service center. Many organizations minimize the importance of change issues, and will try to address them after implementation. This approach will only result in the service center losing credibility from the day it becomes operational. A better approach is to incorporate the above principles from the start.

PART
III

Other Key Trends and Technologies Changing HR

HR Outsourcing in the Internet Era

Thomas Keebler*

FOR A GROWING NUMBER of business leaders, many of whom may have considered HR and HRIS outsourcing in the past and decided against it, the business case for outsourcing has taken on new dimensions, driven by HR technology that continues to evolve at a rate adding new risks to the ownership and internal maintenance of HR systems.

In this chapter, the focus is on the reasons HR departments turn to outsourcing, and the impact of new Internet technology on these considerations. First, however, it is useful to put HR outsourcing in historical and current contexts, and briefly define the major types of HR outsourcing available today, including appli-

*Thomas Keebler is a Principal in the Towers Perrin Philadelphia office, where he assists clients with technology-focused HR and benefits administration solutions. He is also helping lead the Firm's delivery of client-based administration capabilities.

Philadelphia–Centre Square office: Centre Square, 1500 Market Street, Philadelphia, Pennsylvania 19102.

cation service providers (ASPs), business process outsourcers (BPOs), and varieties at both ends of the spectrum.

Evolution of Outsourcing

Outsourcing is not new to HR. Organizations have been outsourcing their payroll functions for a half-century, and for decades have been outsourcing certain administratively complex functions better handled by specialists, especially when complex and changing regulatory requirements affect the function. For example, one would be hard-pressed to find many organizations that retain their 401(k) record-keeping functions in-house. Similarly, as a result of its complex regulations and substantial penalties for noncompliance, COBRA has been a prime target for outsourcing. Likewise, the growth of flexible benefits plans in the past 15 years—with their myriad of options, numerous managed-care offerings, and complicated status change rules—has led to a rise in health and welfare plan outsourcing. Newer laws, such as the Family Medical Leave Act (FMLA), with its elaborate record-keeping, employee communications, and compliance requirements, have also led many to the decision to outsource this function.

For the most part, these are examples of *tactical* outsourcing, which simply moves the activities and tasks associated with a specific, nonstrategic HR function off-site, to be handled by functional experts, using systems specially designed for the administrative activities involved.

Today, these *niche* applications of outsourcing remain popular, but new models are emerging that offer much more. The rapid and accelerating growth of ASPs, also referred to by some as "Managed Solutions Providers," a phenomenon made possible by the Internet, presents the option of putting not only the operation and maintenance of HR systems in the hands of an outsourcing firm, but all other HR activities as well. Similarly, Internet-based outsourcing firms that provide data processing alone, or handle transactions and sometimes employee contact, as BPOs can now perform these tasks for the full spectrum of HR activities.

Further, the pace of HRIS technological change gives added weight to most of the business reasons for considering outsourcing discussed in this chapter. Today's decision to outsource is increasingly driven by the final reason described here: technology access, delivered by a well-selected outsourcing firm, as it becomes available, not when it is halfway to becoming obsolete.

Internet-Based ASPs: The Future?

Today's marketplace is growing, with many areas of HR planning to outsource even more than they have already (see Figure 16-1).

However, in the information technology industry generally, no business category is growing faster than ASPs. Estimates of growth in the ASP marketplace vary wildly, reflecting different definitions of what the term means to the growing number of firms calling themselves ASPs; but all industry analysts agree that growth will be phenomenal. From an American ASP marketplace virtually nonexistent as recently as 1997, analysts are making some startling predictions (see Figure 16-2).

The Gartner Group expects the following:

- ASP revenues, which hit $150 million in 1999, will reach $7.8 billion in 2004 (from IDC).

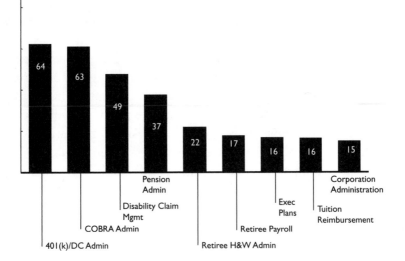

Figure 16-1 Outsourcing HR activities by functional area, per recent Towers Perrin survey of leading companies.

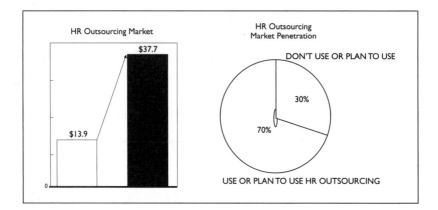

Figure 16-2 Growth of the outsourcing market. The HR outsourcing market is valued at $13.90 and is expected to rise to $37.70 by 2002.

- The ASP marketplace will reach $20 billion in 2003 (from Forrester and Dataquest).
- The total U.S. market for ASPs will reach $48.5 billion in 2003 (from Deloitte Research).

At the high end of these estimates, industry analysts include a broad range of models, from software companies offering their products on-line on a rental basis, to business process outsourcers, treated separately in this chapter. Also, it is expected that, as the ASP bandwagon continues to attract boardroom attention and publicity as the ultimate solution to the costs of owning and maintaining hardware and software, more and more traditional outsourcing firms, software vendors, and Internet service providers will be calling themselves ASPs. This is inevitable and legitimate—usage always determines the meaning of words and terms—but it will require that companies considering an ASP, for HR or any other business application, exercise great care in selecting a provider.

The explosive growth of the ASP marketplace, as well as its being touted as "the outsourcing model of the future" for HR, could not happen without the Internet. Essentially, an ASP is a business that owns and manages applications from remote data centers, and delivers these services to multiple users over the Internet or a private network. With the Internet, this means that ASPs can rent software and services, which are accessible with just a Web browser, to their customers. Users pay on a per-transcription or subscription basis, and typically get these kinds of benefits:

> Access to the latest software and tools of all types, without the costs of acquiring and maintaining hardware and software, or of staffing and retaining in-demand IT professionals

> Fast, relatively painless implementation of new applications needed to address pressing business needs

> Ability to access more powerful and (simultaneously!) more user-friendly data transaction and analysis tools using only a browser, since processing moves to the ASP

> State-of-the-art network and application services, including security, backup, and disaster recovery

The advent of the Internet provides a ubiquitous, inexpensive infrastructure permitting organizations of all sizes to deploy their IT and HRIS processing centers to an off-site ASP. Even though it has been estimated that Internet traffic is doubling every 100 days, total bandwidth—the pipeline through which Internet transactions flow—is increasing by 300 percent per year. In short, there are no limits on how much even the largest organizations can outsource to an Internet-based ASP, and companies of all sizes can greatly reduce the risks, costs, time to market, and staffing requirements of in-house systems.

Types of Outsourcing: A Cumulative Spectrum

One way to look at the types of outsourcing available in an increasingly complex marketplace is shown in Figure 16-3, which presents a typical view of what the outsourcing firm provides at each of the five levels, from basic internal system ownership and maintenance to total HR outsourcing. In this view, each successive type of outsourcing includes the services provided by preceding types, so as the spectrum moves ahead, HR systems work and HR transactions are performed by the outsourcing firm.

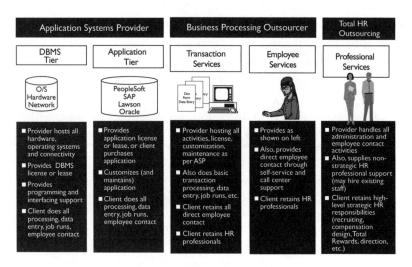

Figure 16-3 Cumulative spectrum.

In-sourced Administration

In this model, long familiar to most organizations, nearly all aspects of HR administration are performed internally by the corporation. Companies may choose to outsource their system's development by virtue of using a commercially available product, but they still retain most of the aspects of implementing, maintaining, and operating that system. Similarly, they retain all activities needed for the "care and feeding" of the data within the system.

Application Service Provider

ASPs are the most rapidly growing and evolving type of outsourcing firm, and now include established HRMS vendors (PeopleSoft, Oracle, and Lawson, among others), as well as vendor-independent ASPs, renting enterprise systems of all types, deliverable anywhere there is a browser. While originally of interest only to small or mid-sized companies, ASPs, for purposes of alignment in this spectrum, are defined as companies that host hardware and systems, provide connectivity, and customize and maintain applications, but let the client handle data entry, processing, job runs, and employee contact.

Basic Business Process Outsourcing

There are two levels of BPOs from the perspective of roles. In basic BPO, the outsourcing firm provides all the hardware and services typically associated with ASPs, and also does basic transaction processing, data entry, and job runs.

Enhanced Business Process Outsourcing

In this form of business process outsourcing, the BPO firm also provides direct employee contact through call center support, for example. This is a popular model for relatively mid- to large-sized organizations with administratively complex HR programs, such as a plethora of different healthcare plans requiring regular enrollment and reenrollment, or a company whose workforce is spread across a widely disparate geographic area and that does not, therefore, have direct access to an HR professional. In this model, the client firm typically retains its HR professionals to plan, develop, and manage HR programs, but most day-to-day administrative tasks (including employee contact) are taken over by the BPO firm.

Before moving on to the next level of outsourcing, we should stop here to discuss the future of these three outsourcing alternatives. While it is true that they are different service offerings with different characteristics (both in actuality and in marketing), it is also true that the increasing usage and capabilities of the Internet will blur these distinctions. For example, before the Internet and its employee self-service capabilities, paper-based processes made it clear where the line was between ASP and basic BPO solutions. Now that Web-based tools allow direct employee access and control of data transactions, this distinction is not so clear. Similarly, with the advent of Internet-based knowledge bases and coaching tools, basic BPO transaction processing and enhanced BPO, with its direct employee contact, also begins to blend together. While no one can say for sure where these models will end up, it is clear that they will continue to meld as the Internet (and HRIS tools) continues to evolve.

Total HR Outsourcing

This model lies primarily in the future for many organizations, and therefore remains on the drawing board for most of its advocates. In this model, virtually the entire existing HR department is moved to the outsourcing firm—which may even hire the same staff—so that all nonstrategic HR professional support is handled by the outsourcing firm. The client retains only senior-level HR strategies for setting the overall strategic direction of HR programs with critical impact on the business—such as the total rewards plan design—or specific staffing and recruitment strategies.

The business objectives or reasons for outsourcing, as described in the preceding section, can and should dictate the type of outsourcing solution selected, and may dictate that more than one model—or even a firm that does not fit neatly into one of these categories—be selected. For example, a BPO firm that handles employee contacts for benefits might be selected, while an ASP hosts the hardware and software for basic HR, providing connectivity to BPO and client through the Web.

Reasons for Outsourcing

While the business objectives or reasons for outsourcing vary among organizations (and within organizations when parts of HR work are outsourced, perhaps to more than one firm), they generally include the following:

- Focus on core business
- Quality improvement
- Functional expansion and access
- Centralized or consolidated operations
- Cost control
- Technology access

As discussed in the following sections, each of these reasons has taken on a new dimension in the age of the Internet. While most of the reasons have been central to why companies have outsourced, the Web and other technologies have vastly increased the importance of technology access as a primary reason to outsource.

Also, it should be clear that these reasons are closely interrelated in the real world of corporate decision making. Cost control, for example, is a key factor in most cases. The organization may want to expand its HRIS services into a new area, such as succession planning, but the costs of acquiring or building this functionality into the existing system is a more expensive alternative than outsourcing. And for technology access generally, cost is always a key consideration.

Focus on Core Business

The most strategic reason for outsourcing HR administration, in terms of its impact on the organization's ongoing and future objectives in attaining competitive advantage, is that it permits the organization to focus on its core business, the reason it exists as a business entity. Whether the company makes cars, provides communications services, or delivers freight, it may feel that it has more important things to spend time and scarce (and highly trained) resources on than basic HR-benefits-payroll transaction processing—especially when these administrative services are seen as adding little value to the products or services the company creates and sells. HR record-keeping and payroll are seen by many managers as nonstrategic, non-value-adding diversions from the real purpose and mission of the organization.

Readers know that this is not always the case, that HR products and services can and do add value to the organization by improving the human capital used to gain and sustain competitive advantages, and that effective HR administration adds value to these products and services. Poorly administered benefit plans diminish the absolute value of benefits to employees, managers who are unable to access those data and processes necessary for the performance of their jobs are less effective, retention rates suffer when career development systems are inadequate, and so on. But often, running a smooth and efficient payroll or HR administration operation is seen by many as merely meeting expectations. It is hard to exceed expectations in this area, but easy to fall below them. An organization must pay its people and meet its compliance and regulatory obligations, but does not have to do so using its own staff.

Quality Improvement

Another main reason for considering outsourcing, especially relevant to organizations where the customers for HR's products and services are being poorly served by existing technology and overworked HR staffers, is the improvement to HR delivery quality that an outsourcing firm can provide. Although *quality* means different things to different people, within the context of HR systems it is almost always defined as including accuracy, timeliness, and consistency. Outsourcing can improve these attributes on a consistent basis.

In general, a well-selected outsourcing firm has the structure, tools, and resources in place to improve and maintain data and administration accuracy. If selected to handle a specialized HR function, such as 401(k) plan administration or healthcare benefits, they have the functional expertise, access to the latest government regulations affecting the function, and a business focus that greatly reduces the risks of inaccurate or inadequately informed programs and policies. They can achieve economies of scale in the application of their knowledge about environmental issues affecting all of their clients, from new laws and regulations, to investment opportunities and the changing landscape of healthcare providers and insurance options.

Perhaps of even more importance, and of increasing benefit in the era of Web-based HR, tools used by outsourcing firms can vastly improve the quality of HR products and services by improving access and timeliness. For example, using the Web for individual portals linked to the outsourcing firm, employees and managers have the full advantage of the outsourcing firm's investment in knowledge base technology, workflow systems, or other still-emerging tools for quality improvement.

Consistency in the delivery of HR data and processes to employees eliminates such problems as "answer shopping" by em-

ployees accustomed to dealing with internal HR staffers with varying levels of knowledge or access to accurate information. When
an employee calls the outsourcing organization to find out when,
and how much, he can borrow from his 401(k) plan, for example,
knowledgeware on the system does the calculations and provides
an accurate answer, based on the individual's own plan. If the same
employee asked the same question of a different customer service
representative later in the day, he would get the same answer—
because it comes from the same knowledge base and case management source (in fact, the same system may even track and/or
record the previous call, so that the CSR can reference it during
the second call!).

Like the other main reasons for outsourcing, quality improvement does not stand alone, but is related to costs. How much can
the company afford to spend on comparable tools, processes, and
expertise? The outsourcer is able to leverage the costs and spread
them over many clients.

Functional Expansion and Access

For many organizations seeking technological support for new
critical Human Resources management functions—from recruitment and leadership development, to benefits cost control and
variable pay—outsourcing provides a cost-effective alternative to
traditional "make or buy" options. By using an outsourcing firm's
specialized software, which today can be integrated by the common "language" and protocols of the Web, the company can
quickly and effectively add applications needed to address HR
issues that have an impact on the success of the business. And due
to Web technology, the access issue, which may have been a bar-
rier to functional outsourcing in the past, need not emerge as a
problem.

Functionally specialized software has long been a characteristic of HRIS, and will continue to be required in the increasingly
complex, multifunctional area known as HR. Most large organizations have at least a dozen distinctly different HR functions, each
with its own data requirements, reporting needs, processes, and
timing cycles. Niche market software designed to address these

unique needs has been both a boon to HR managers responsible for specialized functions, and a curse in some organizations where a plethora of poorly integrated silo systems operate independently. Enterprise resource planning (ERP), client/server systems, and now the development of Web-based HR technology, have all been driven in large part by the need to integrate technology supporting diverse HR functions. But the needs of specialized HR functions and their unique use in some organizations continue, and are not always readily addressed by existing systems. The vendor community for specialized HR software continues to grow, and each new HR issue of the day, such as recruitment in a tight labor market, spawns a dozen new applications overnight.

Outsourcing provides a means for the organization to either add functionality one piece at a time, by selecting best-of-breed outsourcing firms for specific functions, or to outsource the entire HRIS to a firm that can incorporate as much or as little functionality as the company needs. The choice will depend on the overall HR systems strategy (see Chapter 12), but with outsourcing the company has a viable alternative to the "make or buy" options of the past.

Figure 16-4 shows the logic that an organization might use as it decides whether or not to outsource.

The availability of the outsourcing option, which can usually be implemented in a fraction of the time it takes to build or buy-and-customize a specialized application, means that the company can quickly and effectively respond to HR management needs driven by changing business requirements. The following two examples cite some reasons for outsourcing.

A major retailer with company-owned stores throughout the United States, with managers and assistant managers in each, and with scores of regional and district managers above these, found that it was losing many of its high-potential managers to competitors, in part because career progress had stagnated and was not supported by a visible succession planning system. The managers had no access to the existing system, leading many to believe there was no process at all. While there was a process, it was not automated, and the company's home-grown HRIS had no position control or succession planning functionality. So the need for an easy-

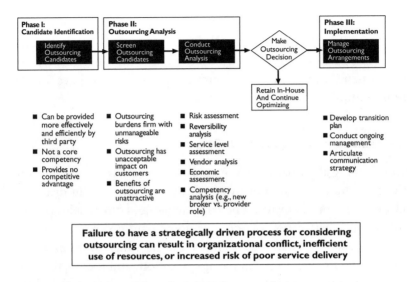

Figure 16-4 Outsourcing analysis.

to-see-and-understand solution was becoming urgent. Further, managers' access to critical HR data and processes needed in other areas (including performance management and compensation planning) was limited. Implementing the needed applications inside the company was an option, but would have taken too long. By outsourcing the entire HRIS to an Internet-based ASP, the company quickly got the technology it needed to both improve existing HRIS services and add new functions that helped to retain key managers.

An organization with under 1000 employees, but with nine benefit plans and seven benefit providers, was spending a disproportionate amount of time and resources just enrolling and terminating employees. Worse, errors were common, affecting both the perceived value of benefits to employees and the company's business relationships with providers. By outsourcing benefits to an Internet-based BPO, and paying a flat monthly fee per employee, the company obviated the need for new software or hardware, eliminated nonstrategic benefits administration activities, and vastly improved its benefits services to employee customers.

For these and similarly situated organizations, outsourcing provides a means of expanding and improving HR services by adding HR functions that can utilize automation to be fully effective (and efficient). Further, Web-based systems that link the outsourced functions to company users via the Internet resolve the access issues of the past, thus mitigating the need to have an HR representative down the hall at each company site.

Centralized or Consolidated Operations

Outsourcing also provides companies with an alternative when considering the consolidation of physically or functionally dispersed HR delivery mechanisms. The cost savings and efficiencies of consolidating a half-dozen or more regional data processing centers, each with its own staff and facilities, can be a huge inducement to centralize HR operations in a single location, and today's technology overcomes past obstacles to integrating payroll and other functions with HR. A large pharmaceutical organization consolidated its benefits and payroll operations, saving millions of dollars a year, and further improved quality by outsourcing portions.

One way to consolidate multiple operations centers is, of course, creation of an in-house HR service center, or shared services center. Typically, these centers evolved in the 1990s with the advent of client/server systems and call center technology, and use workflow, knowledge base systems, IVR, and other technology that makes the center a single source for all HRIS information, transactions, and processing. As discussed in Chapters 14 and 15, however, service center development requires careful planning, the cooperation of numerous constituencies in the organization, and sometimes a major investment in new technology. Staff training issues also escalate in importance, because fewer people are doing more in a typical service center.

Outsourcing provides another means to effect consolidation. In effect, it puts the service center in the hands of the outsourcing firm, obviating the need to keep up with the latest new technology, train and retain key people, and manage the service center on an ongoing basis. Further, an outsourcing solution may also eliminate some of the barriers to consolidation (e.g., attempting to integrate legacy systems, dealing with staffs from different organizations, or political barriers brought on by recalcitrant managers). Even when operational centralization does not include all the functions and features associated with service centers, the consolidation of previously separate, often redundant processing into a single outsourcing unit can achieve huge cost savings and efficiencies, and the Web makes physical location irrelevant.

Cost Control

Very few organizations that turn to outsourcing to handle HR-benefits-payroll functions give cost reductions as their primary reason for doing so, although cost *control* or cost *containment*, and the creation and maintenance of level and predictable costs over time, are often strong factors in the decision to outsource.

Immediate cost reductions, though, may or may not occur, depending on the company's current HRIS and HR delivery environment, and on what it is moving from, or toward, as an outsourcing client. For example, reductions in headcount among HR systems professionals are likely, but in many cases this is offset by fees paid to the outsourcing firm—which may have hired many of the same skill sets that your people may have had. Or headcount reductions among other HR specialists and generalists are possible, but more often a company seeking true HR transformation through outsourcing does so in order to free up these managers and professionals from purely administrative work, and make them more effective partners in pursuing strategic business goals.

However, the costs of going to an outsourcer may be offset somewhat by the expected costs of fixing or replacing an HRIS. If the current HRIS is one that is obsolete or highly cost-ineffective, and needs a complete overhaul, or if the company needs to acquire and implement expensive new HR technology, outsourcing is obviously a less-expensive alternative, with immediate cost savings compared with build-or-buy options. If a new HRIS is not considered as an option, however, the current costs of running the existing system might still be reduced by process improvements and relatively inexpensive technical fixes in concert with the outsourcing arrangement.

More often, outsourcing's appeal to cost-conscious managers and CEOs is based on its ability to *control* costs now and in the foreseeable future, through multiyear contracts that lock in technology and HR service delivery costs. In the past, some of these costs may have soared out of control, and they may be equally be hard to predict in the years ahead. New business imperatives, new government regulations, changing HR priorities, and, most important of all, new technology are among the reasons HRIS professionals say that implementation never ends in HR systems. With outsourcing, the company lets the service provider address changing requirements, while also gaining access to new technology that would otherwise not be affordable, when the costs of implementation and maintenance are included.

Technology Access

In a world of HR transformation driven by rapid and continuing advances in new and more effective technology, outsourcing provides a means for organizations to take advantage of new HR-benefits-payroll technology without long-term implementation cycles or infrastructure investments that may otherwise be required. Just as important, given the pace of technological change, a well-selected outsourcing firm has the resources and business imperative for staying on the leading edge of HR technology. It knows it must not fall behind competitors in offering new and more effective technology as it emerges, and its economies of scale permit continuing investment in enhancements and new systems.

For many organizations, this virtually instant access to new technology and its benefits represents the most important reason to outsource all or part of the HR system. It means that an organization currently at the lower end of the scale in terms of technological advancement and/or HR delivery capabilities, can in effect leapfrog over several stages of capability, landing in an advanced technical environment that might have otherwise taken years to achieve—that is, if the company had the resources and corporate will to do it in-house.

To some extent, technology access has always been a key reason for the decision to outsource. Payroll outsourcing provides timely, accurate processing, and on-time delivery of checks, pay advances, and tax filings, primarily because of the payroll system technology employed by the outsourcing firm. Buying computerized systems to perform relatively routine, rules-driven administrative functions has always made more sense than building and maintaining internal systems. Outsourcing follows that dictum.

Now, in the age of the Internet, technology access made possible by outsourcing has taken on a new and significantly more important meaning. Not only does outsourcing provide efficiencies and relief from purely administrative tasks, but the technology it provides can transform the management and delivery of HR products and services, using remote technology accessible on the Web. Regardless of where an organization currently stands in the technological advancement of its HR systems, outsourcing to one of the Internet-based outsourcing firms can provide:

- Employee and manager self-service, through individual portals linked to the centralized system or site
- Workflow technology embedded in the service provider's system, the enabling technology of business process improvement
- Web-based integration of any number of specialized HR systems, the core HR system, a data warehouse, financial systems, or other enterprise systems linked by the common language and communications protocols of the Internet
- New analytical tools provided by the outsourcing firm, exploiting the integration of enterprise data and reports to support improved decision making and planning

Depending on the organization's current technological environment, the virtually instant access to these and other new technologies can have an impact on HR ranging from a step in the right direction to a revolutionary change. Further, for many organizations, choosing to outsource is also a decision offering a hedge against future technological developments that may lie just ahead. As bandwidth continues to increase, for example, video streaming and audio streaming will become increasingly common, further diminishing the time and space constraints previously associated with remote HR systems sites.

Summary

The ability to have another organization provide needed HR services to your employees has given the HR function a number of new delivery options that they did not have just a few years ago. While the reasons why outsourcing makes business sense might differ from company to company, the HR function and the employees are the clear beneficiaries. HR can focus on the more strategic business issues, knowing that the applications that have been outsourced are in good hands. The customer service will be first rate, and the administration details passed on to the vendor. And with good process analysis, and through the use of Web technology to connect the plans, the actual provider of the service does not have to be resident in the HR function, although it appears to the customer that the services are part of a uniform set of plans and processes. It is a "win-win" for all.

Web-Based HR in an International Setting

Cynthia DeFidelto and Iain Slater*

ELSEWHERE IN THIS BOOK, our colleagues paint a detailed picture, with a mainly North American slant, of how technology is transforming the HR function. But, of course, what works well on one side of the Atlantic does not always translate aptly to the other side. Our aim here is to sketch out the global scene, with a particular emphasis on Europe, where both of us carry out most of our work, so that comparisons with the United States can be made. Use of the Web, though, is growing rapidly, even faster outside the United States, closing any gaps between

*Cynthia DeFidelto is a Principal in the Towers Perrin London office. She leads the European and Asian HR Administration and Technology practice, assisting clients with all aspects of HR transformation and service delivery solutions. She is a member of the firm's global HR Effectiveness Team.

Iain Slater is a consultant in the London office of Towers Perrin where he co-leads the European HR Effectiveness practice. He specializes in assisting clients in addressing the organization design and change dimensions of transforming the HR Function.

London office address: Castlewood House, 77-91 New Oxford Street, London WC1A 1PX, England.

Table 17-1 Percent of Web Users by Region

Region	2000	2005
North America	43.2%	30.2%
Western Europe	25.1	27.9
Asia/Pacific	20.6	24.8
Eastern Europe	3.1	5.9
Latin America	5.6	7.3
Middle East/Africa	2.3	3.8

SOURCE: *The Industry Standard*, 14 February, 2000

non-American usage and that of the United States quickly. In Table 17-1, it shows the changing usage of the Web projected over the next several years.

Europe: Roughly the same geographical size as the United States, has a population three times as large,[1] and at least four languages are commonly used in business: English, German, French, and Spanish. Already the differences between this smorgasbord of a market and the United States become clear, before we even start to touch on the enormous cultural and social divisions within the European population.

Of course, in most large companies, English is readily spoken and understood at the management level, and may even be the language of business, as it is for the French telecom company Alcatel. Whether it is used in Portuguese warehouses or on French factory floors is, however, quite another thing. And despite the fact that the European Union (EU) has, to a very large extent, harmonized much employment legislation and removed market restrictions, the "United States of Europe" is by no means as uniform as the United States of America.

As with any area of European life, understanding what is happening now usually necessitates going back in time, in this case 10 or 20 years, to see how the HR function has evolved.

---

[1] Area of United States is 9,368,900 sq. km.; area of Europe is 10,498,000 sq. km.: population of United States is 248,709,873 people; population of Europe is 749,000,000 people.

The Historical Context

Back in the early and mid 1980s, a large company operating across Europe was probably run by a number of "country kings," the national CEOs. Almost autonomous, these CEOs ran their part of the business according to their perceived market requirements. In most organizations, HR, like all other functions, was run on a one-country basis, with the HR director for, say, France, reporting to the French board. If there was a central corporate HR function, it did not have much say in the way individual countries operated. Figure 17-1*a* shows how the function operated.

Then two things happened. First the costs of research and product development shot up. It was no longer viable for a pharmaceutical company, for example, to launch a drug for just one European market, or for a car manufacturer to come up with a design for a model that would not work across the whole market. It started to make more financial sense to cross boundaries and cooperate on projects.

At the same time, customers were becoming increasingly aware of price differentials across Europe for goods and services. Why should a company operating across Europe pay more for a widget in France than it would in Italy? And why was its accountancy firm charging so much more in Germany for the same business services as could be bought considerably less expensively in Spain?

Client pressures helped to evolve the idea of a line of busi-

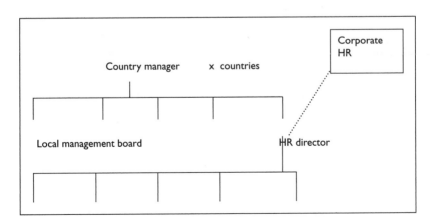

Figure 17-1*a* The 1980s country-based organization.

ness, as opposed to a country-based operation. As the 1980s moved toward their end, most multinationals had accepted that splitting up the HR function by country, when nothing else was divided up this way, was not helping HR to achieve company objectives. However, this split remained for some years, with duplication of time and money, and a lack of any common process. One of the reasons was that companies were nervous about the real or perceived lack of harmony in employment law across Europe.

Never in the vanguard of the new business wave, HR, by the late 1980s and early 1990s, had finally accepted that changes would have to occur to accommodate this function to the changing way of doing business. If HR directors were going to be seen as serious strategic business partners, they had to operate across borders like their corporate clients. However, this awareness did not result in any radical changes. All that happened in many companies was that an extra layer was added to the reporting structure, with a race of Über-HR-directors installed above the existing country positions (see Figure 17-1*b*). As an attempt to reduce costs and duplication, it was a failure.

The situation was untenable. The interweaving of the nuts and bolts of HR operations (the day-to-day administration work) with

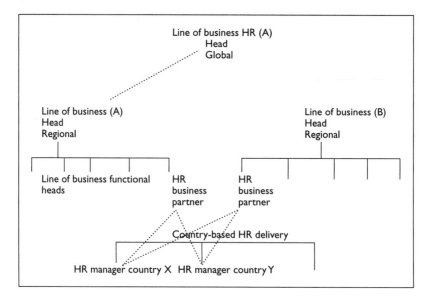

Figure 17-1*b*   Regional-line-of-business organization.

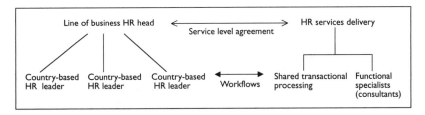

Figure 17-1c Transformed HR function.

the strategic function, for example, led to confusion, and was one reason HR was not contributing more directly to the achievement of corporate objectives. Externally, the position was that the different employment laws in use across Europe had started to become standardized and harmonized, making it easier to operate transnationally. The result was a move toward a structure like that shown in Figure 17-1c. The next section shows how new technology made this possible and forced the HR function to move with the times.

Transforming the HR Function

As always with Europe, every statement must carry a caveat, and here the caveat is that not all these things always happened in all parts of Europe at the same time. A general rule of thumb seems to be that changes follow the Gulf Stream, drifting in from the United States and hitting the U.K. first, then crossing the Benelux countries (Belgium, the Netherlands, and Luxembourg) and Germany and France, and proceeding finally to southern Europe. Central and Eastern Europe are also starting to feel the changes, too, and consultancies have already started to advise organizations from this region as to how they can transform themselves. Eastern Europe presents a particularly interesting challenge, as multinationals typically have lots of small groups of employees spread across several countries in the region. While these organizations have shown a lot of interest in technological solutions, the question of whether it is cost-effective to centralize functions is highly pertinent. Table 17-2 shows how this wave has worked vis-à-vis shared service centers. The U.K. tops the list of locations chosen by organizations, followed at a considerable distance by France,

Table 17-2 Locations Chosen by Companies for HR Shared Services

Country	Percentage of Total
United Kingdom	66
France	8
Germany	8
Republic of Ireland	4
Other Europe	14

NOTE: Some services centers have multiple locations.

SOURCE: Information gained through Towers Perrin's consulting work across Europe in 1999.

Germany, and Ireland. Southern, Central, and Eastern Europe do not appear.

Clearly, changes take place across the continent at different times and speeds, and technology is no exception. One generalizing statement can be made, and this is that legislative fervor, rather than laissez-faire, governs the way in which technology is regarded in most of the region. The desire for a broad, coordinated approach to doing things hampers the U.S.-style entrepreneurial development of Internet and e-commerce services. HR technology is no exception, as shown in Table 17-3.

For example, one of the biggest cultural differences between Europe and the United States concerns data protection. In 1998 Europe passed a directive laying down strict rules about how data

Table 17-3 Country Coverage of Service Centers

Country	Percentage of Total
Global*	17
Pan European	13
National	70

*A number of organizations have global networks of centers rather than one single center.

Table 17-4 The European Economic Area Comprises the Members of the European Union (EU) Plus Three Other Countries

Austria*	Greece*	Netherlands*
Belgium*	Iceland	Norway
Denmark*	Ireland*	Portugal*
Finland*	Italy*	Spain*
France*	Liechtenstein	Sweden*
Germany*	Luxembourg*	U.K.*

* Also EU member

can be used, banning transfers to other countries deemed to have inadequate protection. At the time of this writing, with certain exceptions, transfers of data can take place only between European Economic Area (EEA) countries (see Table 17-4). It is likely that a further group of countries outside the EEA will be designated as "adequate" in terms of the rigor of their data protection laws (see Table 17-5). The bad news for the United States is that it is not included in this group, as it does not have a general data protection law. Obviously, this exclusion makes it harder to send data across the Atlantic as easily as it can be done within Europe.

One ray of light is that the European Commission and the U.S. government may be able to develop a "safe harbor" system whereby data may be transferred to individual U.S. companies if they sign on to the safe harbor agreement, thereby accepting its restrictions and requirements. In the meantime, multinationals

Table 17-5 Non-EEA Countries Likely to Receive "Adequate" Designation by the European Commission

Australia	Isle of Man	Poland
Canada	Israel	Slovak Republic
Guernsey	Japan	Slovenia
Hong Kong	Jersey	Switzerland
Hungary	New Zealand	Taiwan

wishing to transfer personal data to their American offices will have to continue relying on the existing legal ways around the prohibition. The data protection directive does allow individual data controllers some freedom to make their own decisions as to whether an individual organization outside the EEA provides an adequate level of protection for a particular transfer of data. It also lists exceptions that may be made to the law. One of these involves asking employees to sign a consent form allowing the company to transfer personal data to the United States.

Leaving aside the United States for a moment, the Data Protection Act continues to complicate life for those using HR technology within Europe. It places a strict requirement on companies wishing to hold and process personal data to gain consent from employees. Of particular interest to companies setting up an outsourcing agreement with a third party is the requirement to draw up a written contract between the data controller and the data processor, showing that the latter complies with the security requirements of the law.

Even without the Data Protection Act, there are restrictions within individual European countries about the way in which data may be used. As always with Europe, the reasons for these restrictions are often bound up with its complex and often bloody history. For example, the consequences of the racial hatred and discrimination in Italy and Germany in the 1930s and 1940s explain why Italian and German companies are forbidden by their domestic laws to hold data on individuals that list religion or ethnic origin.

To sum up, keeping names of people on computer records potentially causes Europeans more anxiety than it does Americans, and you need only look at the last century's history to understand the reasons for this concern.

Before we look at specific countries, it is worth making another general point, which is that the organization's use of IT across its function is obviously going to determine how strong its commitment can be to HR technology. Obviously, an organization with little understanding of how to use technology in its finance or customer service department is unlikely to be a leader in providing state-of-the-art systems in HR.

Technology and How It Is Being Used as an Enabler

The new HR technologies have been extensively described elsewhere in this book, and our purpose here is not to duplicate this detail. Rather, we will look at what happens to these technologies when they are used in Europe. Do they work in the same way as they do in the United States? What particular problems have to be overcome?

In 1999 many European organizations found themselves grasping the technological nettle of necessity. There was a wave of merger and acquisition activity across all sectors, forcing those affected to look at the technology they were using, and work out whether it could be merged with its partner company, or whether a completely new start was the only practicable option.

Web-Based Service Delivery

The Web and its use outside the workplace has driven many organizations in Europe down the technology route. At first, Internet technology was used as an extension of print form: Texts were simply reproduced into HTML format. Eventually, European companies realized that there was more to it than that, and began to create communications specially for the medium. But as always, there are gaps in how quickly this has happened across Europe (see Figure 17-2). Even in one market, there are huge differences between companies of a similar size within the same sector. Our experience has been that this is particularly so in the U.K. In British companies, there often seem to be personalities on the board who effectively decide how enthusiastically (or not) their organizations embrace the new technology. Even if the personalities throw themselves behind the technology with gusto, it is not always easy to make the same thing work across Europe. Payroll systems are a good example. Europe's differing laws regarding reporting and taxation, and the different currencies involved mean that no cross-European payroll provider has really been able to offer a complete outsourcing service.

Specific technology applications, such as employee-manager self-service centers, are viewed in a very different way in Europe

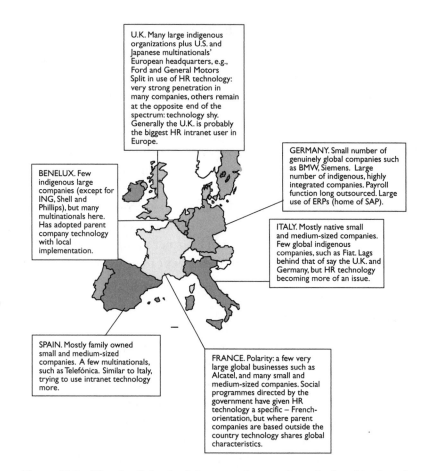

U.K. Many large indigenous organizations plus U.S. and Japanese multinationals' European headquarters, e.g., Ford and General Motors Split in use of HR technology: very strong penetration in many companies, others remain at the opposite end of the spectrum: technology shy. Generally the U.K. is probably the biggest HR intranet user in Europe.

GERMANY. Small number of genuinely global companies such as BMW, Siemens. Large number of indigenous, highly integrated companies. Payroll function long outsourced. Large use of ERPs (home of SAP).

BENELUX. Few indigenous large companies (except for ING, Shell and Phillips), but many multinationals here. Has adopted parent company technology with local implementation.

ITALY. Mostly native small and medium-sized companies. Few global indigenous companies, such as Fiat. Lags behind that of say the U.K. and Germany, but HR technology becoming more of an issue.

SPAIN. Mostly family owned small and medium-sized companies. A few multinationals, such as Telefónica. Similar to Italy, trying to use intranet technology more.

FRANCE. Polarity: a few very large global businesses such as Alcatel, and many small and medium-sized companies. Social programmes directed by the government have given HR technology a specific – French- orientation, but where parent companies are based outside the country technology shares global characteristics.

Figure 17-2 Thumbnail sketch of the types of companies to be found in the principal European countries, and the state of the new technology transformation in each.

than they are in the United States, where people are happier to be pushed toward using new technologies. In Europe, they work only if the curiosity and interest of the employees are sparked to create demand. Consequently, the introduction of the most sophisticated systems, which push employees and managers into making transactions, has been slower, but as Europeans start to bite at the carrot, an acceleration in the use of these systems is apparent. (See Figure 17-3.)

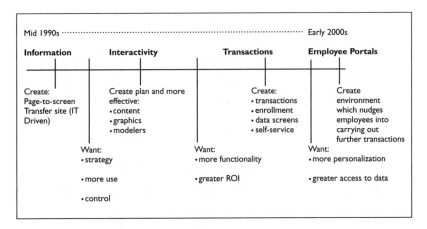

Figure 17-3 How HR is going on-line.

HR Service Centers

In Europe, pulling together HR staff into one center to which employees can telephone or e-mail, is always going to be a more adventurous procedure than it is in the United States. The problems of rigid data protection laws have already been touched on. Employment law can also be a stumbling block: Even though single European legislation has been enacted and built into national laws, there are often different interpretations of these laws among the member states of the EU. And then there is the language issue. As Table 17-2 shows, the most popular site for service centers is the U.K. (even though the British are not regarded as the most linguistically competent of Europeans), because Britain is regarded as a convenient entry point by American companies and because the cosmopolitan nature of the large cities attracts other Europeans, who will go to work for service centers and answer telephones in their native languages. IBM's center at Havant, near Portsmouth on the south coast, is one such example of an American multinational's HR service center. Ireland shares similar advantages. Northern France, Germany, and the Benelux are popular, as they provide access to populations who may be fluent in two or three languages and are flexible about location: It is common for Belgian companies to have commuters from Germany, Luxembourg, or the Netherlands working for them. In this respect, the EU's objective of allowing freedom to move from member state to member state for employment has worked well. The linguistic problem has received four principal solutions:

- *The brave option:* One business language, often English, even in a French company such as Alcatel. With this option you accept that not every employee will be able to understand everything, and that further down the organization this could present problems.
- *The halfway-house option:* Change salient facts on the website or intranet into local languages, but keep the more complex explanatory text in the business language(s).
- *The cautious option:* Run a subset of languages, with websites in the principal three or four European languages (probably English, French, German, Spanish, and Italian).
- *The truly high-tech option:* Change the portal according to the location of the person logging on, just as the large commercial organizations' websites will direct a French user to a French-language portal and a British user to an English-language portal. Again, this is an example of how HR technology relies on the forward strides by e-commerce.

HR Outsourcing

HR outsourcing in Europe entered the twenty-first century well before the clock struck midnight on New Year's Eve 1999. The last year of the previous millennium witnessed a surge toward outsourcing across Europe, and particularly in the U.K. It is now the case that large multinationals in Europe will consider outsourcing for almost every aspect of HR, except strategy. More important, they will allow one service provider to take on everything. (See Figure 17-4.)

In 1999, the British oil company BP Amoco set the trend by outsourcing virtually all its HR functions, except its strategy component. For the first time, Europe has shown the United States how the future appears. This stride forward should not be over-

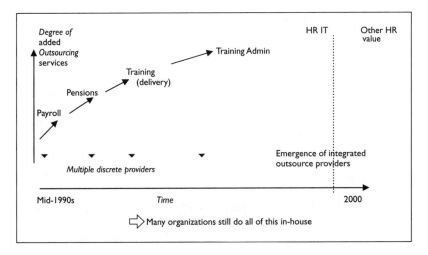

Figure 17-4 How outsourcing is developing.

played, however, as many large companies in Europe still prefer to carry out all their HR work in-house, and at present there is a finite number of suppliers who are able to take on all such functions. All the same, it seems almost certain that many more large organizations will look to HR specialists to remove some of the load and allow them to concentrate on their core business objectives. The choices for those wishing to make a career in HR look interesting: Will the ambitious still want to take the in-house route, or will they decide that going to work for a specialist supplier is where the future lies?

A World of Differences

Europe and its HR transformation have taken up much of this chapter, but the rest of the world presents interesting contrasts with both Europe and the United States.

Culture and history may dictate different routes from those taken in the West, and differences in the cost of employment will certainly play a role in determining the kind of technology adopted. For example, looking at service centers, in most countries in Western Europe, the high level of labor costs acts against the primary objectives of shared service centers—to achieve dramatic cost reduction. In most EU countries, employment regulations are restrictive and the labor force itself is often resistant to change. European companies find it difficult to transfer staff, even to a local shared service center, and increasingly will be forced to look elsewhere.

It is impossible to sum up the whole of the rest of the world in one section, so we shall look at three regions.

Asia/Pacific

Malaysia, Singapore, and Hong Kong have been described as going "Internet mad," so clearly, the mindset of those who live and work in this part of the area is open to using the kind of HR technology described elsewhere in this chapter and throughout the book. Indeed, some businesses here claim that they can transform their economies through the new technology, even skipping a generation of catch-up with the West. Malaysia's Multimedia Supercorridor, Singapore's US$1 billion fund for "technopreneurs," and Hong Kong's US$1.7 billion "cyberport" have certainly set a fast and impressive pace for HR to follow, and indeed, a small number of high-tech multinationals are starting to share service environments, mainly in Australia and Singapore.

Elsewhere in the region, India is a country where employment costs are low, and there is a vast resource of technologically skilled graduates who speak English. Demographics indicate that this will continue for a long time. Many believe that India will become a leading host of the new "Web farms," hosting system applications that will be available on the Internet. This will enable them to take on outsourcing projects for multinationals, but will these projects include HR outsourcing and service centers, as well as other functions?

However, the scope of integration and transactional support in the Asia/Pacific region as a whole is significantly limited by the following "four L's":

- Lack of a common employment law
- Linguistic diversity
- Large time differences
- Long traveling times

Latin America

In many ways, Latin America reminds us of how Europe was 20 years ago. There are a small number of very large organizations, and many locally managed, country-based small- and medium-sized companies. The economies of scale available to companies in the United States and Europe are often simply not an option here. In addition, there are not the same political synergies as in Europe.

A number of local companies, usually subsidiaries of American or European multinationals, have taken the opportunity of centralizing the subject matter experts in HR and using them on an as-and-when-needed basis throughout the region. Miami is a common location for service centers, owing to its status as a transportation hub and to the presence of many Spanish-speaking people. Locating in Florida also avoids the political problems implicit in choosing a central site in, say, Brazil rather than Argentina.

Africa and the Middle East

Similar to Latin America in the size of its companies (i.e., some large multinationals, but a preponderance of small- and medium-sized organizations), Africa and the Middle East, taken together, exhibit very different employment cultures. These two factors make the setting up of HR operations, such as shared service centers, an unlikely proposition. Even in just one country, South Africa, the educational background of many employees would make the use of Internet or intranet technology almost impossible. The cultural background of this and other parts of Africa means that face-to-face contact is vital for the exchange of important information.

The HR of the Future

Our colleague and leading U.S. Human Resources consultant Tom Davenport believes that tomorrow's employees will no longer be regarded as corporate assets. Instead they will be free agents who invest their human capital—abilities, energy, behavior, and time—in companies that give them the best return. As a result, companies will have to create high-return work environments in order to retain workers whose investment is crucial for future prosperity. One of the ways in which they can do this is by empowering employees: setting them up as free agents with control over their own destinies. There is no doubt that opening up the processes of HR by means of the new technologies helps this process. At the most basic level, simply being able to change your address yourself on your company records, without having to resort to telephone calls and internal memos, gives a measure of control. At the other end of the spectrum, being able to access the most sophisticated and responsive technology and use it to plan your own career progression is clearly giving you an autonomy that employees 10 years ago—or even 5—would not have believed they could ever possess.

Elsewhere, author and digital guru Nicholas Negroponte claims that the contrast is not so much between the United States and the rest of the world, but between the swift and the slow. Recent European mergers would seem to back this up. The years 1999 and 2000 have seen a lot of merger and acquisition activity between companies in different technology sectors in Europe (such as that between the U.K.'s Vodafone and Germany's Mannesmann in February 2000), sending an aggressive message to the United States about future ambitions for technology market shares. But can the HR function in Europe show itself equally keen to square up to the United States as the commercial sector? Of course, many of the companies most concerned with embracing technology change around the world are themselves part of American multinationals with no need to fight for position, but the point about leading, not following, stands.

If we had to sum up the 10 most important things to remember when looking at the state of HR technology outside the United States, what would they be?

HR technology outside the United States: 10 key points

- Although roughly the same size as the United States, Europe's population is larger and the diversity of culture and language and history means the regions cannot be treated as an amorphous entity.

- Other regions such as Asia/Pacific are equally diverse.
- The structure of the HR function has evolved from a different starting point than that of U.S. organizations. Historically, the role was a country-based one.
- Data protection laws are stricter in Europe and in some other parts of the world, reflecting current and historical concerns about storing personal information.
- Generally Europeans are not at the same stage of technology usage as Americans and need to be gently urged along the technological path. It's important not to generalize, as the picture varies considerably from country to country.
- However, when they decide to take a technology leap, for example as they have in HR outsourcing, European organizations are acting quickly and decisively.
- Some Asian countries, for example Singapore, are very deeply committed to the new technology and are keen to speed up their implementation of the latest systems.
- The future belongs to the employee-empowering organization, which makes it vital for companies to use the new HR technology to give their people more autonomy.
- Lack of funds and burdens on government social security schemes are shifting responsibility for financial planning to employees and employers.
- Mergers and acquisitions are creating global companies with increased need to capture data on their new employees.

Index